W9-BWP-573

You

can't eat magnolias

edited by H. Brandt Ayers
and
Thomas H. Naylor
with an introduction
by Willie Morris

A PUBLICATION OF THE
L.Q.C. LAMAR SOCIETY

McGRAW-HILL BOOK COMPANY
New York St.Louis San Francisco
Düsseldorf London Mexico Sydney
Toronto

You can't eat magnolias.
"A publication of the L.Q.C. Lamar Society."
1. Southern States—Civilization—Addresses, essays, lectures. I. Ayers, H. Brandt, ed. II. Naylor, Thomas H., ed.

F216.2.Y6 917.5'03'4 73-39499
ISBN 0-07-002635-1

First Edition

CONTENTS

Contents

Contents

INTRODUCTION
Willie Morris

[With the exception of some not-so-old and eminently wise heads such as Terry Sanford and Frank E. Smith, this volume was essentially written by young Southerners, and in this regard there is at least an ephemeral similarity with that esthetically pleasing but exasperating collection by the 1930 paper fugitives (as opposed to the more genuine Southern fugitives, the runaway slaves) called *I'll Take My Stand.* My guess is that this book will invite some comparison with the earlier one. I for one would welcome that comparison, for it is certain to suggest to even the most casual reader the monumental changes in heart and temper, not to mention in politics and society, which have swept the American South from the beginnings of the New Deal to the present.

This book is an act of collaboration among whites and blacks now living and working in the South, writers and editors and politicians and teachers and scholars, who believe passionately in the South and who intend to remain there advancing its most enduring interests, which coincide perhaps more than ever before with the best interests of the rest of the Great Republic. The unifying theme which undergirds this varied collection is that out of a meaningful working partnership between whites and blacks the South stands an exceptionally good chance of solving its old egregious faults and its more contemporary ones, while both preserving the best in its own unique heritage and offering more than a few crucial lessons to other Americans.

Along with their expressions of devotion and loyalty and practicality, I am also happy to see in these pieces, from whites and blacks alike, a certain strain of robust and enlightened Southern orneriness. *You Can't Eat Magnolias* is honestly and quite often penetratingly critical, but it is also imbued with a shared feeling about the South's true and abiding distinctiveness within a mass technological society, and a prideful acknowledgment of the best qualities in its collective past: the indestructible Faulknerian qualities of courage and honor and compassion and sacrifice. At the core of our literature and our thoughts about ourselves has been a perpetual awareness that we are different. From our common inheritance of suffering and anguish we derive some of our deepest strengths. We act from blood and earth and we do not forget; we love the South and we have often despaired of it, and we can never turn our backs upon it.

Robert Penn Warren, in *The Legacy of the Civil War,* wrote that the South used its defeat as the Great Alibi and the North used its victory as the basis for a Treasury of Virtue. In the early 1970s the North faced a dwindling treasury and the South, as this book in part suggests, acted less and less in terms of its alibis. Years of judicial and legal and political pressure from the federal authority and the charged moral energies of its own native reformers, the most dramatic and imposing of whom was a Southern black who grew to maturity in the pulpits and on the campuses of Alabama and Georgia, seemed paradoxically to reach a logical effectiveness in the rather passionless years of a conservative Republican administration. "It was a new ball game as soon as they passed that voting rights bill," Albert Murray, a black writer from Mobile, says in his fascinating book *South to a Very Old Place,* and he quotes Walker Percy: "Changing men's hearts has nothing to do with it. The Negro will vote without difficulty in Mississippi as soon as those who would stop him know they would be put in jail if they try." By no conceivable interpretation is it an accident that eleven of the twelve Southern governors in 1972 were white moderates who largely plead an end to race-mongering and seek to concentrate on some of the problems the region has so long ignored. Under new mandates from the federal courts the states of the old Confederacy have far outstripped the rest of America in the integration of their public schools, and although the segregationist private schools are a continuing financial and perhaps political drain on many communities, an entire new generation of black and white children now eighteen are growing up together and going to school in close proximity. This generation of young Southerners offers one of the enduring hopes of the region. Indeed, from what I have witnessed, I agree with my own elderly grandmother, niece of an early Mississippi governor and daughter of a Confederate major: "*They'll get along fine if older people will just leave them alone.*"

Racism was the primeval obsession. No longer is this so. It will hold out in places, but it will never again shape the white Southern consciousness. For generations immemorial it had misdirected the South from its other elemental problems of poverty and exploitation. This one development could have a profoundly liberating effect; the newer ills facing the region are in many ways a generation or so removed from the ills that beset the rest of the nation. For the South is rapidly becoming an urban society; by 1975 more than half its people will dwell in cities. Reynolds Price, the novelist, writes in this volume:

> *... while neither Atlanta nor New Orleans yet vies seriously with New York, Chicago, Los Angeles as irreclaimable disaster sites, they are trying hard and cheerfully and, given time, may well succeed. Birmingham is nearly as difficult to breathe in as Gary; and dozens of smaller cities—green and clean ten years ago: Raleigh, Richmond, Charleston, Savannah—are imploring not so much their own ruin as*

> *their mortal trivialization, drowning in a sea of carwashes, burgerstands, pennanted gas pumps.... Will the New South prove unrelated to the Old, a petrifying gorgon quite literally?*

That is one of the principal questions raised by this book. What will it take to avoid the pitfalls of the North and create a humane urban civilization out of an agrarian past? In a perceptive essay on page 169, Joel L. Fleishman of Duke University argues that there is still time for the cities of the South, "precious little, but still enough," to prevent the destruction of the land, the decay of the central urban areas, and the flight to the tax-exempt suburbs. "Our cities are still young and pliable.... Because we started later, and because we were poorer than our fellow city-dwellers in the North, we have had neither the time nor the money to immemorialize quite as many of our mistakes as they did." He and other contributors to this book offer concrete proposals seeking to avoid these errors. Curtis Graves, a black legislator from Texas, argues for black-white political coalitions such as have been successful in Houston, and James Clotfelter and William R. Hamilton speak out for the basic economic programs that would appeal to both blacks and poor whites.

It remains for the only non-Southerner among the contributors to speak most eloquently for the kind of salutary example the Southern consciousness might offer our troubled nation. "The history of the South," he writes, "is laced with violence and tragedy. But all America has suffered from the failure to absorb what is best and most liberating in the Southern tradition." The South must

> *not only solve its own problems ... but impart its strengthening values to an America which is confused, divided, and in turmoil. For what America hungers for is not more goods or greater power, but a manner of life, restoration*

> *of the bonds between people that we call community, a philosophy which values the individual rather than his possessions, and a sense of belonging, of shared purpose and enterprise. A South unshackled from distorted memories and present injustices can, more than any other section, open new dimensions in American life, and help shape the American future as it decisively molded the American past.*

It is the effort of this volume to explore some of these new dimensions, for the greater good of the South and the nation.

The southern man

YOU CAN'T EAT MAGNOLIAS

H. Brandt Ayers

[THE compact of isolation between the South and the rest of the nation may not be ratified again. For over a century each has regarded the other suspiciously, agreeing to maintain contact only on the basis of touchy formality. But recent events indicate that the cold Civil War may give way to a period in which South and nation explore each other for the hiding places of lost ideals and manners of life. If the South again moves fully into the commerce of ideas and activities which form American institutions, the experience is likely to prove beneficial in both directions. The Americanization of the South and the Southernization of the nation can be a good bargain if all that is exchanged is what the South knows about the good life for the Yankee's moral impatience and his acquisitive genius.

In many ways the process will help the mass of Southern people on their journey toward material comfort, self-respect, and a touch of joy in their lives. These people, black and white, have come a long way down separate sides of a hard road. They have traveled light out of necessity, carrying only a meager inheritance: gritty patience to bear the hardships and the instinct to listen out for a familiar voice.

Not all heard the same voice, nor did they all hear the same voice in the same way; but, black and white, they listened for the same promise: the gospel of salvation, of escape from something oppressive in their lives and a message of welcome to a place where their worth was recognized. By following demagogues down hell-raising detours the white people of the South have made the journey no easier for themselves. The feeling was good as long as it lasted, but the promise was empty about as often as it was real.

But in the last decade the roads have become easier to travel, and many lead in more promising directions. Now they are river beds built wide to contain the flash flood of rush-hour steel and exhaust: the beltlines, expressways, and interstates. Even the country and state highways are changing. Along the back roads from Atlanta to Alabama the frame shacks are disappearing. In the carports of new brick houses it is possible to see more than one sign of modern affluence: a late-model Pontiac, a boat, or a camper. There is no question about where the road is going nor any mystery about why the people have abandoned their fields to drive on it five days a week. All roads in the South now lead to the city, and, for many, to better jobs.

Measured by the yardstick of the 1970 census the process of transforming the Southern landscape, and with it the Southern man, appears to be going forward rapidly. Much of the change seems to be for the better. The growth of cities means that Southerners are getting more of the profits. There is even reason to hope that in relations between the races the South can expand and enrich the value it has traditionally placed on its sense of community: a caring for place and for the people who live there.

But before the final destination is reached, Southerners must be sure that they have chosen the right road, that they are replacing the old way with something of value.

It is possible that the South will make the right choices, creating a humane urban civilization for the pleasure of its people and as an example for the nation. It is possible that the South can be a full participant, even a leader, in the revival of a happy and useful period of American life. But will the rest of the country listen to what the South has to say? And, for that matter, should it?

[5]

You Can't Eat Magnolias

For well over one hundred years we in the South have managed to hide the elemental virtues of our region from ourselves and from others. A viral weed of mythology has been allowed to grow like kudzu over the South, made up of the oratory at so many Confederate Memorial Days, of so many thousand Confederate flags waved by college undergraduates and borne by high school honor guards, of so many millions of words spilled on the Senate floor in defense of the indefensible.

The average white Southerner does not intend insult by his enjoyment of the symbols of the Confederacy. He feels no shame in showing the flag or singing "Dixie." He sees both flag and "Dixie" as a part of him through the continuum of history and place, and as a tribute to the unvanquished spirit of his own people. "I am a grandchild of a lost war," Katherine Anne Porter has written, "and I have blood-knowledge of what life can be in a defeated country on the bare bones of privation." To all but a few poisoned minds the flag and the song are simply symbols of things which happened to their people along the way. Because they were dramatic and terrible things the symbols state forcefully that "although we have been beaten we will never admit the final defeat, destruction of the human spirit." Such a statement is no more aggressive or hostile in intent than the Black Power salute or "We Shall Overcome." Both sets of symbols speak only of self-respect. Unfortunately, they are not so innocently perceived.

The symbols of the white South have also, moreover, been a barrier to accurate self-perception. Transfixed by the vividness of a violent and painful epoch, the average white Southerner has found it difficult to see beyond the Confederacy. If he could see past it he would similarly revere the symbols of Monticello or the Hermitage—houses built by white Southerners who led the nation—and thus find even better reasons for self-respect.

For in the South we have forgotten that we were Americans before we ever thought to be Southerners. We have not deliberately rejected what is most redemptive in our history; we have been prevented from seeing it by our fixation on the paraphernalia of the

Confederacy and the push-push industrial boosterism of successive New South movements. But if we wish to speak to the nation now, and there is much that is liberating in what we have to say, it is useful for us to remember when we last spoke with authority and what has happened since.

Southerners—Jefferson, Madison, John Marshall—conceived the design of our democracy and found the words to describe it, words we still quote. Up to the time of Lincoln's inauguration the South had dominated the White House, the Congress, the Supreme Court, the cabinet, even American diplomacy. The Jeffersonian tradition encouraged a vigorous and respectable school of antislavery in the South which exposed and attacked the evils of slavery on every level. The slave states contained many more antislavery societies than the free states, furnishing leadership for the Abolitionist movement. But even while a Tennessean, Andrew Jackson, was spreading the participatory power of democracy to average citizens everywhere, the South was beginning to be locked into the paradox from which it is just now showing signs of escaping. From that point until the present, we were never to be thought of first as Americans, but forever apart—usually in a pejorative sense. The Southern estrangement has been often analyzed, and has been traced to many sources. But wherever its source, in morality or economics or politics, it was the region's most durable error. When Southern leaders began to define every issue and eventually our whole way of life with a defense of slavery, we began to go away, retreating behind defensive barricades.

In this one sense the Civil War was a partial victory for the Confederacy. It created something approximating a separate American nation, a satellite following an elliptical path around its parent planet. The South would continue to be held in orbit by America. Intellectual trends originating in other parts of the country, business methods, the federal system of government and the political parties operating under it, all exerted a strong gravitational pull on the South. Geographical proximity ensured that what was happening elsewhere would affect the South, but national standards, instead of being adopted by the South, were absorbed and subtly changed.

Between the Civil War and the turn of the century America was swept by a great burst of material energy which brought it up to the first rank of industrial nations. Reconstruction delayed the process in the South, but in the 1880s the gospel of economic salvation through industry began to be preached by the New South prophets. There was even a tinge of humanism to the movement inspired by Henry Grady and his disciples. "We have planted the schoolhouse on the hilltop and made it free to white and black," said Grady in his famous "New South" oration. The black man, too, was to get a return on his investment through education and participation in the political process.

But things didn't work out so well either for the average white Southerner liberated by Jefferson and Jackson or for the former slaves freed by Lincoln. The "Gallant Cause" had consumed lives, mules, horses, and agricultural machinery in almost equal proportions, leaving a ruined agricultural economy. The crop lien credit system meant that the small farmer usually owed more to the local merchant for his supplies than he could get for his crops. Industrial wages were depressed by the availability of free or nearly free labor under the convict lease system. An Alabama working man in 1880 could labor for an entire month without seeing daylight and make only $8 to $14.

In a rapidly expanding economy wages would have been driven up by competition for the labor of the average Southerner. That was Grady's hope when he issued his invitation to Northern capital at Delmonico's restaurant in New York. "We have wiped out the place where the Mason and Dixon line used to be," he told the New England Society of New York, "and hung out our latchstring to you and yours." Northern capital came, but its mission was not to reconstruct the South by a private-enterprise Marshall Plan. Southern steel prices, for instance, were artificially inflated by Northern owners of Southern mills. They didn't want steel which was cheaper to produce in Birmingham to lower the prices they charged for the same product manufactured in Pittsburgh. Similarly, Northern-owned railroads erected rate barriers which worked against development of the region. The human consequences are expressed by an eloquent set of statistics. The per capita income of the South in 1880 was 49.7 percent below the national average; in 1900 it was 49.8 percent below.

Life, not statistics, teaches a man how to vote. And, for all but a few Southerners, life wasn't good. This was the simple formula for the chemistry of Populism. Populists did not fondle the romantic images of the past. They wanted meat on the table. The only way to get it, they said, was for the people to regain control of the institutions which affected them. Theirs was the language of reform, economics, and self-interest. In the beginning they were not even diverted by the Bourbon Democrats' promise of protection from black domination. Campaigning in the early 1890s for the votes of both races, the Georgia Populist Tom Watson put it this way:

> *You are made to hate each other because upon that hatred is rested the keystone of the arch of financial despotism which enslaves you both. You are deceived and blinded that you may not see how this race antagonism perpetuates a money system which beggars you both.*

The point was—you can't eat magnolias!

Not until the present generation was the South to come so close to making choices that would restore the region to a position of national leadership. Political talk in the Populist era was realistic. Populist rallies exposed the source of legitimate grievances and attacked policies which retarded the development of all, rich and poor, black and white. The politics which prevailed, however, was not the politics of restoration, but of racism. The genteel, landowning Bourbons, under attack in their tax havens, showed they could be as inventive at political corruption as any big city boss, and as virulent in racial rhetoric as any ill-bred twentieth-century demagogue.

[9]

You Can't Eat Magnolias

The electoral process was poisoned by the classical device of stuffing the ballot box. The total vote in some counties the Democrats carried was three and four times the number of eligible males. As important as the direct action taken by Democratic election officials was the way in which the humanism of the New South movement was compromised. Bowing to Bourbon pressure, the New South exponents found it expedient to postpone bringing the black man into full participation until he was ready.

Again, there are eloquent statistics to tell the story. The 1870 New Orleans city directory listed 3,460 Negroes working as carpenters and in other skilled trades. By 1904 less than 10 percent of that number were listed in those categories, though the Negro population had increased by more than 50 percent. By 1902 disfranchisement was virtually completed by state constitutional fiat. Thus postponement of the day when the black man was "ready" for full participation in the Southern enterprise became cancellation of the promise altogether.

The Negro was not segregated from normal society for any crime he committed against it, nor did he get lost out of ignorance. He was made invisible by a deliberate, calculated process of debate and decision in constitutional conventions whose work was ratified by the electorate. But by throwing him over the side, the South did not rid itself of dead weight to lighten its journey. The Negro descended swiftly, disappearing in the political and economic depths—like an anchor.

Putting the black man aside, where he could be forgotten until he was ready, had consequences for the poor white Southerner, too. For take away the rhetoric and what did you have? Pickpocket politics. It is strange logic that proposes to develop a people by anchoring large numbers of them in poverty or subsistence. There are few entrepreneurs either so enlightened or so foolhardy that they would risk their capital building plants and hiring men to manufacture products which an impoverished market cannot afford to buy.

The effect was durable. "It is my conviction," said President

Roosevelt nearly four decades later, "that the South presents right now, in 1938, the nation's number one economic problem." As late as 1959 Southerners who lived in poverty made up 35 percent of the region's population, and, in raw numbers, most were poor *whites*. The income gap between South and nation is narrowing, but it will not close entirely for many more years.

So the white Southerner too was asked to postpone his desires for the ordinary comforts that come with full employment. In return he was given some amazing speeches glorifying the sanctity of white supremacy and reassuring him of his own rank as the preferred among God's creatures. He was shut off from confident, self-respecting contact with the rest of his country. In return he was given the demeaning title "redneck."

The isolation of the South was fixed by 1900, just as the nation's spirit was being happily whetted by the surging reform movement of the Progressive Era. Many of the useful ideas enacted into law at the time were rooted in Southern Populism. The South even led in the adoption of the direct primary, but Southern progressives marched under twin banners: the "New Freedom" of Wilson and the "Bloody Shirt" of Bilbo and Blease. We were denied full credit and participation because we insisted that reform was for whites only. It was part of the schizophrenic struggle to be both white supremacist Southern and progressive American.

Hard-pressed Southern whites found brief solace in Roosevelt. F.D.R. appealed to the same by-passed Southerners whom George Wallace has championed: small farmers, mill workers, mountaineers, all who suffered from their marginal position in the economy and from cultural and political disadvantage. Typical of the response F.D.R. evoked was the reaction of the North Carolina textile worker who sensed an anti–New Deal bias in the questions a reporter was asking him. "What you don't understand," the man said, "is that Roosevelt is the only man we ever had in the White House who would understand that my boss is a son of a bitch." The secret of Roosevelt's success with people who had always tended to approach government on a person-to-person basis was that he regarded the people of the South, not as abstractions, but as friends and neighbors.

The banner of the bloody shirt, which had been flying at half mast, was raised again by Strom Thurmond in 1948 as the threat of tentative civil rights advances became apparent. Thurmond used no code words, gracefully powdered and prettified, to mask what the term "Dixiecrat" meant to him. It was a brazen restatement of the white supremacy theme. It would be repeated again and again for the next two decades by the Faubuses, Barnetts, Claude Kirks, and George Wallaces.

Yet in the dramatic changes overtaking the region now, it is possible to see the destruction of that calculated appeal to the darker mysteries of the mind, that malevolent beckoning to caged instincts which normal men would rather hide from themselves, their wives, and their friends. What is happening is not the creation of a new man. There is no reborn Southerner, no wholly different creature risen out of the skin of his old creed. The Southerner of today is the same man reporter-pollster Sam Lubell has talked to in every election since 1948. "The Southerners whom I've met are decent people," says Lubell, "a lot better than their leaders." The Polish-born New Yorker is on to something important about the Southern man. Racial bigotry is no more the dominant fact of his life than it was in the life of the Irish Catholic construction worker in Queens who in the 1969 New York mayor's race chose the rough, familiar working man's face and language of Mario Procaccino over the stylish liberalism of the handsome incumbent, John Lindsay. Nor can race explain why the single-family farmers and wage-earners of the South followed Jefferson and Jackson or Wilson and F.D.R. It does not account for the grip Huey Long had on Louisiana without resort to the race issue. How does it explain the reelection of Alabama's James E. (Big Jim) Folsom who, in the bad-tempered aftermath of the Dixiecrat movement, delivered a Christmas message to his people in which he declared, "As long as the Negroes are held down by deprivation and lack of opportunity, all the other people will be held down alongside them.

Let's start talking fellowship and brotherly love and doing unto others; and let's do more than talk about it; let's start living it."

To hold that racial animus is the consuming passion of ordinary people is to maintain that life itself is an abstraction, to be experienced on paper, in speeches, books, and committee reports. Only those who have lost contact with ordinary citizens could cling to such a belief. Such a view of man insists that the black welder on the assembly line in Detroit is sustained in his monotonous daily work by anticipation of quitting time when he will be free to get whitey, or that the girl behind the department store counter in Selma secretly plans some atrocity against the niggers on her day off.

Although historical conditions and recent events have put a severe strain on the everyday ethic of life in America, it is still the dominant fact of life in this country. A man wants to buy his own house, to do with as *he* wishes, to furnish so his wife will be proud to invite the preacher to Sunday supper or the parish priest by for a cup of tea. He hopes he can get a little overtime to help with the payments on the new sofa or the draperies or his boat. When prices rise, putting an additional burden on his already heavy payments, he lives in dread of an economic slowdown that will reduce his shift or eliminate it altogether. He also persists in the belief that it is *his* government, too, whether he is black or white. And he demands that his worth be respected. He will, eventually, always return to these habits of thinking and doing.

Human behavior is always contradicting the most confident predictions of the articulate, upper-income segments of American society. At the same time that the intellectual elite decided that George Wallace was a permanent caricature of the average Southerner's preoccupation with racial bigotry, Southerners elected a succession of moderate governors who proclaimed an end to racial discrimination. By 1971 moderate governors ruled eleven of the South's twelve Statehouses.

Light must be poured into the perceptual gaps that made such a development a surprise if we are to understand what is happening in the South in relation to where the nation is and where it wants to go. One barrier to understanding is the different time frame through which different segments of society view the national commitment to civil rights. Professors of constitutional law can trace the inevitable defeat of legal segregation back to 1938 when *Missouri v. Canada* was decided. Journalists normally use 1954, when *Brown v. Board of Education* was delivered, as the yardstick by which to measure progress. Regrettably, the national commitment has been of much shorter duration, dating from about 1963.

The agents of consensus about major change in America are not professors or journalists. They live deep in the Maine woods or on Iowa farms; they work in Massachusetts factories and steer their Chevies and Fords along Los Angeles freeways. Until they move in concert, the Congress and the President are mired in compromises and postponements and nothing very big happens. The agents of consensus moved in 1964 and 1965.

To the mass of white Southerners it all happened very fast. They had been taught that segregation was normal, the way things are, by their leaders in Congress and state capitals and by practice in Sunday school, the classroom, at the movies, on the radio, everywhere. There had been rumors for a long time, but Southerners experienced nothing but the sameness of life as it had always been. Then, suddenly, in massive proportions in every county and small town, change swept over the South.

Social revolution at the cutting edge of change is not a normal environment, one which encourages people to go about their routines, thinking about conventional things as if nothing out of the ordinary is happening. A revolution of that magnitude puts unaccustomed stress on people. They long for peace, to be left alone, for an end to the lash of criticism or, at least, for encouragement. Instead, Southerners found that television provided access to their homes to reporters and politicians who told them they were racist redneck bigots living in a corrupt, racist society. If a man is trying to adapt to a new way of life, or if he has been educated so the new way is almost impossible for him to follow, he won't tolerate talk like that in his house. He will punch the reporter or the politician in the nose. Later, when things have calmed down, he will cool off and regret he swung. George Wallace was that punch in the nose. But it is later now and things have calmed down.

While the South was undergoing its short but elemental struggle with its own conscience the rest of the nation experienced the stunning realization that it had lost its innocence. Non-Southern America had always occupied the favored position of exporter of moral concern. Self-doubt had never inhibited its crusades to save other Americans or the free peoples of the world from foolish and perverse refusal to become cultural replicas of the industrial society. This bright, bully self-image was abrasive, but it had produced some good and had done no great harm. Southerners, too, have fought losing battles with history by trying to prove themselves above the actual human condition. So, many of us watched with a special sense of tragedy as the cocksure Yankee's image of moral superiority perished in the fire-storms of Watts, Chicago, Hough, and Newark, and in what came to be the pointless sacrifice of Vietnam.

But it is later now, North and South, in the cities and on the campuses; the whole temper of national life has calmed down. The events of the past few years have put the country in a reflective mood. There is little evidence that we lost interest in 1971. We are simply approaching our problems in a more deliberate, thoughtful fashion.

The process by which the nation reached this point and the original issues which propelled us, sometimes at dangerous speeds, recall another time in our history. Events and conditions at the start of the decade of the 1970s recall those at the start of the new century in 1900. The similarities encourage cautious optimism that national morale can be restored and usefully channeled in a repetition of the Progressive Era.

Richard Hofstadter, historian of the Progressive movement, described it as "an attempt to develop the moral will, the intellectual insight, and the political and administrative agencies to remedy the accumulated evils and negligences of a period of industrial growth." He added, "Since the Progressives were not revolutionists, it was also an attempt to work out a strategy for orderly social change."

At the end of a thirty-year burst of productive energy the nation in 1900 found itself relatively prosperous, freed from purely material concerns and ready to examine what recent physical changes had done for its citizens. In the 1890s Populist demands for economic and political reform had drawn attention to the human consequences of industrialization. Populism presented much of the agenda for change but could not lead the nation into implementation of its program. The movement was weakened, first, because it drew away from political allies, insisting on going it alone as a third party. Further, its spokesmen clouded the legitimacy of their demands by the apocalyptic militancy of their statements. An example of the ideological overkill which frightened away potential friends was Ignatius Donnelly's novel, *Caesar's Column.* The picture of a continental mass murder of the nation's elite, some perishing in the flames of a huge pyre they had been forced to build, appeared to be purposeless savagery, totally unrelated to the honest plight of the working man, farmer, and tenement dweller.

The agenda was taken up by more respectable forces. The validating authority of many in the intellectual, professional, and opinion-making occupations—professors, lawyers, the clergy, the muckraking press—was drawn into the reform movement. Their presence gave reform such legitimacy that public interest organizations sprang up around every problem needing correction: the National Civil Service League, the Pure Food Association, the Child Labor Committee, and the Consumer's League. By 1895 over seventy organizations were working to improve urban conditions alone.

Real victories, some only temporary but others permanent, grew out of the impressive catalogue of concerns that the surge of reform presented to the nation: power to the people through direct election of United States Senators, the breaking up of the impersonal and oppressive power of monopolies, passage of pure food and drug laws, improvement of conditions in tenements, conservation of natural resources, economic relief for farmers and laborers, and support of the Negro in his struggle for rights and of women seeking the vote.

Today, after another thirty-year leap of technological progress, we are asking similar questions about the condition of our people. The list of concerns is almost identical: the dehumanized corporate state, Congressional and legislative reform, civil rights and ecological movements, wars on poverty, consumerism, urban blight, the drug problem, and, inevitably, Women's Lib.

We find ourselves again in a time of relative prosperity, when we are free to look around and ask, "What has happened? What have we become?" The agenda of negligence was presented first by the civil rights movement. Its tactic was direct action of clarity, related to visible, supportable goals: the right to eat a hot dog in a dime store, seated; the right to register and to vote; the right to get a good education and better jobs. The country understood and responded; the agents of consensus moved.

Eventually the tactic was taken up by young whites whose perceptions had been expanded by education at good colleges and by television. But beginning in the spring and summer of 1965 the clarity began to drain out of the direct action movement. Watts exploded in a confusion of violence that, to mass America, seemed to have no definable origin and no clear objective. And a widening war, hard to understand from the beginning, began to press down on the minds of young Americans with incredible, maddening weight. Even those who thought they knew were not exactly sure what the crowds of students were trying to say when they shouted "Kill the pigs!" from the dean's office or outside the Democratic convention hall. The excesses of our recent past, when we screamed at each other in language meant not to convey meaning but as another form of direct action, have left us with a national hangover.

There are many reasons to believe the decade of the 1970s may be a good moment in our history. Ironically, the war itself may be the best reason. World War I killed the first Progressive movement. But this generation's war is ending. Americans in this decade are likely to be free from the insane distraction of war and the anchor, weighting them down, of economic hard times.

The agenda is still before us, and we are reflecting on it with earnest concentration. Organizations like Nader's Raiders and John Gardner's Common Cause are asserting the right of people to be better served by the huge economic and political institutions which have accumulated irresistible power over their lives. They are not likely to let our attention wander from the page.

In the South, where our energies have been so long caged by the defense of segregation, we are free to become equal partners in seeking a worthy national objective. There is strong evidence to support the South's place in this new reformation. In addition to such old-line human rights organizations as the Southern Regional Council, a new, more broad-based organization is growing. The L.Q.C. Lamar Society is a regional progressive movement in microcosm. Its membership is composed of the same intellectual, professional, and opinion-making elements which legitimized the original Progressive movement. Presidents of great universities, Governors, United States Senators and Representatives, attorneys, professors, newspaper editors and publishers, business leaders, bank presidents, and students—black and white—have come together out of the same instincts which produced the election of a succession of moderate governors. Their mission is not to promote a particular political ideology but to define and seek practical solutions to regional problems too long overlooked.

But, despite all the hopeful signs, no one in the fall of 1971 felt the breeze of forward momentum in his face. There was no sense of good-natured, orderly, and optimistic progress toward attainable goals. America was not yet in the grips of a unifying restoration of the spirit.

To revive a Progressive sense of the possible in our people, we must look to the place from which we draw inspiration, direction, morale, and national purpose—the White House. Whoever occupies the office of the Presidency, from either party, during the 1970s and beyond will not evoke from the country what it is ready to give if his appeal is rooted in the belief that the nation is hurt, angry, or afraid. We appear to be divided and polarized while every organized effort and inarticulate voice—even the political fringes of the Wallace Right and the New Left—seems to be saying the same thing: that we want to regain control of institutions that are not or seem not to be producing the benefits we have a right to expect. The President who leads us into a new Progressive Era must do more listening, more hard and deliberate thinking, so he will understand how things are with the people. Only then can he speak with the clarity that will illuminate the dark misconceptions which make the plurality natural in a large nation seem to be threatening polarity. He must appeal to that plurality in ways that show the healthy interconnection of our interests. This means not only the avoidance of rhetoric which divides different classes and conditions of men, but the avoidance of habits of speech which set geographical regions apart.

The South should be told in no uncertain terms that it is a welcome partner in the national enterprise, not because its people are more virtuous than New Englanders or Californians, but because they are neither better nor worse. The men whose names are now in the news or some man not yet discovered in a national sense must come South and learn our people, white and black, giving them a place equal to that of their neighbors, North and West. The South deserves such a place because its people are trying. True, the white South was so taught that it resisted, flaring against the critics who made change harder to bear, hating the changes at first but trying to learn new people and new ways and, to a greater degree than many thought possible, accepting them. The fact that its schools are more integrated than those of other regions, that its politics is turning from race to reason, may mean no more than the reluctance of its people to relive the ugly, turbulent years just past.

You Can't Eat Magnolias

We have not become overnight a nation of philosopher-kings who have banished meanness from the realm, but neither did we invent that sin. The approach that presidential leadership should take to our people is the same approach it should take to all people. Southerners, black and white, locked together in yet another uniquely Southern experience, should be addressed with the humanity that teaches wise and just men to hate the sin, but love the sinner.

> *I remember watching the Diamond Jubilee procession myself as a small boy. I remember the atmosphere. It was: well, here we are on the top of the world, and we have arrived at this peak to stay there—forever! There is, of course, a thing called history, but history is something unpleasant that happens to other people. We are comfortably outside all that. I am sure, if I had been a small boy in New York in 1897 I should have felt the same. Of course, if I had been a small boy in 1897 in the Southern part of the United States, I should not have felt the same; I should then have known from my parents that history had happened to my people in my part of the world.*
>
> —*Arnold J. Toynbee*

North and South we have now been reduced to the same historical dimension. Vietnam and the nationalization of racial problems have shattered the Yankees' innocent illusions that they have been ordained by God to trample out immorality and that His truth marches with them into every war. They have even discovered that His bounty is not sufficient to feed the incredible hunger of their cities. The South has been closer to the actual human condition, knowing for a long time that anything is possible: defeat in war, calculated injustice, poverty, hunger, disease, suspension of civil rights, even occupation by a victorious army. But the South has not always used well what it has learned. It has had to be reminded that a tragic history does not make it immune to the consequences of complacently perpetuating an unjust way of life.

Now that we are finally equal—only fallible humankind, no better—we can learn from each other if we are wise. There is a duality in the South which the nation could well heed. It is not the warring impulses to be both American and white supremacist Southern: that is dying and good riddance! It is the dual allegiance among Southerners to a spiritual as well as a material god.

We have never worshiped industrial progress exclusively. As each wave of industrial boosterism swept over the South—Gradyism, the Atlanta Spirit, and the Chamber of Commerce Movement—each has been met by an answering tide which emphasized the humane virtues of a leisurely, agrarian manner of life. Sometimes the reverse current has been sustained only by the thin, piping reed of garden guilds and federated women's clubs. Once it was stated so eloquently that it was raised to the level of philosophy.

The agrarian manifesto, *I'll Take My Stand,* was published in 1930 by twelve Southern academicians and writers clustered around Vanderbilt University. It was an outspoken rejection of industrialization and a celebration of the rural life as a means of accumulating wealth, extracting pleasure from life, and nourishing the arts. Some of the questions it asked about where we were being led then have application today. Contemporary city dwellers might agree with a critique of willy-nilly development through which "we receive the illusion of having power over nature, and lose the sense of nature as something mysterious and contingent."

Unfortunately, *I'll Take My Stand* was also chauvinistic, elitist, and unrealistic. The Agrarians' uncritical devotion to the agrarian ethic doomed their argument. We were asked to believe that the agrarian way of life would nourish the arts in the South. The scrabbling existence of South Georgia tenant farmers provided neither the leisure nor the spacious means to organize a symphony or a ballet company. The Agrarians' other visions were equally ludicrous. It is hard to imagine how subsistence farming could eliminate poverty and two other rural Southern blossoms, pellagra and hookworm. How much damage would have been done the national dialogue if we had not had such pastoral creations as Bilbo, Blease, and George Wallace?

The gift the Agrarians had to give did not interest the real people whose life and death were measured only by so many seasons trying to coax cotton from fields of dead clay, the men, women, and ragged children who, from Vanderbilt, were perceived romantically as the virtuous yeomanry. Their sons aren't interested either. They feel no regret at leaving those fields to drive on good roads to city jobs and back to their new brick houses before dark. They were following the hard-driving Yankee dream that says self-respect cannot be had without enough material comfort to rise above subsistence. The Yankee dollars which built the new houses along the road have validated the worth of that philosophy for an increasing number of Southerners.

But some of what the Agrarians had to say lingers, a permanent sediment on the Southern consciousness which may, if anything can, redeem our cities and offer some hope to city dwellers elsewhere.

Urbanization in the South is inevitable, but the duality of the Southern consciousness, fed by both the desire for material comfort and the spiritual outrage of the Agrarians, may be at least a partially saving grace. That hope was implicit in a recent long-distance call between two Southerners, both born in small towns. A freezing snow was falling outside as one, the vice provost for urban studies at Yale University, picked up the phone in his New Haven office. At the other end of the line, a small Alabama city, the temperature was 68.

The two men were discussing plans for a symposium in the South on an urban topic. When the Alabamian admitted the comedy of a small-town boy's having anything to say on such a subject, the urban affairs authority answered evenly, "You know more about the good life than we do." He is right.

There is room for the accidental in a small town. People meet casually at the bank, the supermarket, the PTA, the churches, schools, and parks. Out of these unplanned encounters grows a feeling of community, of people sharing trivial news about people they know, of common interest in each other and in the place where they live. They are rooted in that place and touched by it, and they are therefore caring.

Nothing seems too large, distant, or foreboding, not even government. Their legislators and city councilmen are known, visible, and approachable. All the business they have with government can be accomplished easily at the courthouse and city hall, across the street. Many can walk out of their houses and, in five minutes, be in a stretch of silent pine woods. All can drive downtown to the movies with relative ease.

These easy graces of the small-town South could be partially recreated in large Southern urban centers. It is possible to design new towns and humanize a few major cities for the pleasure and convenience of people by breaking them down into small-town districts. Such a design would cluster parks, schools, housing, and commercial, financial, and amusement centers in such a way as to create unified communities, each of which would elect its congressman, state legislators, and city councilmen.

We can decide to do these things in the South, or, aping the Northern model, we can abandon our cities to development by random fits of the real estate economy. We can have government that is distant; we can wall up our people away from each other in high-rise filing cabinets built on top of the last green living spaces.

The concrete desolation of such cities pushed those who could afford the journey on a great crabgrass stampede to the suburbs where they hoped to recapture the good life. That the stampede hasn't worked is now plain to many. Family and community are in one place and the urgencies of occupation are in another; between lies the centrifuge of the commuter train or the fuming rapids of steel we euphemistically call expressways. Having attempted to plant new roots, many suburbanites find their lives to be totally rootless, without a sense of belonging anywhere. Behind them they have left a city starved by the exodus of taxes to Scarsdale and Cannondale, a dying shell populated by armies of hostile strangers. Yet it is much easier to make similar cities in the South. We can have them by doing absolutely nothing.

It will take a heroic act of will to create a humane urban civilization in the South. It will not be the meek who inherit Southern land before it is bulldozed and buried under miles of concrete. It will take mean and protracted political battles in city councils and state legislatures. It will take taxes and new instruments of government to apply human intelligence to the process of creating cities designed not exclusively for profit but for people. It will also mean that the white South must learn to regard the black man not as someone to be despised or feared and run away from. Both blacks and whites—viewing each other with almost immutable suspicion at the end of a history of hating and loving, of atrocities committed and borne—must learn to see each other differently. We must recover our sense of humor and recall that we are both members of an imperfect tribe. Together, we must restore and enrich the traditional ways that we have valued because they improved contact among people, the Southern virtues of community, neighborliness, and courtesy.

Is the dream big enough? Is it big enough for the young who reject both the obsessive materialism of the Yankee way and the lilac-scented artificiality of the jejune brand of Southern courtesy? The dream is not big enough for the tough, cold-eyed young who want the instant, cathartic consensus of revolution. So be it, for there is no humanity to redemption through blood and fury.

The vision may be big enough to attract the susceptible young who yearn not for the barricades but for gentler, softer, more enduring ways of improving commerce among people. It may recapture those vulnerable youths who flee the warring tribes of adults, searching for a true sense of community and family in communes, just as their mothers and fathers did when they fled to the suburbs.

Sir Kenneth Clark eloquently stated the essence of a humane

civilization when he said, "I believe in courtesy, the ritual by which we avoid hurting other people's feelings by satisfying our own egos. . . . I am sure that human sympathy is more valuable than ideology." If the South has something to give which the nation seems momentarily to have lost, it is these simple virtues: a manner of life which stresses courtesy, neighborliness, and community over the ruthless competition of the lonely crowd.

It is not unrealistic to catch a lively sense of the possible from the new mood now running at tidal proportions through the mind of the South. We may be entering a postracial era in which the nation can find hope and an example. But Fate is no special friend of the South. Our final destination will not be reached by the friendly intervention of any omnipotent and unseen force; what we become will be directed by the hard, deliberate choices we make. As Toynbee observed, history has happened to our people in our part of the world. Only from that longer perspective will it be known whether or not the South invested the conscience, commitment and effort that can yield a humane society.

MY GRANDFATHER AND THE CYCLONE

Reese Cleghorn

[My Grandfather Reese would have been a hundred years old. He died, still ruddy-faced and pridefully careful about his splash of white Edwardian mustache, less than four months short of the mark. Some of us thought he did not really want to make it; if he did, there would be a commotion. And he had seen enough. When he was born, it took three days to get from Boston to New York, traveling fast, because the transportation on that route was the same kind Nebuchadnezzar had used. In his youth people lit lamp wicks for light, as the Druids had lit torches made of faggots. Water was drawn from wells about the same way the Assyrians had drawn it. Only one lengthy life span earlier, there had been no United States of America.

He was born near Madison, Georgia, on February 16, 1867. Not so long before, Madison had been a wilderness. A man named Booth Fitzpatrick, hunting game in 1795, had crossed the shoals near where the Apalachee River flows into the Oconee and admired the rich flatland beyond. The next day he brought his brothers back with him. They were the first whites to settle. By 1807 there were enough settlers to form a separate county, and so they split off a part of Baldwin County and called it Morgan. Lands acquired from the Indians by treaty were distributed by lotteries to the new settlers, and the town of Madison, named for our fourth President, sprang up on the site of Round Bowl Spring.

Madison was different from the start. It seemed eager not to be a frontier. It wanted grace, The Virginians came in, some of them in wagon trains loaded with well-packed English china and Napoleon beds. And then there were new people from those coastal enclaves of culture and Old World manners, Charleston and Savannah. By 1815 people were building handsome mansions in and around Madison, from timbers cut and fitted at Augusta and hauled inland by oxcart. Out in the South's hinterlands at about the same time, farmers were putting up crude box houses as they cleared their first land. As years passed they would add rooms and façades, and finally, triumphant, they would erect the columns that announced they had ceased to be frontiersmen and had become gentlemen. But Madison's houses were intact from the start, models of Georgian or colonial beauty, furnished not with frontiersmen's pine and oak but with rich mahoganies from France.

The stage line helped make the difference, and later the railroad. (The first locomotive to reach the crossroads that was to become Atlanta, hauled overland to be put on the new Western and Atlantic tracks running to Chattanooga, came from the tracks that ended in Madison.) Early in the 1800s *White's Statistics* called Madison the "most aristocratic and cultured town on the stagecoach route from Charleston to New Orleans." If you traveled from New York to New Orleans, or, later, from Savannah toward Chattanooga, you went through Madison. Money came in, and a combination of Mr. Whitney's cotton gin and slavery made the lands nearby heavy with the currency called cotton. Shortly there were three colleges. And there was music. In the 1830s Madison had its own opera house. My great aunt, the most regal woman I ever knew, and a spirited *femme* who believed no woman should demean herself by voting, had been young in Madison in the 1880s and she liked to recall the older ladies playing their guitars made of rosewood and adorned with mother-of-pearl. (Only a few years ago, moments before her death, her mind left us and went back to those days, and we heard her say something about "the musicale." We listened in wonder then as she softly spoke of some remembered performance that had brought friends to a drawing room. She was hearing again the music that had gone with the wind.)

When our country was on the verge of civil war, people in Madison, like those all over the South, were divided about what to do. That turned out to be fortunate. One of the most outspoken opponents of secession was a famous son of Madison, Joshua Hill. When the Confederacy finally was collapsing and Sherman was scorching the earth of Georgia, federal forces under General Slocum approached Madison and were met by three emissaries from the town. They wanted to surrender Madison and ask that it not be burned, they said, and they wanted to remind the general that this was the home of Colonel Joshua Hill. Most of the town was spared.

My grandfather arrived shortly after that, a war baby, born two years after his father had returned from history's bloodiest conflict up to that time, a war in which my grandfather's uncles had been killed. Madison was foundering. There was no money. Big plantations were broken up and commerce was shattered. After a time this family moved off the farm and into town, and its home place was sold for some trifling sum, $1,200, I believe. But Madison was to have another day: after its postwar disasters and the depressions of the seventies and eighties, King Cotton got on his feet. The town began to prosper again. By 1900 Morgan County had 15,000 people and, by 1920, 20,143. Then, at the peak of this new prosperity, the boll weevil came, like the immutable hand of some angry Jehovah, and stayed to devastate the cotton fields of Middle Georgia. The great droughts in the mid-1920s did the rest. By 1930 Morgan County was Depression-poor again, and its population was down to 2,488, with more people leaving. The nearby towns that had been little way stations in a cotton empire began to dry up. In the 1930s the stores were closing in Bostwick, Swords, Buckhead, Apalachee, and Godfrey, most of them not to reopen.

You Can't Eat Magnolias

You may drive through that country now and see rolling green fields much prettier than the cotton fields ever were. That is so because in the thirties the tractors came and made dairy pastures, and farming became neater and more predictable. The fields that had been left rutted, down to red clay and bedrock, had gained new life with the new Roosevelt. We recognize now, of course, the bitter residue of the New Deal's agricultural programs, as they were manipulated in the South to make the land a middle-class property, sending millions of the poor and black into the cities. But the plow-under programs, with bonuses for people who would lime the old cotton fields and turn them into pasture, did make the land live again. In truth, these federal intrusions made Madison itself live again.

Nevertheless, the world my grandfather had been born into was dead, for he was a man of that older century, though born just this side of The War. Cotton might revive, for a time, but all that was associated with it before was gone, never to return. Like so many others of his time, he was an awkwardly transitional man. The stuff of his childhood—the spirit, the fondnesses, the values, the allusions, the stories picked up from his elders in a time when everyone talked, perhaps even the cape jasmine smells and the surrey sounds, and surely most important the pace and tone of an older South—all this stayed with him and kept emerging, though it was strange to most of those around him. He was a son of privilege born after the privilege was gone. The wealth of an older Madison that had its armoires sent from France and its unalloyed silver from Liverpool was never there for him, though a few of the physical remnants were. His own grandfather had gone from Madison to Yale and then on to study law under John Randolph in Virginia, and his aunts, like many other Southern girls before there were many schools in the South, had been sent to the old Connecticut College for Women. But when he came along, there was nothing. So he went to what in those poor times in Madison was called a school, an institution grandly styled "Colonel Butler's Academy for Young Men," but in truth it was not much of a school. (If you were black, you had not even that.)

If you were white, you learned what you could at home and you listened to somebody talk about law and absorbed a little. You might read the books of the old household libraries and Henry Grady's *Atlanta Constitution* (and, later, Tom Watson's magazine); many people simply read the Congressional Record, which could be had free. And the lack of further education notwithstanding, you did not feel deprived or inferior, ever. If you were a young man always surrounded by men in law and politics, you developed a titillating, vital, escapist, useful, consuming interest in politics, and forever retold the anecdotes of big Bob Toombs, "Little Alec" Stephens, and others of Georgia's Confederate pantheon, already being canonized.

I can hear him now telling how Little Alec, whom he recalled seeing, had quieted a hostile crowd by coolly taking two little black derringers from his pockets and placing them on the podium, and I can hear him laughing irreverently about some grand insult one politician had hurled at another in a race everyone now has forgotten. No wonder that generation was so creative with invective and so awesomely disastrous with government and compromise. No wonder my great-uncle, another son of Madison, an editor and a printed-word stylist of the first chop, had to be rescued more than once from duels of his own hasty making.

Shortly, there was a great impatience with all this. After all, the old world was gone, wasn't it? It should be put in a pretty package, with Robert E. Lee romance as the ribbon and a latter-day, magnolia-blossom fantasy as the wrapping paper to cover the awful truth, and put aside, perhaps to be identified with, somehow, but not to be allowed to get in the way. The youth of the early part of this century, the up-and-coming youth, was born of the modern world, and it was not thinking planter or hillsman or cropper or Southern iconoclast: it was the wave of the future, and it already was thinking middle-class in a country rapidly becoming middle-class. It said, by implication, that it had had enough of this backwash of the older South and the poverty that went with what was left of it. It said business is king, and, for the first time, the old ways of that South of lazy afternoons, front-porch talk, and casual community came to seem backward and old-fashioned, or just inept. And all that was right, surely. What lingered from the old world seemed to lack a sense of schedule and accounting. If you were to be in business, you couldn't be getting so personal about everything; you certainly could not be doing anything that would cut into the profits because, you know, "you've got to make a living." It was, of course, mainly the worst part of that older South that lived on: the awful hangover that emerged as modern racism to continue to warp the South and, finally, the whole country. But the better part began to die in the crudities of thought that came with the march of new-rich tradesmen's values into a frontier and plantation land. Go now into Madison and into the other small towns all over the South and you will see that while many of those crudities have now been polished, the Yankees did, in fact, win: not the Northerners, generally, but the Yankee traders. Efficiency came after The War, efficiency and schedule and accounting. That was what finally turned Southerners into Americans.

Most Southerners. But my grandfather never got reconstructed. Please make no mistake: he was not one of those "unreconstructed rebels" who kept refighting and rearguing The War. It seems important that I cannot recall hearing a word from him about the legal correctness of the right to secede, the propriety of Jefferson Davis's position as opposed to Abraham Lincoln's in regard to the exchange of prisoners, the infamy of Thaddeus Stevens, or the treachery of General Ben Butler. I heard words about these matters of state from others, but I think I never heard it from my grandfather because, actually, he preceded most of that. All that talk, full-blown, I mean. It was the next generation down, the one that came along in the 1890s and the early 1900s, that went heavy on such Southern apologetics: the whole apparatus of theoretical defense of the Old South and the Confederacy, a complete litany that we were learning in youth as late as the

1940s, and which was explained as "the truth you can't get in the textbooks because they are published in the North." No, my grandfather didn't seem to need all that. Heavy doses of Southern apologetics came back into style only when there was clear reason again to feel guilty, at the time when Negroes once more were forcibly put down and back, through disfranchisement and the formalization of white supremacy about the turn of the century. That reversion to the South of slavery necessitated defensiveness. It gave birth to elaborate and extraordinary theorems and legal distortions, all designed to justify the new suppression and to prove that it was the *white* South that was being mistreated. It all became obsessive, almost paranoiac. (We hear the strange echoes of it still.)

My grandfather was unreconstructed not because he clung to some sort of fierce and destructive animosity but because he never did become modern man, though the old South he was born in died and the new South became a land of modern men. He must have thought they were all frightfully serious, and though he maintained a posture of courteous respectfulness toward all who were busy achieving around him, he made no move to join them. I cannot imagine him serving with zest as president of a civic club, though his sons did. Nor can I see him organizing either a fund drive or a sales campaign or going to a convention. (I can't imagine that anybody in his right mind would ask him to do any of those, either.)

There was something about people of his generation that seemed to defy the neat compartments we feel compelled to put everyone in. Our obituaries, for instance: name, age, place of residence, business and professional positions, schools attended, civic and church positions held, fraternal organizations. Any awards? Key man in other civic endeavors? What about fraternal associations? He could be forced into the first four of those on the forms, but none of the rest. Those other categories are, for us, the Achievers. Take the blank space for schools attended. He studied at home? What do you mean studied with his grandfather? And it would not sound good if you really answered the one about fraternal associations. You can't just say, "None, but all his life he was strong on goodtime friends and cronies." Civic and church positions held? Well, I know he was privately pious, with simplicity and strength in his faith and I have seen him on his knees by his bed after he was in his eighties; and I could not forget how his parting advice to me invariably went word for word, over a span of twenty years: "Remember to trust in the Lord, write to your mother, and vote the Democratic ticket." But I am sure he was never a deacon or the head of a church building drive. And certainly that mischievous soul was never touched by pietistic admonitions against John Barleycorn and poker playing. Though I did not know him to overindulge, I am sure he had decided on his own behavior before anyone had ever discerned the inherent evil in the fermentation of a grape. His generation looked upon that process with kindlier eye than did the next; and I do not wonder that many of them overdid it, being intensely social creatures who liked to talk and visit, and living, as they did, through the disintegration of the only world that they could be at home in.

Cut back like a dying bush, fading, discolored, that old world lingered in little bits and pieces in certain spots all over the South for a long time. It did in Madison. (Bits of it are there even now, for the old ladies of Madison self-consciously keep stirring and preserving the fallen leaves and still live out the past that others have forgotten.) But my grandfather left that world physically, if never spiritually, in 1891. A young man had nothing to stay for. So he took his delicately pretty wife, who had grown up in a wonderful house already old then but standing even now on the main street of Madison, and moved westward to Rome, Georgia, population 2,500. People in Madison said they had gone "out West." And it was true that Rome was frontier country. But it had a river to keep it in touch. Its streets had been made of cobblestones brought up the Coosa as ballast (and sometimes the Coosa itself invaded the main streets, in times of high water before the levees, so that once a riverboat had steamed up Broad Street, passing, in full glory, the stores it supplied). In 1891 Rome was on the rise, and Madison on the decline. In fact, Rome was where Madison had been seventy years earlier: it was a city with a future, on the edge of rough country still being developed. Georgia had moved on. This was a better place for a young man. So the young man stayed, for seventy-five years.

The telephone, the telegraph, the electric light, the airplane, radio, television, Charles Darwin, Karl Marx, Sigmund Freud, P. T. Barnum, Henry Ford, Bismarck, Queen Victoria, the first explorations of the Arctic and Antarctic and some parts of Africa and the Pacific, Grover Cleveland, Teddy Roosevelt, Woodrow Wilson, the vacuum tube, Joseph Stalin, Adolf Hitler, nuclear energy, Martin Luther King, Jr., a social revolution, travel into space: they made their mark on the world during this one lifetime. For tens of thousands of years the speed of man's progress had increased relatively little. (It had taken four centuries for the art of pottery-making to travel a hundred miles in Europe.) But all of a sudden, within this hundred years, the pace had quickened more in the realms of science and technology, not to mention the speed of social change, than in all the one million years of human life that had gone before. We grow up seeing this speed and expecting more of it, and so we are seldom surprised. Our world was never static, and the basic conditions of rapid change were obvious all about us the first time we looked. But this was not so when my grandfather's century of life began. Men and women could look around and most of what they saw and did was the same as men and women had seen and done for centuries. Then, suddenly, history turned into a cyclone.

The South has not escaped the cyclone. Cash was right, of course, in finding some continuity of the Old South's ugliness in the new, and we still find it; but even that artificial entity we call "the South" so that we may better define ourselves could hardly fail to blow with winds that whip a whole world. More than porch talk and verandas are gone, and the South no more knows where it is headed than a child going to school at Hiroshima on the day of the poisonous mushroom. Our consciousness is troubled, or, if not, we are even deeper in trouble than others; and our transitional time, already well under way when my grandfather was spending hours in his last days searching the "personals" of his newspaper for signs of friends, makes us people who cannot know, as people used to think they knew. We cannot even know whether the South is, ultimately, of any significance. We can only *think* we know it is, and that its very change, animated by some of the best of its past, will make it so.

Well, my grandfather, as I knew him during only the smaller part of that long life, did not concoct ratiocinations and help design new breastworks for continuing the battles; did not, in fact, struggle at all with the change. Confronting the twentieth century, the gentry of the South, it is said, held on grimly, retreating a little when it had to, but getting off a few more rounds from behind each rock. As for the yeomanry (somehow it is always just the poor *whites* the writers have in mind when they use that word), it is said to have continued to "stand to its captain" and to fight alongside him all the way, to its own loss. Those are useful words, "gentry" and "yeomanry," but they have been *too* useful in forging our New-Southerner thinking about what has gone before.

I don't know whether my grandfather was gentry or yeomanry; in fact, he was some of both. There was his boyhood on a farm which Middle Georgia townspeople, perhaps pretentiously, liked to call a "plantation." There were early years as a merchant, at a time when some old-time Southerners still scorned that calling, and years during his eighties when he was a United States commissioner, holding the preliminary hearings for federal courts in North Georgia. Just as he did not fit into the neat categories of modern obituaries, neither did he fit into neat categories of "gentry" and "yeomanry," with those words' special meanings to the definers of history. What I saw in him in this bizarre twentieth century was not the gentry's determination to get off another round against change or the yeomanry's loyalty to the leader. Rather, it was a kind of special grace in accepting, and an ultimate humaneness. Of course, there were those who saw him as too soft. Even so, no one could dismiss him as a charming and mindless old fellow; there was too much spleen and not a little subtle cunning, used, almost always, to improve his relations with somebody. It was a loving cunning.

If there is a South in the future, and if there is a civilization, it may be because we got soft enough and subtle enough and loving cunning enough to make do during the cyclone. Who knows whether the South has some special gift for the nation, a hand-me-down from a gentry or a yeomanry? If it has, the Lord again was working to confound the prognosticators of Southern history, for we have seen it best personified publicly not in a descendant of one of that white gentry or yeomanry we hear about, or in some wielder of established temporal powers, but in an unexpected Martin Luther King, with his capacity to combine passion for justice with a loving cunning that made some people call him soft. *There* was a subtle Southerner, one who acted out on the public stage some of the virtues that the better part of the past South honored privately. If the South now has something extraordinarily good to offer the world, that must be it, and that must be all. "Tell I tried to love somebody." Words from the Black Emancipator of enslaved Southern white folk.

Here, though, I celebrate a much simpler expression of the virtue of loving cunning, observed in a man whose life spanned the first cyclonic century. He clearly could be faulted, if we want to be flint-eyed analytical about it, for not helping much to right the major wrongs that existed all around him. But he was on another frequency. What I finally will remember best about him, and with most awe, is that he made it through with such easy grace. All the world may change, but the human spirit in its best forms endures much the same always. I think if he had been taken to some inhabitable planet in a far constellation at the age of twenty and there had found human beings to live with, he would have been very much the same as he was here in our strange world, though I doubt that I would be. He wouldn't have fought with life, or conquered it or turned away from it; he would have softly turned with it as if possessed of an Eastern wisdom, emerging victorious through nonstruggle. On that planet, after all, the familiar touchstones of his childhood would have been not much further removed than they were in the Georgia of the mid-twentieth century. He would have charmed all the ladies on the front porches there, attended all the funerals, and raised hell if any of the boys spilled beer on the poker cards and made them too soft to back-shuffle. In the end he would have been as unaffected by that planet's harsher and stranger ways as he was, in truth, by the more invidious aspects of what was going on around him in our own brave new world of strivers, achievers, competers, sales pace-setters, and hungerers-after-identity. He never did understand all that stuff of the modern South, or even pay much attention to it. I think it was because, all along, he knew who he was.

Will we learn from the likes of him? If we do, we will be rejecting just enough of the twentieth century to learn to covet, even as it was about to evaporate like mist on the meadow, the South's own special residue of personalism and its lonely communion with sin and defeat. Of course, the juggernaut of modernity will continue to move on, and Southerners will be an urban people, no longer frontier folk of the land. Perhaps they then will cease to be Southerners in any but the geographical sense; no longer the leading ethnics—native ethnics—of America. If so, we, black and white together, will have accepted a cultural genocide. But, on the other hand, we could resist. We have had ample experience at that, resisting the wrong things, to be sure. The Vanderbilt Agrarians wanted to resist the twentieth century, perhaps even the nineteenth. They were like England's Luddites of the 1830s, who broke into mills to beat the power looms with sledge hammers while shouting, "Death to the machines." A law-and-order Parliament then made it a felony to hit a machine, and the march of industrialization and mechanization continued. So will our own march of urbanization and the technology of cybernetics and automation, with all their impersonal aspects. We can't stop that with sledge hammers and slogans, and, anyway, not many people would want to give up the benefits.

The task, of course, is somehow to keep it human. Sledge hammers will not help much with that, although if we do not change we may see violent rebellions by affluent urban dwellers in the future very much like the rebellions of blacks in the urban ghettos in the mid-1960s: wildfire revolts against inhuman conditions. Rather than sledge hammers, some recapturing of an old, soft wisdom can serve us best: what was good in the South of my grandfather, which helped make him as he was, and which he conveyed as if with secret signals to those around him. He even seemed to calm the cyclone.

BEYOND THE BRIAR PATCH

Curtis M. Graves

[FORTY years ago, twelve Southerners published a volume of essays entitled *I'll Take My Stand.* The essays included a piece by Robert Penn Warren called "The Briar Patch," concerning the place of the black man in the South of the 1930s.

Things have changed a lot since then. For one thing, it's clear now that the agrarian setting in which the Fugitives wrote has changed drastically, and that these days not only the black man, but the white man as well, must define his identity by reference to some other system. For another, *this* essay is by a black man writing about the future of his brothers. Few blacks would have been credited with the intelligence to do that forty years ago—indeed, few blacks would have had the education necessary to articulate what they felt.

And yet, at the same time, a lot of things are much the same as when Warren wrote his essay. The black man is still the object of social, economic, and political exploitation and discrimination. And "Separate But Equal," Warren's ideological stance in "The Briar Patch," dies hard as a rallying cry for conservatives in many parts of the deep South. So we cannot begin to be complacent about the progress that we've made—but neither can we overlook our great strides forward since the agrarian heyday.

There are really only two alternatives open to the Southern black in the seventies: he can go North, or he can stay put and fight the battle on his home ground. When the Southern black goes North, he thinks that he is leaving for the Promised Land. When he arrives, he finds the situation worse than in the Southern communities which he has fled. The jobs he thinks are readily available are nowhere to be found; the money needed to go to the places he can't go to in the South isn't there; the education he thinks he is providing for his children by moving is, in many cases, just as bad as Southern education, because he is forced to move into ghetto areas. He thinks that Northern whites will be waiting with open arms, encouraging him to join their country clubs, move into their neighborhoods, be friends with them; instead he finds the same kind of discrimination and mistrust he thought he'd left behind. But it isn't obvious and open; it is subtle, subdued. So blacks have started coming home again.

The second alternative, staying put, is the one we're working on now. Staying put, however, means first of all coming to terms with ourselves. In recent years, we've made a lot of progress in that way, too.

We spent the decade of the sixties developing a sense of community among ourselves. One expression of it was the development of black-owned and -operated business enterprises, designed to serve the black community's needs. On the negative side, however, was the obvious fact that we didn't navigate in the mainstream. We were never able to deal in banks or higher finances, establish industries, or construct large buildings. But this isolation gave us a great feeling of closeness, a sense of brotherhood; we even refer to each other as brother and sister. Similarly, the attitude of separateness has come to make Southern black men more aggressive and positive individuals. It is not strange, then, that most of the outspoken and outstanding blacks have come from the South.

These outstanding people have come not only from the South, but more specifically from middle-class black families, the segment of American society which sociologist E. Franklin Frazier refers to as the "black bourgeoise." Dr. Frazier saw these people as escapists or, to use the vernacular, "honorary white-folks." I suppose in the main he was right, because most of them considered themselves superior to their hungry brothers, and therefore developed into a new breed of "house niggers." They found themselves in limbo between the whites who rejected them and the black have-nots whom they would not accept.

Ironic as it may seem, the freedom fighters and leaders—the Martin Luther Kings, Whitney Youngs, Thurgood Marshalls, and Julian Bonds—all came from that same middle ground. They were compassionate enough to tie themselves to their impoverished brothers yet articulate enough to communicate their problems to white America.

After the Meredith march, the black sense of community strengthened into a black sense of power. *Black Power*—these two words have caused more unity on one side and more confusion and polarization on the other than any other two words I can think of in American history. When Stokely Carmichael uttered them he was not talking about looting and burning and chaos; he was referring to the numerical power blacks have in the South. In many places blacks constitute more than 50 percent of the population in the political subdivisions, but they have little political, economic, or social power to show for it. If 45 percent of the population of, say, New Orleans, is black, then blacks should be represented in approximately that proportion in city halls, parish boards, and courts, and also among the district's representatives in state government and in Congress.

And, indeed, blacks are finally beginning to reap the benefits of the power inherent in our numerical strength. The election of Charles Evers as Mayor of the little city of Fayette, Mississippi, is not just an isolated case of a black taking control of a black city; it is also one step up the long ladder of blacks taking political control of the districts where they numerically predominate. If blacks can be politicized to the point where they can file as candidates for public offices, they can, where the numerical advantage exists, elect their people.

Beyond the Briar Patch

In Atlanta, blacks have been elected to eleven state offices: they have elected a Vice-Mayor, two members of the city council, school board members, and other city officials. For the first time blacks are realizing that they are in the numerical majority in political subdivisions and as such should take control politically. I suspect that within the next ten years Atlanta, Houston, New Orleans, Jackson, Montgomery, and Tallahassee—to mention only a few of the larger cities—will be controlled by black people.

It's true, then, that we can have, and have had, a certain degree of success in electing blacks to political office. But there's another thing that hasn't changed much since the thirties. Our real potential strength lies in coalition politics. Forty years ago Robert Penn Warren wrote, "The fates of the 'poor white' and the Negro are linked in a single tether." It was an abstraction then; today it's an irrefutable reality, and an imperative to action as well. And today, for the first time since Reconstruction, real, viable coalitions between progressive whites and Southern blacks are being formed all across the South—coalitions like the one in Houston, which is comprised of the community of organized labor, the Council of Black Organizations, the Mexican-American community (represented by the Political Organization of Spanish-Speaking People), and the liberal Democratic groups. In 1966, they merged forces and nominated slates of candidates from different legislative, congressional, and senatorial districts. Because of the efforts of this coalition, I was elected. Without the consensus of all these groups, it would have been virtually impossible for the coalition to work. But our slate won, and the history of politics in Houston, Harris County, was changed by that victory.

Comparable coalitions are forming in many major cities throughout the South. These coalitions are extraordinarily significant because of the positive and constructive action emanating from them. For the first time, whites and blacks in the South are working together in mutual trust. Realizing that things in the South are not as they should be for either blacks or whites, the two groups are beginning to talk over their common problems; they are joining forces to see that a better South is created. For the first time, businesses owned jointly by blacks and whites are springing up all across the South. Rather than functioning as "front men" or in menial positions, blacks are being accepted by the white-collar business community, working with whites in trust and confidence, to the benefit of everybody concerned.

These social, financial, and political coalitions are the harbingers of the new South, the forerunners of what is to come in the very near future. The history of the South has been unfortunate, but right now the tide is turning—new ideas and new concepts are being tried, people are finally realizing that the Civil War is over and dead, and that the funeral has lasted too long. As a result, we've already begun the process of building the kind of South that all of us want to have in the future.

The Southern white man is beginning to understand that the politics of bigotry cannot be a politics of progress. He is beginning to understand that as long as politicians are elected on the basis of promises to keep the races apart, then his economy, industry, education, and total life style remain in a rut. There are even Southern white men who are growing in the belief that perhaps they can be better represented politically by blacks than by whites. This is not the pipe dream of a black politician, but a growing reality across the region.

In New Orleans, a significant coalition of whites and blacks joined for the first time to elect a black man, a former civil rights attorney, to a major district court judgeship. Because of his prominence in the community, and because he stood firm on just causes for blacks and whites, leaders from nearly every political subdivision supported him for the judgeship. The net result was overwhelming victory over two white opponents.

In the wake of the 1968 Democratic convention, another interesting coalition was formed in Texas. Texas delegates who had gone to Chicago as McCarthy Democrats came back and decided to establish a liberal wing of the state Democratic party. They organized themselves into what eventually became the New Democratic Coalition of Texas. Its unique structure is significant in the development of coalition politics. Individual caucuses representing factions of blacks, whites, Chicanos, and young people convene. Each caucus elects three representatives to serve on an executive committee. The executive committee then elects a chairman for the entire organization. All four groups have equal representation, so young people have equal voice with the other caucuses. Blacks are franchised because they aren't given second or third place as a token "to show good faith." This is the kind of participatory democracy that's coming out of the South. The new coalition front in the South is not necessarily liberal or conservative, not necessarily right or wrong, not necessarily black or white or brown. Political ideology has been superseded by a more general concern with getting the South out of the rut that it's in, upgrading the entire region, and, above all, helping people.

As one of three black people elected to the Texas State Legislature in 1966—the first black state officials in Texas since Reconstruction—I think I have a unique insight into the specific problems of blacks in Texas and the South, plus a unique awareness of what white Southerners are all about. This experience has given me a raw, undiluted impression of what the average Southern white man is made of, and from that I believe I can ascertain some possible solutions and directions for the problems that besiege the South at this point in history. I have learned that the white man's oft and loudly professed assertion of the supremacy of his race is only a cover-up, not only for guilt but for fear. As a white friend once said: "The average white man thinks to himself, 'What we did was monstrous, but it's nothing compared to what the black man will do to us if we ever let him get up and gain power.' " Our biggest problem today, our mutual problem, is to replace the centuries of hatred and suspicion with a new era of respect and trust. The burden, unfair as it may seem, is largely on us. We must teach the white man that there is no reason to fear us —that no one could be better trusted with power than we who have felt the punishing blows of its misuse. We must forget our anger and bitterness and reach out with our humanity and intelligence. Given that people are basically more forgiving than vindictive, and more concerned with the future than with the past, it is still possible for the South to become the model for a sane and human relationship between the races.

The crucial thing that has happened over the last forty years is a transition from abstract speculation to concrete implementation. We can no longer afford the luxury of quibbling over the definition of "equality." We have long since learned that "separate but equal" is a self-contradiction. Equality—meaning "same"—has become a given in the new problem we're working on: the problem of implementing it.

We can see this change reflected in many ways, even in the way people *talk* about problems. In "The Briar Patch," Robert Penn Warren comments, "With the accelerated process of Negro education a question will certainly be asked again. For what is the Negro to be educated?" The implication is that different categories of people are peculiarly and naturally suited to different types of work. Traditionally, it was thought that the Negro should be limited to the artisan trades, equipped for survival by what his hands, rather than his mind, could produce. Today, the very phrasing of the question is obsolete. We would no more think of asking "For what is the Negro to be educated?" than "For what are people more than six feet tall, or people with naturally curly hair, or people from Rolling Fork, Mississippi, to be educated?" The question today is, "For what are *people* to be educated?" Our economy has changed, and therefore, so have our jobs. But the answer, in the words of Booker T. Washington, is the same as ever: "I am constantly trying to impress upon . . . our people throughout the country . . . that any man, regardless of color, will be recognized and rewarded just in proportion as he learns to do something well." The only difference today is that it's a different thing we, blacks *and* whites, must learn to do well.

Someone once said that a chain is only as strong as its weakest link. As blacks in the South are educated, the quality of life for *all* Southerners is enhanced, and the entire chain is strengthened. The South at this point in history has a definite advantage because it can look at Northern examples and see the mistakes that have been made; it can look at overcrowded conditions in the cities; it can look at the pollution problem; it can look at the total destruction of property which has resulted from riots—it can look at all the things that have happened in other parts of this country and benefit from others' mistakes. The people of the South are now standing at the crossroads where we can move into the mainstream and gain access to the political and economic opportunities which we deserve.

Sure, George Wallace was reelected Governor of Alabama; sure, Preston Smith, a West Texas movie operator, was reelected Governor of Texas; but also more than two hundred blacks now hold public office in the South. In 1965 that number was less than twenty. The South is on its way. We are now in a position to move out of the ideological backwoods and into the mainstream of national life. This must happen, and will happen, if we set our minds to it with the same degree of fervor that we used to perpetuate the racial illusions of the past.

The southerni- zation of the nation

THE SOUTHERN CONSCIOUSNESS: A SOURCE FOR NATIONAL RENEWAL

Ronald S. Borod
and
W. J. Michael Cody

[THE South is under siege. There are forces at work in the land which are threatening it with extinction. This, of course, is nothing new. The South has felt embattled since before the Civil War, and Southern history is marked with numerous attempts to stave off alien forces, real or imagined. Agrarianism and white supremacy could be looked upon as two such attempts, although the former was too visionary and the latter too morally corrupt to be successful. But despite the failures of the agrarians and the segregationists to preserve their respective versions of the Southern Way of Life, there has remained an abiding faith among most Southerners that there is something about the South which is permanent. With landmarks of the old South crumbling all around them in astonishingly rapid succession, Southern people, as well as many students of the South, have nevertheless remained confident that there are some qualities about the South which are immune from outside forces. In an essay first published in 1958, C. Vann Woodward suggested that it was the South's history which would provide its continuity. Out of their collective past, he wrote, with its military defeat, economic want, and direct confrontation with a great and intractable social evil, the Southern people had forged an historical consciousness which had set them off from other Americans, and which would enable them to resist the powerful conformist tendencies of national life. The poet-novelist, James Dickey, had something similar in mind when he referred to "something important and mysterious that passes between the generations [of Southerners], a kind of thread of continuity."

But despite these intimations of immortality, there are recent signs that the South is in real danger of losing its identity. This time the danger is all the more insidious because it is the Southern consciousness itself, which for so long has been thought to be the South's one indestructible link with its own past, which is being threatened. If present trends continue, it will soon be meaningless to speak of "the South" in any sense but the geographic one.

Many, of course, would rejoice at this prospect, seeing in it the end of sectional divisions which have plagued our country throughout its history. But if the Southern consciousness were allowed to expire, much would be lost, both to the South and to the rest of the nation. The historical position of the South never evolved beyond the negative one of resistance to national trends. In its protest, however, the South was responding, perhaps unknowingly, to a complex but strangely unified set of values, biases, and historical premises fundamentally different from those of the rest of America. The Southern people have historically placed more faith in the simple amenities of social living, such as friendship, civility, and common courtesy, than in the abstract principles of "progress" and "success." The opposition to industrialism, which has consumed so much of Southern thought over the past century, is a reflection of a deep appreciation of human values and a perception of the dehumanizing influence of industry and technology. Although many Southern proponents of agrarianism suffered no lack of material goods themselves, they understood, as few others did, the debilitating effect of materialism on the human spirit. The South's resistance to racial change was morally indefensible; but there was some truth to the repeated claim of Southerners that they were possessed of insights into the race problem which "outsiders" could not comprehend. The South, unlike the North, had lived with racial injustice for all its history, and it alone was capable of seeing the race problem in other than abstract terms. Southerners had lived for over a century in the abiding presence of a great social evil; and even if they were not willing to admit it was an evil, they did acquire an intimate knowledge of human imperfectibility which made them skeptical of the naïve American belief that every evil has a cure.

Both of these themes—the reverence for human values and the belief in the imperfectibility of man—are deeply embedded in the Southern consciousness; and the tension between them has produced a profound ambivalence throughout Southern history. It was the reverence for human values, and the fear that they would be smothered by the onslaught of industrialism, which led the agrarians to take their futile stand for a subsistence agricultural economy in the South. And the belief in the imperfectibility of man supported and reinforced the segregationists in their ardent but morally untenable struggle against the Northern solution to the race problem. In each instance, questions were being raised about American society which were not only valid but also crucial to its future vitality; but in each instance the questions were raised in ways which rendered them unfit for Northern consumption.

The agrarians were attempting to warn their fellow citizens of the dehumanizing tendencies of industrialism; but in their belief that man's humanity could be preserved simply by keeping him down on the farm they were guilty of the same facile thinking which characterized the rest of America. And the segregationists were uttering an important truth when they said that "laws cannot change men's hearts"; but in being faithful to one Southern theme they totally abandoned the other, which valued man's humanity as the most cherished of his possessions.

Southern humanism was not allowed to become a viable national force because of its identification with utopian visions of an agricultural nation, and Southern skepticism was denied Northern acceptance because it was identified with the South's inhumane racism. It is one of the central ironies of American history that the Southern themes of humanism and skepticism, which could have provided important counterweights to the American themes of materialism and moral innocence, instead became a source of the South's alienation from the rest of the country.

THE PRICE OF MODERATION

Long before the time of the agrarians, Southerners were raising doubts about Northern industrialism. It was largely unnoticed at the time, and it is largely forgotten today, that many Southern intellectuals before and immediately after the Civil War were not only defending the institution of slavery, they were also asking some searching questions about the economic system of the North. Because their racial position was so untenable, however, it was assumed that their critique of the North was infected with a similar degree of moral obtuseness.

Toward the end of Reconstruction a fateful bargain was struck between the South and the North. In return for the tacit promise of the North to let the South handle its race problems in its "own way," many Southerners began to shed their fears of Northern industrialism. Henry Grady and his New South group energetically set about remaking the Southern economy in the Northern image, and, in the words of Henry Nash Smith, "The ideas of most articulate Southerners became indistinguishable from those of official Republican spokesmen." It has been for others than ourselves to show the brutal impact of this bargain on the Southern black, but equally brutal in its end result was the fact that many eloquent critics of the dehumanizing excesses of industrialism were coaxed into silence.

Of course, the South continued well into the following century as a symbol for preindustrial values. But while Herman Melville was using a Southern narrator to decry mill owners who destroy children for the sake of profits and to warn of a "civic barbarism" with "man disennobled—brutalized/By popular science," the effects of this bargain were causing a subtle but real erosion in the Southern consciousness. By 1930, the agrarians were bemoaning the fact that the South was becoming an undistinguished replica of the industrialized North, and increasing numbers of Southerners were absorbed in pursuit of the American standard of living.

Just as preoccupation with race initiated this trend, so it hastened its culmination in the 1950s and 1960s. This time, however, a new type of Southerner was added to the cast of characters—the Southern liberal. In many ways, the strident and often violent resistance to racial integration which during that period riveted so much of the nation's attention on the South was a mere distraction from another more significant development that was taking place simultaneously. While the confrontations in Montgomery, Birmingham, and Selma were stealing national headlines, an informal but powerful alliance was being forged between Southern businessmen and those who were genuinely shamed by the violent resistance of their fellow Southerners to racial integration.

On the one hand, there were Southerners who had formed a sincere commitment to equal rights for Negroes, and who began to look upon industry as a possible cure for the South's racial illness. Broadening the economic base of the South would, after all, mean more jobs for Southern blacks. Moreover, it was believed that the more the South became economically integrated with the rest of the country, the easier its racial transitions would become. On the other hand, there were Southerners who felt no moral commitment to the civil rights movement, and who in fact were not sympathetic toward it, but who also were practical enough to see that some progress for Negroes would have to be tolerated for the sake of economic growth in the South. Tax incentives and bond issues were not always adequate to lure national industries; sometimes at least a patina of racial respectability was required.

The short-range achievements of this coalition were obviously beneficial. Overt appeal to racial bias is no longer the assured route to political power in the South that it used to be, and the rhetoric of even the worst Southern demagogues has become more civilized. Moreover, no one can dispute the benefits of cross-fertilization between the South and the rest of America which has accompanied the South's industrial growth.

But these improvements were purchased for a price. Asphalt and instant food franchises soon covered the Southern landscape, and the chamber of commerce became the spokesman for the new New South. Even more important was what was happening to the Southern consciousness. Human values were forced to take a back seat to the mandates of business and technology, and even some of the old Southern skepticism was giving way to the belief that all the South's racial problems would be solved through economic growth. Although it was an isolated instance, the reaction of the Mayor of Memphis to the efforts of a group of citizens trying to prevent the construction of an expressway through the city's only wilderness park speaks eloquently of the change that has come over the mind of the South. "The road must be built," he said. "We are doing everything we know how to keep from budging from our position of building the road where the engineers say to build it." It is irony of a most tragic kind to hear the Mayor of a large Southern city, who prides himself in his allegiance to traditional Southern values, repudiate in those two sentences much that was redemptive about the Southern past.

Some have suggested that the humanizing influences of the Southern consciousness were so closely intertwined with its racial prejudices that moderating the evil of one would mean losing the good of the other. But we question whether racial moderation had to be purchased at such a price.

THE SOUTHERNIZATION OF AMERICA

While Northern industries were expanding below the Mason-Dixon line, there was an equally important movement in the opposite direction—the mass exodus of Southern Negroes to the big cities of the North, the East, and the West. Just as the black man had played a major role in the history of the South, so did he begin to play a major role in the great urban centers of America. Again, a trend that was begun much earlier culminated in the 1960s. Thrown into crowded and unlivable slums in the decaying inner cities, and cut off from the Southern soil which had formerly sustained him, it was not long before the urban black began to lash out at his grim surroundings the only way he knew—by trying to destroy it. The Watts riots in the summer of 1965, followed by riots in Chicago the following summer, and culminating in the riots in Newark and Detroit in the summer of 1967, brought a wave of fear and resentment over the entire nation. Up to that time, the Negro had been primarily the problem of the South alone; race had not, generally speaking, been thought of as a national problem. These three summers suddenly thrust the "white man's burden" upon the shoulders of all Americans; and the racial tolerance of the nation as a whole did not prove to be as durable as many had thought or hoped.

The politicians were, characteristically, among the first to perceive this. Richard Nixon's "Southern strategy" is more than an attempt to carry the states of the old Confederacy. It is instead an acknowledgment of the fact that recent upheavals have reduced the political preoccupation of all Americans to a common denominator. And the success of George Wallace's march northward in the past two Presidential campaigns bears grotesque witness to Lincoln's prediction over a century before that the nation "will become all one thing, or all the other."

As preoccupation with race weakened the South's resistance to the dehumanizing influences of the North, so the North's uncritical worship of industry and technology rendered it ineffective in averting a racial crisis of grave proportions. The institutionalized brutality of life in its teeming ghettoes is in many ways more oppressive than the overt racism of a "Bull" Connor or a Leander Perez. And the political institutions of urban America have grown so unresponsive that men of good will of both races have thus far been powerless to bring relief. In their eager pursuit of the American Dream, Americans have created a society which Charles Reich likens to an autonomous machine, "ordered, legalistic, rational, yet utterly out of human control and indifferent to human values." In the short span of one decade, Americans have been rudely divested of their belief that there is an easy cure for every evil. In losing their innocence, they have also come close to losing their humanity; and if this were not a sufficient threat to the nation's equilibrium, America has experienced its first military defeat, in a war which proves that moral crusades—when pursued with uncritical devotion to our own mythology—can have unintended and even tragic consequences.

It is another of those many ironies of American history that the South, with its heritage of humanism and skepticism which could be a source of renewal and salvation for the whole nation during these times of national travail, is instead on the verge of forsaking its heritage in its blind conformity to national norms. This need not be so. The unhurried approach to life, the sense of place, the intense feeling of community, the profound sense of the absurd, all attributes of the Southern consciousness, could do much to redeem a torn nation. Despite many failures, and despite the current period of retrenchment, the South is making rapid strides toward racial reconciliation. The migration of the race problem into the Northern provinces has, perhaps indefinitely, removed a chief cause of Southern isolation. The South is now in a position to speak to the rest of America, and to be heard. Its voice should be neither one of reaction nor one of complacency; it still has much to learn from the rest of the nation as well as much to teach. But it is uniquely equipped by its own historical experience to show the rest of America that greatness depends not on the Gross National Product but on fidelity to human values, and that goodness comes not from winning every moral struggle but from knowing the permanence of evil and striving nevertheless to transcend it.

THE END OF RECONSTRUCTION

Richard N. Goodwin

[ALTHOUGH I have traveled through the South in two presidential campaigns and have worked with Southerners throughout my political career, I am not a particular student of, nor expert on, that section of the country. Yet as a native New Englander I feel a certain familiarity when I am in the South. It is almost as if New England and the South are the only parts of America with a history—where the roots of culture and tradition strike deep into our country's past. They yield a sense of continuity, places where the generations are born, remain, and die, in the midst of the frantic, rootless motion that characterizes so much of American life. This sense of place, of belonging, is, I am convinced, why so much of the best in American culture—from Jefferson of Virginia to Faulkner of Mississippi—has flowered on Southern soil. The history of the South is laced with violence and tragedy. But all America has suffered from the failure to absorb what is best and most liberating in the Southern tradition.

My mission is not to convert but to discover, not to teach but to search—to see if one can glimpse the expanding self-confidence and strength which will permit the South not only to solve its own problems, but to impart its strengthening values to an America which is confused, divided, and in turmoil. For what America hungers for is not more goods or greater power, but a manner of life, restoration of the bonds between people that we call community, a philosophy which values the individual rather than his possessions, and a sense of belonging, of shared purpose and enterprise. A South unshackled from distorted memories and present injustices can, more than any other section, open new dimensions in American life and help shape the American future as it decisively molded the American past.

However, I do not want to ask for unity and reconciliation, but to call for resistance and rebellion—not to evoke the sweet illusion of comradeship but to submit the need for determined and unremitting hostility against the ancient and continuing conspiracy of Northern interest and a small band of Southerners which has been designed to retard the growth of the South, divide it from the rest of the country, and deny its people their full share of American abundance. Only when that conspiracy is exposed and broken will the period of Reconstruction be ended.

Let me try and explain by briefly sketching a very complicated history. The principal issue of our first century as a nation was the struggle to establish a territorial union. This was not just a Southern issue. In 1814, for example, the New England states called a conference at Hartford to consider secession. And when South Carolina nullified a federal law, it was Andrew Jackson who said South Carolina could do whatever it wanted, but he would personally see that the first person who broke the law would be hanged from the highest limb of the tallest tree. And he meant it. How fortunate for George Wallace and Claude Kirk that the tradition of Tennessee does not still occupy the White House.

Finally, after a hundred years, the issue of territorial union was sealed in blood.

The principal task then was to rebuild Southern society and reincorporate it in the newly emerging industrial society. Without reviewing the endless mythology of Reconstruction there is clear evidence that—despite injustice and corruption—progress was made.

Then, in 1876, the crippling compact was made. In the disputed election of that year, a few Southern leaders agreed to support the Republican candidate—the representative of what we now call the robber barons—in return for a promise that the North would remain indifferent to any enforcement of the rights of black men. It is only after this date that the blanket of segregation descended on the South. It is a date commonly referred to as the end of Reconstruction, but it really meant that the South was never to be reconstructed. Its people and economy were to languish in the backwaters of American progress.

The result of this compact is that by the time of the New Deal the entire South was an underdeveloped country. President Roosevelt proclaimed that the South was "the nation's No. 1 economic problem." With a third of the people the South received less than a fifth of the national income. In 1938, a presidential investigation reported that two million Southerners were infected by malaria each year, and pellagra was a Southern epidemic. More than 70 percent of all low-income families—and that meant most families, black and white—could not buy enough to eat.

The advent of the New Deal illuminated the Southern reality. Southerners had been allowed to maintain their way of life, to keep the black man in bondage, as long as most of them also shared the enslavement of material deprivation. They could do what they wanted with their share of America as long as they did not ask for a share of the profits.

The result of this new Southern awareness was the growth of a powerful, indigenous Populism ranging from Huey Long—the true prophet of the New Left—to men like Lister Hill, Hugo Black, and Walter George. For a brief moment, it seemed as if Reconstruction would be renewed and completed, that the South would share in the creation and blessings of the American dream.

Tragically, however, in the 1950s, men from North and South began to renew the old oppressive compact and for the old oppressive reasons. Progress under Roosevelt had taken the edge off Southern poverty; and the immense black migration to Northern cities had focused national attention on racial injustice and compelled Northern leaders to take a strong stand. Demagogues, opportunists, and those of a more calculating malevolence saw their chance and took it: the appeal to racial passions would be a springboard to political power and a shield for the dominant economic interests. It would divert the demands of the Southern white away from higher wages and better education toward protection from the aspirations of the black man.

Meanwhile, the racial problem had moved North. And events were quick to demonstrate that no section of the country had a monopoly on racial hostilities or a capacity for injustice.

Since 1950, in less than two decades, America's black urban population has increased by more than seven million, more than the total immigration by any other single ethnic group—German, Italian, or Irish—in the entire history of the country. No longer could Northerners indulge in pious proclamations at the expense of the South, or deal with racial problems by passing laws designed to eliminate formal legal barriers. Poverty and the ghettos would not yield to so simple and painless a technique.

I do not underestimate the real and powerful nature of racial feelings. They have scarred our course since the first slave landed at Jamestown. Nor can I retreat from the belief that any action or relationship between men that does not involve full recognition of our common humanity is unjust in American terms and a wrong committed before God. It is part of our tragedy that men, North and South, are so fragile they must reinforce their own worth by degrading all that lies outside. Racism, then, is terror—not of black, but of one's own existence. It can only be overcome by widening the community. It can only be dissolved in an America more confident of itself, its power, and its future. In that sense the black future is tied to the welfare of the rest of us. Meanwhile, with all their scars and burdens, one must also envy the black man who has a cause, definable adversaries and a growing brotherhood of comrades, and the chance to make a clear moral commitment.

The fact that racial feelings are real and powerful, that they are rooted in social tradition and the deepest mysteries of the mind, does not mean we must yield to exploitation. It only makes the job harder. And the first step is to understand clearly what is happening. Not only is the old, oppressive compact being renewed in the South; there is now an effort to extend it across the country. The *status quo* is to be protected, the rich and powerful secured, by persuading people to forego their just demands and disregard their real needs in the name of a common front against the black man.

It may very well be that Southern poverty resulted from the exploitation and neglect of the North. But it would not have been possible without powerful Southern allies. And the same thing is true today.

For the harsh fact of the matter is that the Southern white man has less opportunity to develop his talents, earn a decent income, participate in the national affluence, and develop the full resources of his humanity than his fellow citizens in any other section of the United States. Of the ten states with the lowest per capita income in the country, nine are Southern states. The median family income for the entire South is $6,700, about $2,000 less than the family income in every other section of the country. Because their income is at the bottom of the scale, so are the resources devoted to education; the Southern pupil, black and white, has less spent on his education than his counterparts in the rest of the country. And as for poverty, there is not only more of it in the South, but there are 50 percent more poor white families than poor black families. And the median income of the poor white family in the South is actually 20 percent less than that of the poor black.

Why is this? Is it because Southerners are less enterprising or unskilled or intelligent than other Americans? To ask the question reveals its absurdities.

The South is the birthplace of liberal democracy. Southern giants such as Thomas Jefferson and Patrick Henry established the standards of freedom and the value of education which still guide us. From Tennessee came the Jacksonian Democracy which re-created the nation. It was a Virginian, John Marshall, who gave life to the Constitution and established the principle of judicial review to safeguard our liberties. The essential technology for mass production was invented in the South. More of our greatest writers have come from the South than from any other section. And if any should doubt the stamina and bravery of the South, the military history of this country gives ample and conclusive refutation. If capacity and potential were the only issue, the South would be leading the nation, not lagging behind.

The answer is that the huge skill and vitality of the South have been imprisoned in a web of illusion. Make no mistake: a so-called "Southern strategy" is not simply in opposition to the blacks, but to the legitimate and just demands of the entire South. Those who oppose school integration also oppose every measure to give a decent education to white children. Those who identify poverty programs with race, and oppose them, are also stripping millions of white families of the opportunity to learn skills and get a job. Those who are offering the hand of friendship to the South are supporting economic policies which are depressing the economy, reducing real income, and which strike hardest at the middle class and the small businessman.

Take high interest rates, for example. They do not damage the Chase Manhattan Bank which collects them. They do not harm the corporate giants who can finance operations and expansions from earnings. They hardly touch the very wealthy who can deduct the interest payments from their taxes. Rather, they strike directly at every consumer who must pay exorbitant rates of interest on payments for his house, his car, and his television set. And they can cripple the small businessman who now finds it difficult or extravagantly expensive to borrow the capital he needs.

Stripped of the rhetoric, the hypocrisy and flattery, this is what the South is being told: Give up your desire for rapid economic development, the dream of a decent education for every child, forget about the poor, the sick without medical care and the elderly; have your representatives in Congress vote against every measure which might benefit the people of the South at the expense of the leaders of finance and industry—few of whom are in the South. And in return we will go slow in enforcing the rights of the black man, and we will make some wonderful speeches attacking the very establishment whose treasuries we are filling. What a wonderful deal—for someone, but not for the South, and not for the great majority of the American people.

Let me be clear that this accusation is nothing so trivial as a partisan attack. It is true that such a policy has not been sanctioned in the highest reaches of the Nixon administration. But now, and over the years, it has required cooperative effort by men of both parties.

Even in its newest form it had its beginning in the closing years of the last Democratic administration. And it was Woodrow Wilson who resegregated the government cafeterias in order to win Southern support. In both parties there are enlightened men more concerned with improving the welfare of the people than with deceiving them to act against their own interest. And one also must have a sort of perverse admiration for officials who loudly enact in the brightest sunlight a policy which, by conventional moral standards, should be pursued in crowded woods in the depths of a starless night.

In fact this policy has nothing to do with politics at all. Politics is only an instrument for imposing it. It is, rather, an alliance of interests—of those who seek to safeguard, enhance, and not to share their own position of economic power. And you can be sure that every time a Southern senator votes against tax reform or measures to improve medical care or education there is far more reason for expressions of satisfaction in the plush clubrooms of distant Northern cities than in Memphis or Atlanta or Jackson. And what contempt must lie behind the superficial flattery and the obvious attentions to think that an entire section of the country can be persuaded to give up its hopes for the future and its right to an equal share of the present in return for slogans, a few appointments to high office, and the illusion that the black man can be permanently suppressed.

It is especially tragic that division should be widened at a time when America urgently needs the best in the Southern tradition. Let me explain why I think so.

As I traveled across the country in the campaign of 1968 one could sense what is now obvious to all who follow events: something was wrong. There was restless uneasiness, a discontent—not just among the poor or the blacks or the young—but suffusing the American middle class: those who had made it and were members of the Affluent Society. I saw workers in Indiana who voted for Robert Kennedy and then for George Wallace, suburbanites in Oregon who supported McCarthy and Wallace. That was my first clue that the trouble lay deeper than ideology or race. For what these men had in common was not policy or conviction, but they all seemed to stand a little outside the system, a little apart from conventional politics. This confirmed what I had first sensed in New Hampshire. For President Johnson was not defeated there because of the war. Had that been the only issue, McCarthy would have received 20 percent of the vote. The amazing fact is that the solid, cautious, moderate citizens of New Hampshire were voting against the leadership of America and the entire course of American life. They didn't quite know what it was or why, but they did not like what was happening in their country.

Ever since then I have been trying to understand the source of the public unhappiness. At the moment I can do no more than hint at a few of the ideas.

The Civil War brought the triumph of the industrial society over the agrarian dream. With the New Deal came the belief that rising wealth more fairly distributed was the key to the good life. That belief is now fading. For despite our enormous growth—despite the wealth, the power, the invention—our society is diminishing human freedom.

By freedom I do not mean legal rights and constitutional guarantees, but freedom in its largest and truest sense—the liberation and enrichment of the human spirit, the uncaging of human possibilities, the development of man's capacity to realize his full humanity. That freedom requires that men be able to live in sustaining contact with the natural world, and in the intimacy of community with his fellow men. It requires that he be able to use his inward powers to work, to play, to engage his sense in a way which yields him satisfaction as well as money or position. It is what Thomas Jefferson summed up in the phrase "pursuit of happiness." And later Walt Whitman elaborated, "I say democracy is of use only that it may pass on and come to its flower and fruits in manners, in the highest form of interaction between men and their beliefs." In this sense, the true human sense, we middle-class Americans are less free than our ancestors of fifty years ago.

The twin causes of our dwindling freedom are the oppressiveness of our world and our powerlessness to change it. Modern man is confined and often crippled by the world he lives in. A city dweller, he is cut off from sustaining contact with nature. It is almost impossible for the individual to escape the vast and frenzied throng of strangers, stripping him at once of isolation and a place in the community. The dissolution of family and neighborhood and community deprive him of those worlds within a world where he once could find a liberating sense of importance and shared enterprise as well as the security of friends. His job often yields merely income or status, rather than the satisfaction that comes from the fullest use of his talents and he would be in a small minority if he believed that his work makes an improving difference in the lives of others. His children go to schools which stifle imagination and creativity, and then to universities which are designed to provide, for all but a handful, nothing more than a set of irrelevant credentials to an occupation which could have better been mastered through actual work or apprenticeship.

And as we look about us we ask: Who decided that men should live this way? There seems to be no answer. Our cities grow, factories are built and inventions proclaimed, all powered by forces few can understand and no one seems able to control. Decisions affecting the quality of life, and even the prospects for life itself, are made by remote officials in distant places. And, more terrifyingly, no decision seems even to be made at all.

This mounting sense of powerlessness is transforming every aspect of American life. It is this that the young are protesting and it is the moving force behind black power. We must also be aware that when people lose confidence in their ability to shape the future, they also become fearful of the present. Their impulse is to protect what they have to, to hold on, and to defend. When men are insecure and fearful, then every threat to security becomes a monster.

There is no room here to discuss the manifold causes of this condition. Yet I believe that despite the adversities of the South and the wrongs of which the South can justly be accused, there are powerful elements of Southern life which can serve to liberate the entire nation. There is a sense that life is more than the accumulation of material goods; a belief in the individual, not as a solitary wanderer, but as a person whose place among his fellows is to be secured and respected; and, above all, a fierce desire that people be able to shape their own destiny in their own way. The incredible weight of race—the fruits of America's original sin—has blurred these virtues. But I believe they are there, and I know the country needs them.

Thus if Southerners work to liberate the South from the cant and demagoguery and hypocrisy which have imprisoned their energies for so many years, they will not only serve the people of the South, but they will enrich and even save the Union. Again, Walt Whitman, writing of America, said: "The Northern ice and rain that began me nourish me to the end, but the hot sun of the South is to fully ripen my songs."

I cannot tell Southerners how to accomplish their objectives. I have no Southern strategy of my own. I believe the truth is on the side of the South, and the truth is a powerful weapon. But weapons don't win battles. Men win battles. That means the South must organize, set forth its goals clearly and without equivocation, raise money and men to carry the message to the people—not to the enlightened but to those who are still acquiescent victims of the old conspiracy.

The End of Reconstruction

I leave the Southern tactics to the South. But I do know that the North, Northerners, and even Northern political leaders, have often accepted all the stereotypes and fictions. They are unaware of the new forces and of the vast potential for populist change. They rarely come to the South, and, when they do, they often do not know how to communicate. Not only does this deprive Southerners of valuable allies, but this same ignorance pervades the mass media which reach from New York into every Southern home.

And if I may be partisan for a moment, Southerners must work to persuade Democrats not to "write off" the South, as they are on the edge of doing. That will mean another one-party system—only this time with a party which I believe is destined to be a conservative minority. Only in a highly competitive political system does the opportunity arise to challenge accepted views and to demonstrate the popular strength of new ideas.

Can the South succeed? Or rather, can we succeed? For the land Southerners inhabit is mine as well as theirs and has been from the moment I was born an American. I am not sure. But I believe we can.

Finally, there are only two kinds of politics—the politics of fear and the politics of trust. One says: You are encircled by monstrous dangers; give us power over your freedom and your future so we may protect you. The other says: The world is a baffling and perilous place, but it can be made to yield. . . .

It is the second, the politics of trust, that strikes the deepest response in men. However, they must be able to see and understand the choice. That is our responsibility—those of us who have been privileged in background and education, endowed with sympathy, gifted with a passion that molds all change. If we can show—in terms which are clear and which spring not from abstract sentiment, but from the specific and concrete demands of daily life for a man and his family—if we can show there is a course to liberation, then I believe most men will take that course. And not only in the South, but everywhere.

I base this hope not on philosophy but on experience and observation. I am a politician and in 1968 I traveled across this country working in the primary campaigns of Eugene McCarthy and Robert Kennedy. Everywhere I went there was the sense I have described of discontent and frustration, a desire for individual assertion and community power. Whenever people had a real choice they voted for the forces of liberation. They supported those who attacked the war, the militarization of our foreign policy, and the immorality of poverty and racial injustice.

I believe they form a potential majority for fundamental change. For 1968, with all its sorrows and failures, was finally a voyage of rediscovery, a journey to the springs of American hope. We did not find it in Washington or in the pages of learned journals. Rather, it was waiting for us in Nashua and Concord and Manchester; in Madison and Racine and Eau Claire; in Oregon and California: the people of this country—decent, sure of instinct, desirous of peace, grateful for honesty, willing to face obstacles and willing also to strive against them—the repository of our strength, the source of our faith, the fiber of our will and high expectations.

Who will change America? Given a chance, the people will change America. Certainly, nothing else can.

Southern culture

DODO, PHOENIX, OR TOUGH OLD COCK?

Reynolds Price

[WHITHER the Southern novel? Anyone who has lived and tried to write fiction within the bounds of the old Confederacy in the last ten years has heard that question, and been asked to answer it, only slightly less often than "Whither race?" No one imagines that the first question is more urgent than the second—though even in the deepest South there are sane men who suspect the two questions to be intimately and secretly related, perhaps symbiotic—and few serious novelists have the time or need to answer such idle, hilariously unanswerable questions as the first (knowing, like artists in any art, that *the novel* has never existed, only *novels,* and that Southern novels will proceed, if at all, not by anyone's diagram or battle plan—there are whole careers, whole magazines devoted to making nothing else—but as they always have: by miracle). By the unpredictable, so far unmanageable but apparently not accidental births of babies who will in their teens and twenties—because of the specific weight of their experience upon certain cerebral and coronary tendencies (genetic? or even more directly God-given?)—begin to produce long works of narrative prose fiction. Any plans or diagnoses which advance beyond that bed-rock, however sane and studious the planner, are no more than sibylline mutterings-amongst-the-offal (or self-justifications, screwings-up of courage or face: *whither me?* or *whence my silence?*)

You Can't Eat Magnolias

So—my own answer (or a sketch for this week's answer), my own justification, quick calisthenics as I poise at the brink of a sixth book of fiction (Southern: by a Southerner; set in the South and *about* the South, among other places). But first a little brush-clearing to state at least an intelligent question. I've suggested that there never was a Southern novel (though there are already sober-looking guides to The Novel in North Carolina or Mississippi or Georgia). I'll go further—there was never a flood of good novels out of the South, though there was and still is a thick torrent of prose fiction, no better than most—and my question will be something like this: will strong fiction (attentive, passionately perceived, freshly and honestly built, useful beyond the Mason-Dixon) continue to trickle out of a geographical region defined as the old Confederacy, a country larger than France? If so, will it come from natives and long-term inhabitants or, indiscriminately, from writers who, in an increasingly mobile population, happen to pause there?

First answer: why wouldn't it?

Two strong reasons maybe: (1) that the Old South is used-up, worked-out, as a vein for novelists and (2) that the New South will prove unworkable, not a vein at all but a Medusa.

To consider the question of exhaustion—and for a change, from the point of view of a novelist, not a reader or a literary journalist: I've never heard a Southern novelist, good or bad, speak more than momentarily about the South-as-exhausted-vein. (I've spoken of it momentarily myself, usually after a bout of reading journalists on the subject, journalists who assume that because *they* are exhausted, with a quantity of reading, which they have after all volunteered to do, therefore the South is—or the Midwest or urban Jewry or, tomorrow, the black ghetto.) But I do hear the lament from everyone but writers—"Oh, you're a Southern novelist. How brave!" (and, *aside,* "How sad! how touching!"). But then how brave to have been a painter in fifteenth-century Rome, a composer in nineteenth-century Vienna.

For surely what is exhausted is the *reader* of Southern fiction of the past forty years, not the South or its novelists. And exhausted by what?—as always, by quantity not quality. The publicists of any renaissance—especially among an oppressed people (ex- Confederates, Jews)—can hardly be blamed for their early delirium; but any publicity is doomed to sate an audience very quickly—and in our case, to sate it with what amounted to a serious inaccuracy: that the South swarmed with genius. It didn't, though considering its size, the length and range of its history, the South can come honorably out of a cool examination of its fiction in the past forty years. In fact, its record as a country can stand with the simultaneous record of any other country—with France, Britain, Germany, the rest of America. For since 1930 the South (as literal cradle and crucible) has contained the careers of three novelists of world stature—William Faulkner, Robert Penn Warren, Eudora Welty—and of two masters of the short story—Katherine Anne Porter, Flannery O'Connor. Three women, two men—four of them from or concerned with the deep South, one from Texas.

Unquestionably there have been in the same period other distinguished Southern novelists and story writers, not to speak of poets and dramatists; and in another ten years the list may well bear another two or three names (there are strong visible candidates). But I think my point is clear. Insofar as there is any sense of exhaustion with the South-as-literature, that exhaustion is felt only by readers (and by professional readers, at that) who have forced themselves to consume large quantities of the fiction (first-rate or fifth-) emerging from so peculiar, so high and gamy a culture as that of the Old South.

The situation is radically different for young Southerners who think of themselves as novelists and are beginning their work now. If they have read widely in the fiction of their region (by no means a certainty; I hadn't until I had written two books of my own), they may indeed feel that certain objects and themes have been handled so frequently and obsessively, well and badly, as to be dangerously worn, the comic-Southern stereotypes—odorous ladies with memories of the War in mansions by swamps hung with moss and moccasins where dead blacks are dumped for misdemeanors. And yet, and yet—most Southerners my age (b. 1933) and thousands born in 1971 have had, or will have early, intense and formative encounters with a number of living originals of the types. And more—bellied sheriffs, beloved and loving retainers, revival preachers, claustrophobic families, tottering rhetorical childhoods drowned in lonely backwaters fed by books (not Southern) and dreams of escape.

If these Southerners have had their very educations as writers determined in part by realities which now arouse conditioned boredom in a small overread audience, what are they to seize as their themes and subjects when their experience requires, compels, the order of fabulation? Their experience, of course; the matter on which they can speak with authority, their lives, their literal visions, the mysterious inventions and combinations which their imaginations extract from, force into, that experience. For any serious novelist who is sane enough to ignore book journalism will know, as cornerstone of his work, that if the compulsion to write fiction continues in any one organism, then the exhaustion of a portion of a given decade's journalists with a given subject or region is precisely meaningless since it is produced by the unavoidable plethora of lesser work summoned by a local genius's call and promoted by the hucksters of a free economy, work whose memory and force will survive (twenty years hence) only in the author's family and in graduate English departments. The man who can and must merely proceeds, trusting the heat of his own vision to vaporize accretions, dissolve patinas, reveal the thing itself. In any case, time—if time continues—will winnow the products. Whoever wrote for less than time?

And no one maintains that the past forty years have seen no changes in the old South—its look, sound, smell, the charge in air and objects. Enormous changes, apparently, though most of them so recent (since 1945) as to be beyond measurement or tests for permanence, influence, direction. Industrialization, urbanization, integration, uglification. Yet however great their threat to all that has been meant by "South"—and the first two would seem the great threats, as they did to the Agrarians in 1930—the fact remains that vast stretches of the old South remain untouched by the twentieth century. *Survive* is perhaps more accurate, but *surviving* as opposed to *flourishing* has always been the supreme Southern specialty, black and white.

When Eudora Welty's *Losing Battles* was published in 1970, several of the more serious reviewers (I saw a handful of the old "What?-more-hillbillies?" groans; my own two earliest novels got a fair amout of hillbillying when in fact they dealt with characters who live two hundred miles east of the nearest hill and are as distinct from hillfolk as from Brooklyn cabbies) suggested that, strong as it was, this was clearly the last Southern novel, since the South that had fueled Faulkner and Miss Welty was gone and good riddance.

Nonsense. The old South—the Confederacy, still spiritually intact, with the difference only that the slaves were called servants —continued in alarming good health into the late 1950s and throughout the whole huge region, Mississippi to Virginia, country and town. And today I can leave my house, midway between Duke University and Chapel Hill, walk five hundred yards, and be in houses and among people, white and black, who could today conduct mutually intelligible, agreeing dialogues with their resurrected great-grandparents and who, for all that, do not see themselves as isolated islands of the past but as typical of the world around them. I can drive sixty miles to the house where I was born, in a town of two hundred; visit my aunts (whose mother—my grandmother whom I clearly remember—was kissed by General Lee in 1870); submerge with them gladly in days of memory —the sacred hilarious appalling past reeled through us again in the sacred forms (each word as rigid in its place and function as a phrase of the Mass, as productive of promise, release, joy). And not only I—my niece, age three, already listens closely to the same ceremonies; and though she is a visitor, how can I guess what strata are slowly, immovably depositing in her? Or the millions of children who live, not visit, in the rural/small-town South and turn from television to the oral tradition many times each day, who are fighting again this afternoon in hundreds of public schools the final lost battles of the Civil War, a gray line of six-year-olds in the van? If such encounters do not, in fifteen years or so, prove to have been intense, mysterious, scarring enough to produce their own novelists (whose work will feed at the same dugs as Faulkner's or Warren's or Welty's), *then* claim that Southern fiction is dead. For whatever new subjects, new forms of life the new South is offering (and to me they seem either developments of the old or copies of standard American types), the old South will go on offering its life as subject for another fifty years at least —the working life of those who are children in it now. Not *offering* but *imposing,* and those apprentice novelists upon whom it imposes itself must invent new tools for seeing and controlling its intent on their lives or smother in silence—or turn to the fiction of game and puzzle which is presently cranking up in younger regions already gone to desert.

But these children, like their parents, are also experiencing various kinds of new South—almost half of them are chiefly if not exclusively experiencing an urban South (North Carolina plans to have a 51 percent urban population by 1980); and while neither Atlanta nor New Orleans yet vies seriously with New York, Chicago, Los Angeles as irreclaimable disaster sites, they are trying hard and cheerfully, and, given time, may well succeed. Birmingham is nearly as difficult to breathe in as Gary; and dozens of smaller cities—green and clean ten years ago: Raleigh, Richmond, Charleston, Savannah—are imploring not so much their own ruin as their mortal trivialization, drowning in a sea of carwashes, burgerstands, pennanted gas pumps. So the next question is, as I said at the start—will the new South prove unrelated to the old, a petrifying gorgon quite literally?

Unanswerable of course, and in any case not a peculiarly Southern question—though a look at simultaneous American fiction of other regions gives serious pause. Insofar as the twentieth-century novel in this country has consisted of the South and the Jews (with the odd Midwesterner), it has been the product of two profoundly similar cultures—God-and-family centered, oppressed and oppressing (the old ghetto Jew being his own Negro), gifted with unashamed feeling and eloquence, supported by ancient traditions of sorrow and the promise of justice, a comic vision of ultimate triumph. But with one large difference—the classical Southern novel is rural; the Jewish, urban. I can think of no exception (maybe Malamud's *New Life*?). And while the moral resources of Judaism have irrigated the work of Malamud, Bellow, and Roth, a great many other specifically Jewish novels have suffered the predictable pressures of their scenes—frayed nerves, self-absorption (through urban isolation), ghetto smugness, *noise.*

Surely, in fact, the great dilemma of an American Jewish novelist is not, again, exhaustion (the unimaginableness of certain repetitions after *Portnoy,* say) but the far more daunting fact that the modern novel, from its eighteenth-century origins till 1922 (*Ulysses*), was a bilocal form—city and country. It is difficult to think of any great European novelist before Joyce whose every novel is not intricately strung between the mutually nourishing poles of city and country—Fielding, Stendhal, George Eliot, Tolstoy, James, Proust, Lawrence, Mann. Dickens and Dostoevsky (the supreme urban novelists, the first and richest students of city nerves) send their plots and people for frequent and indispensable visits to the country; and I'm not the only man who thinks that *Wuthering Heights,* entirely rural, is the greatest single novel of a nineteenth-century England already locked in the mania of urbanization, nor the only one to notice that not one of the classic American novels through Hemingway and Faulkner is exclusively, even largely, urban in setting.

Why this oscillation?—a simple reflection of earlier life when populations were mostly rural and writers could afford villas, cottages, dachas for clearing-the-head, flushing-the-pipes? the remnants of nineteenth-century nature worship? All that and a good deal more. Chiefly this—such a range of geographical movement has, until the past ten years, been the novelist's technical strategy for expressing what was an early and strengthening perception of the occidental novel: that the European and American city of stone, asphalt, traffic, harassed parks cannot provide an anima of imagery sufficiently rich or varied to support long fictions concerned with emotions other than hate, rage, anxiety. Why?

Wordsworth knew, in 1800, the preface to *Lyrical Ballads* (and the fact that he speaks of conditions for poetry seems to me no objection)—"Humble and rustic life was generally chosen . . . because in that condition the passions of men are incorporated with the beautiful and permanent forms of nature." *Permanent.* You might argue that a city is a form of nature (even that, as recently as ten years ago, a few of them were beautiful forms); and I'd join you in affirming that the suggestiveness-to-art of a Rome or an Athens is largely a function of its longevity, its *apparent* permanence, the long scale it offers for the measurement of our brevity; but even the most resigned city-dweller would not contend that permanence is a feature of any American city—oh, a few square blocks of Charleston, Savannah, a few other "heritage-squares" in chloroform. The deepest principle of American cities as opposed to European or Oriental is precisely their impermanence, mutability (and surely one explanation of the present state of horror of our cities is that our premise has always been, "It's awful; never mind; we'll get it right next time"). Now, add to that basically economic impermanence a new and perfectly feasible threat—nuclear destruction—and anyone can see that, for the first time in history, a city the size of greater New York is literally easier to destroy, to vaporize in every stone, than any one man within the city. Given five minutes' warning, the man can take shelter; the city cannot. Neither can the country, of course; but the threat of destruction against, say, the Appalachians or any given rock, field, or tree has thus far seemed less credible than that against clustered buildings. (The current revival of fear for the environment, overdue as it is, is essentially a fear for man—man may succeed in destroying himself, the tuna, the plankton;

but does anyone seriously suppose that nature—the earth—would not survive us? The earth has been hell and desert several times before.)

So rocks and trees condemn our folly and our virtue, chasten our fret as buildings never can—scratch a farmer and find the tragic sense of life—yet they still can console us because they will submit to the pathetic fallacy, will absorb all our emotions, not simply our destructive emotions. Or—if consolation is impossible or irrelevant—illumination, clarification; because they offer us the only objects of meditation in the presence of which the literally human qualities of man can be distanced, comprehended, calmed, controlled. That is not merely the experience of Wordsworth and all the novelists of the world till 1922 but of Aeschylus, Jesus, Oedipus at Colonus, King Lear.

Will Southern novelists then—undaunted by their native horrors, unintimidated by general misapprehension—be finally silenced by urban din? or galvanized into nerves and jitters? or forced into cave art (the scared cottage industries mentioned above)? Maybe. Why not? Maybe I've answered that already. Literally because many more than half the people of the South still live in close proximity with a nature that beautifully, grandly asserts its permanence. If that nature—its organic killable members—is killed, as it may be, then its memory may well survive in a few of the human survivors and work for generations (the Garden of Eden has lingered nicely—as dream, implied condemnation, blueprint). And if, in twenty or fifty years, Southerners all huddle like the rest of the nation in cities of dreadful night, there will still be what there has always been (often all there has been for the South, always all there has been for the novelists)—the past, as dream, condemnation, cause of the present. The past which, for all the stunning raids upon it, all the muffled hobbling obeisance to it, refuses to die or yield for more than the space of one novel in one man's life but grows, proliferates in each new life and demands early treatment, desperate remedy. Perhaps, indeed, as readers we *have* had the Civil War, the lavendered ladies, preachers and sheriffs, bare-souled adolescents; but as the stuff of life in a huge and long-inhabited country, they have no more been plumbed than the Marianas Trench. And other central traumas and figures are untouched—the great Depression (my father's Civil War), the manless years from 1941–45 when many of us grew up in the midst of a war three thousand miles away yet hooked into our hearts, the black-rights struggle of the fifties and sixties, the present agonies of school and housing integration, another war, thousands of others unknown to me; and Southern blacks (having given us our best poetry) have only begun to write their pasts, their visions of self and of us, into novels that may yet tell us, and in time, so much we need to know. And what Jeremiahs we could make among the ruins. Our credentials are impeccable—the only people in the nation who have claimed from the start that graceless man, even *Homo americanus,* was damned and doomed, would botch all jobs, and that we in the South were the damnedest of all.

So—given an imaginably livable world and the survival of memory—the next fifty years seem as safe as years get for anyone born in the South whose life here demands control in the form of what we have agreed in the past two centuries to call fiction. Beyond that—well into the twenty-first century—even I won't peer. First, children must be born with the genes, the senses (though maybe all that will prove manageable). Then the world must remain an observable world, one that human eyes and ears can bear to study, can conceive reasons for wishing to portray, a world that will hold pose long enough. If these conditions vanish, so probably will the novel. Forms with longer lives and achievements as grand are dead as pterodactyls—epic, pastoral, dramatic tragedy. And not only the American Southern novel—all fiction, everywhere. Not to speak of organisms far more gravely threatened, of far greater weight in the life of the race.

And yet, and yet. If the race survives in some recognizable form, if language is employed to communicate emotion and acquired experience, if men spend large tracts of time in one place (however man-ruined or man-made) and if one of those places remains the ground we now call the South, it is all but inconceivable that one man at least (white, black, red, yellow; whatever new mixtures) won't be compelled to retire to private space and, helpless to do otherwise, invent some means of saying what he knows, having had his life. The novel, for instance. A Southern novel.

ARE THE BOZARTS BLOOMING?

Roger Griffin Hall

[It is a half century since H. L. Mencken characterized the South as "The Sahara of the Bozart"—a region of worn-out farms, shoddy cities, and paralyzed cerebrums; a vacuity so vast as to defy contemplation. "One would find it difficult," he wrote, "to unearth a single second-rate city between Ohio and the Pacific that isn't struggling to establish an orchestra, or setting up a little theater, or going in for an art gallery, or making some effort to get in touch with civilization. . . . You will find no such effort in the South."

Remember, this is the young Mencken speaking, the supreme Whangdoodle, the rollicksome, raucous gadfly who built a reputation by hurling caustic grenades at every sector of the American cultural stage; take what he has to say at ten cents on the dollar. Then consider: fifty-one years later, even if the particulars of Mencken's breach with the South are no longer current, isn't there a distressing aptness to its tone? Have we really grown any less susceptible to the cynic's eye? It's true, the South of the 1970s has her community orchestra, she has her little theaters, her civic ballets, her galleries and her arts councils; but, by and large, these developments exist at the amateur and semiprofessional level. In the professional ranks, where the ultimate responsibility for the highest level of creative output in the performing arts lies, the cultural landscape of the South, now as in Mencken's day, is relatively barren.

Now, whether or not this places our region behind other sections of the country is an open question. The "cultural boom" so boldly trumpeted in the past decade has perhaps been more the child of wishful thinking than hard reality. Quantitative analyses in this realm are difficult to come by and suspect to begin with. Whether there are "more piano players in this country than fishermen, as many painters as hunters, twice as many concert-goers as major league ball fans and more theater-goers than boaters, skiers, golfers, and skin divers combined" (as held by a Stanford Research Institute study in 1962) may not be verifiable; but this much is true: despite the recent phenomenon of governmental support of the arts, virtually every professional performing organization in this country is in a perpetual state of economic crisis. One reads constantly of disastrous rises in costs, of emergency fund drives, of desperate pleas to foundations. It is an endless process of leaping from deficit to deficit, of crawling out of one crisis only to be beset by another. For the performing artist, the financial picture is even drearier. To cite one statistic: 95 percent of the membership of Actor's Equity is currently unemployed. When work does come, it is often seasonal and of short duration. The pay is demeaning. The hours are endless. Job security, fringe benefits, health plans, *et al.*, are nonexistent.

What is worse, things may never get better. A 1965 Twentieth Century Fund report, the standard treatise on the economics of the performing arts, strongly suggested that the financial woes of arts organizations will prove to be a chronic, not temporary, affliction. Since production costs will continue to rise faster than revenue from admission, the report held that arts organizations cannot be supported by the box office alone. This is particularly true of experimental and *avant-garde* groups—groups which by definition cannot always command the security of a substantial following. Clearly, if our age is to be remembered as one which not only kept alive the universal heritage of the arts, but also made a contribution to it, these organizations must not fall victim to the tyranny of the market place.

There are some hopeful signs. In 1964, Congress created a public funding source for performing organizations and artists, the National Endowment for the Arts. With that, our government finally, belatedly, accepted the argument that despite their "elite" appeal, the arts are a public good, a national resource, if you will, and as such merit public monies. If the pleasures of this generation's few are not allowed to flower, they will surely not possess the vitality to compete for the interest of the next generation's many. The arts in no small sense represent a legacy to posterity—to all posterity—and for this, they are a profoundly "public" good. One is reminded of the gardens at Versailles. "How are they kept so luxuriant?" the visitor asks. "Simple," the groundskeeper says. "Water daily for three hundred years."

Unfortunately, Congressional appropriations to the National Endowment in the six years since it was created have been so niggardly as to suggest that government aid has been embraced in principle, not principal. The 1971 executive budget includes a request for $30 million for the Arts Endowment, the highest figure allowed by law and a figure more than double the sum of all appropriations in the first five years! Even at full funding, however, federal government contributions to the arts will amount to little more than a drop in the bucket. What really supports the arts in this country is neither the box office nor the government; it is philanthropy, and despite increases at the private, corporate, and foundation level, less than 3 percent of the American philanthropic dollar goes into the arts.

Why? Perhaps the time has come to square off against the old bugaboo. As a nation, we have traditionally possessed a meager appetite for music, dance, and drama; if anything, we have inherited a suspicion that the practice of these arts is superfluous and the practitioners are unmanly. Attribute this predilection to a puritan heritage, a hard-nosed utilitarianism, a fascination for technology (the antithesis of art), a taste for doing rather than contemplating, or an implicit suspicion of the aristocratic, the elite, the intellectual—the arts have never been rooted in our national life style. De Tocqueville saw it nearly 150 years ago: "Democratic nations," he wrote, "will habitually prefer the useful to the beautiful, and they will require that the beautiful shall be useful."

Only a small percentage of Americans—the figure usually cited is 3 percent—are willing today to accept the beautiful on its own terms. Many more, perhaps even a majority, might grudgingly concede the arts are a "good thing," but something for their children to enjoy, not themselves.

The problem for the South is not so much that the 3 percent all live in New York-Philadelphia-Boston-Chicago-Minnesota-Los Angeles-San Francisco, for they do not; but rather that 3 percent of New York City constitutes a large enough potential audience to support a major symphony orchestra, two major opera houses, three major ballet companies, a half dozen modern dance troupes, all of Broadway (on, off, and off-off), and the most exciting collection of art galleries in the country. But 3 percent of Valdosta, Georgia, or Little Rock, Arkansas, or Columbia, South Carolina, or the scores of other small and middle-sized cities that comprise the South can support very little. For obvious reasons, the performing arts have always gravitated to the big city, to the area where 3 percent means a potential audience of 100,000, not 3,000. Recent reports that the South is the most populous region in the country notwithstanding, our demography is working against us. We are not a region of big cities.

Nor, alas, are we a region of big money. Concentrated wealth is every bit the draw of a concentrated populace; put them both together, in an Atlanta or a Houston or a Dallas, and it is reasonable to expect professional performing arts organizations. Wealth (tempered with a sense of *noblesse oblige*) without a vast megalopolis, as in Winston-Salem, can generate remarkable activity. But these cities are the exception, not the rule, and for the most part, today as a century ago, the major concentration of private, industrial, and foundation wealth is in the North. Together, these wellsprings of philanthropy provide performing arts organizations with something like 85 percent of their budgets, and not surprisingly, the beneficiaries of this good will, like their benefactors, are mainly up North. Even the few "national" philanthropists in this country, the Ford and Rockefeller foundations for example, have no qualms about bypassing whole regions. Their interest lies not with geographic parity but with national quality—the strong shall be made stronger.

Given these circumstances, federal support of the arts is particularly important to the South. Here is the source of funds that should and will minister to the needs of the nation's culturally deprived areas. Nancy Hanks, director of the National Endowment, has issued an agencywide directive: Look South!

The bushes have been beaten, her program directors reply, there's little to be found.

Are we really all that culture-poor? Is it a fair index that, of the twenty artists awarded individual grants from the National Endowment in 1970, only one came from the South?

Yes and no. When I suggested earlier that the plaintive tones of Mencken's essay still haunt us today, I did not want to imply that nothing is happening here at all. Plenty is happening. Since 1950, somewhere in excess of 180 cultural centers have been built in this country (perhaps the most concrete evidence of a "boom" yet produced by its exponents), and this is a surge in which the South has carried its own weight. Cultural complexes are going up everywhere, in every conceivable way; Huntsville, Alabama, paid for theirs with a municipal liquor tax. Too often, of course, these supposed citadels of culture are little more than all-purpose convention centers/exhibition halls/sports amphitheaters in which "the lusty passions animated by one night's bout with wrestling seem to trouble the next evening's session with Brahms" (as one Britisher wistfully noted).

Another caveat should be raised here—against the false hope that exteriors of mortar and brick will necessarily spawn interiors of truth and beauty, or, for that matter, an audience that cares if they do. Atlanta is the classic case of a city that tried to superimpose vast cultural activity onto a populace all at once. In 1968, amid a flurry of national publicity, the city opened the doors of a $13-million Memorial Arts Center, dedicated to 122 Atlanta arts patrons who died in a plane crash while making a museum tour of Europe. NBC's *Today Show* devoted a full hour to the center, and to "the arts in renaissance in Atlanta." It may have been the briefest renaissance in history. Overambitious productions ($250,000 was poured into "King Arthur," the inaugural presentation) and disappointing public support put the Municipal Theater (an amalgam of professional dance, drama, and opera companies) out of business in three months. Impresarios in Atlanta have recently taken on a new vitality, and the tenants of the lavishly colonnaded structure—the symphony orchestra, the High Museum, the Atlanta School of Art, the Alliance Theatre Company, and the children's theater—seem to be thriving. Professional ballet and opera companies in Atlanta are also in the works. Yet the lessons of that city should be well taken: we must, as Robert Brustein has written, shift our concern from cultural complexes to cultural complexity.

Leaving aside the physical earmarks of cultural progress, the South still has some significant advances to point to, though most are either at the amateur or semiprofessional level. It has been estimated that amateur productions in this country are five times better attended than professional ones; in the South, the ratio may be closer to ten to one. Arts Councils have sprouted in every Southern state in the past twenty years, with the city of Winston-Salem and the state of North Carolina leading the nation. Little theaters, community orchestras, commercial art galleries, yes, we have them all. But the question ultimately suggests itself: "To what extent does proliferating amateur or quasi-professional activity build audiences for professional performances?" Is it possible that a deluge of amateur productions will satiate the thirst of the unsophisticated audience for cultural enrichment? Or, worse, is it possible the mediocrity of many of these performances will diminish that thirst? The answer is yes, both these dangers are real. On the other hand, it is just as legitimate to propose that the audience hearing Bartók and Brahms played acceptably will be excited by the prospect of hearing them played superbly.

As a general rule, the consequences of extensive amateur activity depend upon the extent of exposure to professional productions. At least a small diet of professionalism is desirable, lest the tastes become dulled. In the past, regions such as the South which lack professional companies of their own have had this need met by intermittent exposure to national tours and road shows. As recently as a decade ago, most of this country's major performing organizations spent a good part of their season on the road, hop-skip-and-jumping from one-night stand to one-night stand. "The South was our bread and butter," a Ballet Russe dancer of the 1950s recalled. Today, the national tour has all but disappeared, a victim of spiraling travel expenses and stronger artists' union negotiating committees. Who, then, is to provide Southern audiences with performances good enough to elevate and expand the cultural appetite of the region?

There is only one conceivable answer: somewhere, somehow, professional arts organizations must grow out of Southern soil. There are already some, but not nearly enough. A brief rundown:

In drama, the Alley Theater in Houston comes to mind, perhaps the highest caliber performing arts institution in the South. The Alley is one of the oldest resident theaters in the country, founded in 1947 by Nina Vance and a troupe of amateur actors. By the mid-fifties the Alley was ready to turn professional, and by the early sixties it began to attract national attention. It has since become a pet beneficiary of the Ford Foundation, which has poured an astonishing $3.5 million into it in the past decade. With the completion of a new theater (two auditoriums, capacities 800 and 300) in 1968, the future for the Alley looks bright.

Other reasonably healthy professional theaters include the Dallas Theater Center, created and sustained by the energy of Paul Baker, a minister's son from the Texas Panhandle; the Front Street

Theater in Memphis; Theater Atlanta; Repertory Theater in New Orleans; Actors Theater in Louisville; the Asolo Theater in Sarasota; and the ageless Barter Theater in Abingdon, Virginia. To varying degrees, all are struggling to survive, casting melancholy glances at foundations and corporations, and turning out productions that are occasionally brilliant but more often not. The kindest words one visiting critic could summon to describe one better known Southern theater were: "Clearly, it is better than no theater at all."

In music, there is a similar mix. Not one of the country's Big Five symphony orchestras (New York, Philadelphia, Boston, Cleveland, and Chicago) is located in the South, yet we have approximately a dozen "metropolitan" orchestras (to use the classification of the American Symphony Orchestra League) of varying quality. These are located in Atlanta, Birmingham, Dallas, Orlando, Houston, Jacksonville, Louisville, Nashville, Chapel Hill, Richmond, San Antonio, and Shreveport. As universities and conservatories turn out increasing numbers of talented musicians, and as places in the prestigious Northern orchestras grow ever more competitive, doors are opened up for orchestras in other regions. Two of the South's finest orchestras—Dallas and Houston—are located in Texas, where arts patrons are literally buying a heritage. With enough money, or enough moxie, or both, talented musicians can be coaxed Southward. Here again, Atlanta is a case in point. Two years ago, they lured Robert Shaw, an international legend in the choral field, away from his position as associate conductor of the Cleveland Orchestra and gave him free reign to fashion their orchestra in his own image. He has since built perhaps the finest musical organization in the South.

In opera and dance, the situation is bleaker. Nearly all major dance companies in this country, both modern and classical, are based in New York City. There are only three thriving regional troupes (Boston Ballet, Pennsylvania Ballet, Ballet West), and none is within five hundred miles of the South. What the South does have is SERBA, the oldest and most sophisticated regional ballet association in the country. SERBA (Southeastern Regional Ballet Association) presides over the scores of private ballet schools scattered throughout the region. The productions these schools give are primarily amateur, but of a different brand of amateurism from their counterparts in music and drama. Community orchestras in this country offer performing opportunities to hobbyists, music teachers, and a small core of resident musicians; little theaters exist principally as an outlet for the avocational interest of businessmen and housewives who "always had a yen." Civic ballets are something else. By the nature of the art, training starts young and careers end early. The mainstay of the civic ballet production (aside from the visiting prima ballerina) is the sixteen-year-old starlet who, if everything breaks, will be off to New York next year. The tragedy of it all for the South, of course, is that from then on things will be breaking or not breaking in New York City. There are no outlets for her professional aspirations in the South.

Actually, that is no longer completely true. Two young and potentially vital dance companies are now emerging in the South—the North Carolina Dance Theater, based at the North Carolina School of the Arts in Winston-Salem, and the Atlanta Ballet. Both, as we shall see, are in the process of developing a regional audience.

In opera, there is little activity. Most opera productions in the South are put together by community and metropolitan orchestras which somehow find the money to bring a half dozen singers down from New York City on a one-production basis. There are some moderately successful opera companies in New Orleans, Mobile, Houston, Dallas, Miami, and Louisville.

There remain the visual arts, and here the deck is more heavily stacked against the South than in any other art form. This has more to do with the nature of the medium than with the nature of the region. In music, opera, theater, or dance, the great literature of the past is everyone's property, for better or for worse. With art, virtually all the master works are locked in galleries and private collections, few of them in the South. Two notable exceptions are the North Carolina Museum in Raleigh and the High Museum in Atlanta. But for the most part, all we have, laments one museum director, is a collection of commercial galleries dealing mainly "in what I call the 'dead house' school of art. For some reason, Southerners seem fascinated by decrepit old barns, houses, and buildings. This is traditional, decorative stuff." Tastes are slowly changing, with corporations, particularly banks, going into the business of speculating with modern works, partially as a public relations device. But aside from several good university art departments (Virginia Commonwealth University's in particular), there is nothing to keep a serious artist in the South.

This then in brief is the region's cultural landscape—some scattered areas of fertility surrounded by a vast Sahara. Keeping in mind the economic and demographic conditions of this desert, it seems to me the best way for professional arts organizations to flower is through the concept of regionalism.

Trends have a way of turning back on themselves, of going full cycle. In politics, the liberal who ten years ago lobbied for expanded federal authority has recently come to proselytize community control. In the arts, the same set of circumstances that a decade ago reduced the feasibility of the "road company" may now be bringing it back to prominence. Or, if not the road company, the regional company.

Nowhere is this development more evident than in drama. The American theater has undergone a profound redeployment. Broadway, a generation ago "the" professional theater in America, today is increasingly the purveyor of a single form: light musical entertainment. In the past decade, off- and off-off-Broadway have taken up the slack in reviving the classical repertory and providing a stage for serious new plays. Outside New York, a similar development is taking place. A headline in a March 1966 issue of the trade magazine *Variety* said it all: "Hinterland Legits Top Broadway." For the first time since the heyday of stock, there were more professional actors working in regional theater than in Broadway or touring productions. What kind of theaters are they? Julius Novick, in his book *Beyond Broadway,* describes them as follows:

> *Professional theaters they are, but not commercial theaters. They do not compete with the road-company houses, where those exist; for the most part, they do not bother much with Broadway commercial comedies; they are interested in art, not money (though they try not to be self-righteous about it). They are all incorporated as non-profit institutions, and most of them operate on deficits. They survive by going to the public as Good Causes; they enroll ladies' auxiliaries to help out in annual subscription campaigns; they solicit funds from foundations, from government and from private donors.... These theaters aim to become permanent institutions. Most of them have permanent premises. Usually they try to assemble a resident company of actors who remain together from play to play throughout part or all of a thirty or forty week season, with guest performers to play roles that cannot be cast from the company. A core of actors is usually retained from one season to the next, in the hope of developing a genuine ensemble. Always there is some continuity of management and policy, some attempt to create something more than a lot of single, separate, unrelated productions; some effort, however timid and tentative, to stand for something.*

The regional theater is not an altogether new development. The older ones (Alley, Arena, and Actors Workshop) are pushing twenty-five, and most of the three dozen (give or take) others are well into their teens. Already, there are symptoms of middle age. Once the honeymoon with audiences and financial backers is over, two hard realizations sink in: people will no longer come to see productions just because the theater is an intriguing novelty; financial backers with enough money to start a theater do not necessarily have enough to sustain it.

Some partial answers, both in terms of money and audiences, lie in the notion of a truly "regional" theater (until now, "regional" has been the generic term for any theater outside New York City which is not commercial)—that is, a theater group that spends part of its season at a home base and part of its season on the road. This is not the road in the old national sense, but the regional road. Why can't we have professional drama, ballet, music, and opera companies in a dozen of our larger Southern cities, affiliated wherever possible with educational institutions or performing arts schools, serving whole sections of a state, whole groups of states? If we are talking about a dance troupe, make it one which works with portable scenery, simple props, a small cast—with productions, in other words, geared to smaller audiences. Base it in a reputable School of Dance, use advanced students to supplement a core of resident professionals and faculty members, spend the off-season building a repertoire and lining up dates in every town of 30,000 on the map. Go out on two- and three-week bus-and-truck tours several times a year. Bring down an occasional "name artist" for publicity. Use the company as a means of attracting students to the school, the school as the channel of talent into the company. It is the New York City Ballet that keeps the American School of Ballet at the top of its field, and vice versa. Why not effect the same symbiotic relationship, admittedly on a less exalted scale, in the South? Why tolerate a situation in which our potential saviors—the young Southern artists—are forced to spend their most creative years elsewhere?

This is, of course, precisely the formula the North Carolina School of the Arts has followed in the formation of the North Carolina Dance Theatre, a professional dance company, which was launched in the 1970–71 season via the sponsorship of the Winston-Salem Civic Ballet. This unique training institution in

Winston-Salem can be the wellspring of a cultural renaissance, not only in North Carolina, but throughout the Southeast. This, in my judgment, is the ultimate mission of the school.

Of course these companies cannot expect to be up to the caliber of the best, but they would, at the very least, be collectives of performing artists trying to create. In this simple proposition, there is infinite appeal. Not all college football teams can be number one, not all can be nationally ranked, but virtually all enjoy an enormous local following. Obviously, the arts will never have the mass popularity of sports; but the point is simply this: locale is a tremendously important factor in generating interest, sympathy, and support.

"Flexible" is the key word for these organizations. Suppose civic leaders in a city of 20,000 want to bring a professional symphony orchestra to town, but cannot afford the cost of the entire ninety-member orchestra based in the city of 300,000 some 75 miles away. That orchestra should be responding to their problem —offering a thirty-five-member chamber orchestra, a string quartet, and a wind quintet. Here you create a situation in which not only the smaller cities can be served, but, since ensemble playing is attractive to most musicians, a more talented artist can be serving them. In the event that union contracts for musicians ease somewhat, constraints on this kind of flexibility could be eliminated.

Here again, with the aid of a Rockefeller Foundation grant, the North Carolina School of the Arts is in the forefront of this regional innovation. The school year 1971–72 marks the fourth season for the Piedmont Players, an ensemble made up of the top professional artist-instructors at the School of Music. With a flexibility ranging from a chamber orchestra of twenty-five to a wind quintet or a string quartet, the Piedmont Players present adult concerts, children's concerts, and seminars in a five-state area, in communities ranging in size from Wilmington, North Carolina, to Chatham, Virginia.

It all sounds very nice, very much of a pipe dream, but two questions, the old questions, remain. Money? Audiences? These are two questions, unfortunately, with no firm answers. At the very hour established performing arts organizations are struggling to maintain their grip on both, how can a region with limited community enthusiasm for the fine arts expect to attract either? It is easy to be pessimistic, yet I can't help thinking that because we have a modest cultural heritage, because we are not restricted by what has gone before and what now exists, we as a region have a unique opportunity to develop new, winning combinations in the fine arts.

One "natural" is a marriage of the university and the professional performing arts. Many Southern universities already have fine art, drama, and music departments, and the practice of bringing in visiting professionals on a short-term basis is becoming increasingly well-established (as is the more permanent arrangement of the artist-in-residence). Artists Affiliates, a New York–based outfit with funds from the National Endowment, is in the business of matching performer with university. Why not go beyond this and bring whole groups of artists into the academic community, create resident companies? The few American universities to effect this kind of arrangement (Brustein's Yale Repertory Theatre, for example) have had notable success. It makes simple sense. The university starts out with advantages it may take a new company several years to attain: physical facilities, a fund source (though in these troubled times, this is dubious) and an established name. The potential benefits to the university are no less alluring. If the resident company is good, it will attract interest and publicity, and serve as an effective recruiting aid. For the academic community in general and the fine arts major in particular, the intimate exposure to professional productions would enrich the college years. Further, this combination makes it possible to tap the energy and imagination of students without suffering corollary consequences of amateurism.

But keep one biblical fact in mind: in the overwhelming majority of cases, those talented youngsters who actually "make it" on the stages of this nation—the graduates who actually embark on careers and remain competitive as professional performers, *who earn their living as performers*—come from professional training institutions like Juilliard, the American School of Ballet, and the Academy of Dramatic Art. The academic community should house professional companies and develop arts educators and arts administrators and taste in public entertainment. But it is the dedicated conservatories and professional schools like the North Carolina School of the Arts that will breed the performers.

In addition to a partnership with the university, the performing arts should aim for a greater partnership with the land. Perhaps it is time for our stodgy bearers of high culture to emerge from their self-imposed exile in aseptic concert halls and theaters and try their hand at more outdoor drama, lawn concerts, symphonies in the streets. Our cultural centers—while they probably add a certain glamour and excitement—may in the end symbolize "not the majesty of the arts, but their increasing isolation" (as Martin Mayer has written). The high arts would do well to follow the lead of such vastly popular Southern institutions as fiddlers' conventions and outdoor dramas with such presentations as chamber music conventions, ballet festivals, serious summer repertory theater, and so forth. The more widespread and varied the outlets for exposure, the better.

I am not proposing that our cultural organizations emigrate *en masse* unto the hills, for there is something a trifle preposterous to this notion; I am proposing that the high arts let down their hair a little. It is a curious thing that a region so rich in the "popular arts"—in jazz and spirituals and folk music; in outdoor drama and fiddlers and folk tales; in pottery and weaving and glassblowing; in furniture making and all the crafts (the Penland School of Crafts in western North Carolina has no equal)—has been so empty of influence on the high arts. Clearly, the South has something that sets her apart. In the face of the homogenizing, mediocritizing effects of mass culture and mass retailing, this is the one region which to a degree has retained its own identity, its special mores, its separate life style. This is the region, more than any other, that has a present link with its past. Look at those marvelous twentieth-century American novelists who bear a distinctly Southern imprint—Faulkner, Wolfe, Warren, Styron, McCullers, and Welty. Clearly there is some common thing—a sense of paradise lost perhaps—that has shaped their writing.

But where are the Southern choreographers, the Southern composers, the Southern playwrights? Admittedly, these forms are less susceptible to regional flavoring. For one thing, unlike writing, where the creation is simultaneously the performance, the performing arts separate these into two mutually dependent processes: first the creation, then the performance. The creative activity of a composer or choreographer or playwright therefore is unlikely to come to full fruition in a region where the possibilities for a performance are scarce. Accordingly, most of our creative people in the arts have gone to the Big City, been acted upon by the Big City, and have sacrificed a measure of their Southernness.

Yes, but didn't many of the Southern novelists also migrate North? Indeed they did. Writing, though, more than dance or music or art, is a medium sympathetic to the portrayal of a region. Music and dance can deal with emotions with equal or greater force, but in the elusive business of capturing a life style, a history, mores, nuances of the written word are more effective. Drama—in all its forms—is similarly equipped to depict the essence of a region, and there is no reason that dramatic dance, dramatic opera, and dramatic theater cannot bear a Southern mark.

I have a suspicion and I have a dream. My suspicion is that within this country's mass culture, performing arts organizations are not the outgrowth of pockets of creative composers or choreographers or playwrights, but vice versa. My suspicion, further, is that once broad and humane and permanent professional performing arts organizations are established in the South, the creative people in this region will be drawn to them.

My dream is that the creator and the performing organization can together bring about something no other region in this country, through history, has produced—a truly indigenous high culture. The possibilities for a fine arts which draws content and theme from the Southern experience are stirring to contemplate. What a vast, untapped potential lies within our Sahara! Isn't it time for a flowering?

RELIGION IN THE LAND OF COTTON

Wallace M. Alston, Jr.,
and
Wayne Flynt

I

[THE impact of religion on Southern society and thought is an essential question, though it does not lend itself to glib analysis. The function of religion in producing and sustaining the social and economic values of society makes it imperative that any attempt to understand a people come to terms with their religious institutions and thought. Religious ideals produce values which determine the nature of society, and the culture thus produced in turn alters and shapes religious institutions. The interaction of culture and religion puzzles both the devotees of religion and the uncommitted social analyst. The problems are innumerable. What is cause and what is effect? How should one evaluate the gap between theory and practice? How does one distinguish between mainstream traditions and smaller but nevertheless important minority movements?

A complete list of references and data sources for this paper may be obtained from the L.Q.C. Lamar Society, P.O. Box 4774, Duke Station, Durham, North Carolina, 27706.

To complicate the issue, Southern religion has attracted considerable attention, much of it from critics intent on attributing most of the South's problems to its evangelical Protestantism and unaware of any deviation from the fundamentalist norm. Many Southerners, sensitive to such attacks, have dogmatically proclaimed the South's fundamentalism to be the only road to an idyllic—and definitely segregated—Paradise. As in so many terrestrial squabbles, neither side of this controversy has a monopoly on truth.

Critics of the South's religious ideals and institutions have dissected its shortcomings with stiletto precision. Samuel S. Hill, Jr., professor of philosophy at the University of North Carolina at Chapel Hill, has analyzed the region's other-worldly emphasis on soul-winning and its relative exclusion of social concern. Noting the homogeneity of religious life in the South, he concludes, like H. L. Mencken before him, that a region so overwhelmingly Methodist and Baptist, and so obviously backward, must be backward partly because it is fundamentalist.

A recent study by Rufus Spain of Southern Baptist social thought between the Civil War and the end of the nineteenth century concludes that, although a small number of Southern Baptists developed a social consciousness during the last years of the "Gilded Age," most remained staunch defenders of the *status quo.* They were provincial in outlook and poorly educated, shared the prevailing Southern attitudes toward the inferiority of blacks, and reflected the predominant social views of their society.

Nor is this the end of the indictment of fundamentalism. Southern counties in which lynchings were most frequent were 75 percent Baptist and Methodist, and these occurrences were lamentably ignored in both local pulpit and district meetings. The fundamentalist sects also suppressed free thought, most notably the teaching of evolution in public schools. With few exceptions, Southern Protestants ignored the social problems of the poor and the working class. While one may quibble over the extent of some of these judgments, the recent history of the South has demonstrated their regrettable accuracy at least in broad outline. Pastors and laymen alike have been prominent in the defense of segregation, the censorship of denominational colleges, and the nativist prejudice against religious minorities, especially Catholics.

While American society has been grappling with the problems of war, race, and justice, Protestantism in the "Bible Belt" has rarely extended itself beyond contemplation of such purely academic issues as the morality of dancing or the literalness of the Genesis account of creation. Ever sensitive to vilification by "outsiders," hard-pressed Methodists and Baptists attributed sacrosanct meaning to the term "Bible Belt," for if they were negligent in their concern for social salvation, they were at least Bible- and salvation-oriented. Northern churches might follow the false gods of sociology, but the South would adhere to the traditional ethereal Jehovah of its fathers. Biblical literalism, salvation of souls, and ethical negativism ("Thou shalt not . . .") became the battleground chosen by many Southern Protestants to halt the apostasy of theological "modernism," the spread of the social gospel, and ecumenism. The Reverend W. A. Criswell, pastor of the largest Southern Baptist Church in the world (The First Baptist Church, Dallas, Texas), and president of the Southern Baptist Convention (1968–70), delineated one great danger to his denomination in his 1969 publication, *Why I Preach That the Bible Is Literally True.* That danger was "theological liberalism that denies the [literal] Word of God [and] . . . will destroy us." After a frontal assault on evolution as "the big lie of the modern era," he concluded:

> *We think we free ourselves from the bondage of religion and the burden of an inerrant Bible when we turn aside from the truth of God in Genesis to accept the so-called academic freedom that is offered us in the world of evolution, but this freedom is a freedom*

> *that shuts God out and leaves man a slave to his brute ancestry. It is persuaded that the whole meaning of life ultimately comes to nothing.*

When Criswell's tome came under fire from the Association of Baptist Professors of Religion in 1969, Criswell responded by saying that diversity within his denomination was destroying it; and he invited any who did not share its traditional doctrinal statements to get out.

The major problem with both critics and defenders has been their monolithic view of Southern Protestantism. Despite the ample evidence of Southern political, economic, racial, and philosophical diversity which has been unearthed during the last forty years, even knowledgeable Americans have stubbornly refused to acknowledge religious diversity in the South. Only in the decade of the 1960s did historians focus on this richly variegated Southern Protestantism. They found here an influential Southern Protestant tradition of intellectual openness and social involvement. They even discerned a smaller tradition of religio-political "radicalism." Though eddies within the mainstream of conservative fundamentalism, these minority attitudes flourished during certain epochs of Southern history. We shall investigate this tradition of liberalism later in the paper.

II

Surprisingly, the pervasiveness of religion in the South is a relatively new phenomenon. In the colonial period, of course, there was no "South" as such, but rather three distinct societies: the already old Chesapeake society, which had been erected on a tobacco base; the young Carolina society, established on the profits from rice and indigo; and the hearty Back Country, which was still in the process of taking shape. Though several denominations were at work at this time, there was no clear indication until about 1740 of the direction religion would take in the South. In that year a spontaneous revival grew up in the country around Hanover, Virginia, and, under the leadership of the Reverend William ("One-Eyed") Robinson, the revival, a uniquely American phenomenon, was brought onto the religious scene. The Presbyterian Church, with the techniques of revivalism, made great gains in all three colonial societies, but revivalism itself made gains far greater than any single denomination. The Presbyterians were handicapped as far as numbers were concerned by the high educational standards which they required of their ministers. The academies simply could not produce enough clergymen to serve the established congregations, to say nothing of the new Presbyterian communities that were coming into existence through the good offices of revivalism. Before the end of the colonial period, the Baptists had taken the numerical lead in the South, a statistic which has remained unchanged to the present day.

During the Revolutionary War, the public mind had been so preoccupied with the state of the country that all religious institutions languished and some were actually suspended temporarily. No sooner had the war ended than a great multitude of pioneers turned their faces toward the cheap, unoccupied lands of the West. By the end of the eighteenth century, most of the mountain area of Virginia was settled, as well as practically all of the western part of North Carolina.

Life on the frontier was rough. Murder, thievery, and robbery were commonplace, as were land-jobbing, litigation, and feuds in and among families and communities. The mainline denominations of the Old World were neither emotionally nor physically equipped to cope with frontier life and religion was at a low ebb not only in the South, but in the entire land.

Then, just when the French infidelity seemed to be subverting religion and society on the continent of Europe, a great new wave of revivals began in America, "the second Great Awakening," and for the next two generations these revivals were almost continuous, reaching out into the new frontier settlements to convert individuals and organize them into free voluntary associations. The movement spread like wildfire throughout the land and established the revival technique, first through the camp meeting and then the "protracted meeting," as the dominant characteristic of American religious life.

Voluntarism was the essence of the spirit of revival. Revivalistic preachers confronted men with the urgency of decision about where they would spend eternity. The whole sweep of the biblical revelation was compressed into one demand: to "get right with God" before it was too late.

To be sure, revivalism was not an exclusively Southern phenomenon. Earlier in New England, then on the early frontier, in western New York, later in the old Northwest Territory and beyond, the technique of revivalism and the message it preached were basically the same. The important fact, however, is that the mainstream of American religious life began to broaden in the nineteenth century, departing from revivalism as its primary method of presentation, while Southern churches institutionalized that frontier tradition, making it normative rather than exceptional in the life of the church. What had been a transitional phase for mainstream American Protestantism became the characteristic emphasis of Southern Protestantism. The liberal tradition of dissent, the social ferment in the North and East, the openness to new knowledge, led the American Church outside the South to constant reappraisal and modification. Southern religion before the Civil War, however, was guided by a leadership class that was singularly unsophisticated and provincial. Especially among the Baptists, who were steadily moving into the forefront of the regional religious picture, informed and aware leadership was sadly lacking. Education was low on the list of priorities held by Southern churches, being absolute anathema in the eyes of some. Southern churches grew in membership, but the growing institution was far from prophetic, being rather a reflection of the culture, isolated from the intellectual and issue-oriented dialogue going on in churches of other regions of the country.

Then came the Civil War, and, although churches gained in influence through the War by a series of revivals and carried on certain limited philanthropic activities, the War itself presented an ethical issue which measured the Southern Church and found it far too small for the task set before it. The individualism, voluntarism, and moralism that stemmed from revivalism and had become the norm for Southern religion had little to say about the problem of how man should live in a tragic situation in which each alternative is partly good and partly evil. Even the way the South fought the War, the late James McBride Dabbs suggested, shows the flaw in its religion. For a short while, Southerners fought as fiercely as men have ever fought; some so fought even to the end. But, when the end came, half the Southern army was absent without leave; and, curious fact, General Lee did not take to the hills for continued warfare.

The reason for this, according to Dabbs, was that, although the life of the South was extremely rich in many ways, it was not deeply rooted. It lacked a prophetic religion which would not only ground this world in the next, but would provide a kind of prophetic criticism of this world in the light of the next.

> *They had all the religious words, they were defending Christian righteousness against modern paganism, and these words carried them fiercely to the top of Cemetery Ridge, but they couldn't stay there. Even as they went, it was a better show than a battle: the South at its most splendid, a sight to thrill forever the heart of a fighter, but not quite right.*

The South had sought to live by a highly individualistic religion which lacked a prophetic perspective. It produced neither poets nor saints to tell it when and where it had gone wrong. "So it kept on trying to make politics serve the purpose of religion, until politics ended in war, and war in defeat, and still the South did not know why it had been defeated or what course might lead it upward again."

III

The Protestant hegemony in the South and the resultant homogeneity of the Southern Church are absolutely unique in this country. The South is a strongly Protestant region and it is so without great competition. Yet even more significant is the fact that Southern Protestantism is overwhelmingly a Baptist-Methodist Protestantism. In many Southern communities, it makes little difference whether one worships in the Baptist, Methodist, or Presbyterian churches of the community, for it is all basically the same. The liturgy varies only slightly. The theology varies even less. Instead of representing different historical and theological traditions, denominationalism in the South is generally of one piece, divided far more significantly along political, economic, and social lines than along lines of doctrine or polity. The Episcopal and Presbyterian churches have struggled to an extent against the pressures that would have them join the Southern Protestant amalgam. But, taken as a whole, there is a "Southern Protestant Church" which cuts across denominational lines and espouses a common theology, though it is yet unable to transcend the lines of race and class.

The theology common to the Southern religious expression is fundamentalism, a belief in the verbal inspiration of the Bible, and thus of the inerrancy and infallibility of the biblical message. These "fundamentals" are so widely assumed by the Protestant layman in the South that deviations on the part of either pulpit or pew are immediately obvious. Moreover, a reasonable percentage of these laymen are aggressively articulate in bearing verbal witness to these fundamentals of their faith. Visitors to the South often comment on how close to the surface religious language is in Southern conversation and how often "the Good Lord" is invoked in the midst of an otherwise technical conversation or debate.

Further, there is a common theological heritage which lies close to the surface of the Southern Protestant, and it includes ethical as well as doctrinal assumptions often held by an individual despite the stated position of his particular denomination. For example, in its lead piece covering the abortion debate on the floor of the North Carolina Senate, the *Durham Morning-Herald* reported that one legislator argued, "I'm a Presbyterian, a Calvinist . . . I believe in predestination. I cannot play God"; while another concluded, "I do not know when life begins . . . when the soul is born, and under God I'm not going to decide." The Presbyterian Church in the United States, some ten months before the statement quoted above, had taken a strong stand in favor of precisely the kind of state law which this Presbyterian legislator was opposing.

It is impossible to calculate the influence of theological fundamentalism on the social and political attitudes of this country. Alfred O. Hero, Jr., investigating the influence of Southern religion on United States foreign policy, notes that the fundamentalism of Southern religion has historically been so interwoven with other influences—such as poor education, rural underprivileged childhoods, low social status, passive resignation to fate, *laissez-faire* economics, political conservatism, and a general pessimism concerning human nature—that it is often difficult to distinguish fundamentalism from the whole ethos of the region. But fundamentalistic attitudes have intensified the effects of these other influences by encouraging people to think in dogmatic, oversimplified ways, to apply black-and-white moralism to social and political issues, and to press for clear-cut "solutions" and "victories" at home and abroad. The frontier individualism of the sects and of the more theologically conservative congregations in the Southern Baptist Convention, and to a lesser extent among other Protestants, has helped to foster similarly individualistic frames of reference of an extreme free-enterprise sort in economics, social relations, and political affairs. Due to the politics of the one-party South and the seniority system in the Congress of the United States, the nation as a whole has felt Southern influence in the realm of social and political policy. It has been this vehicle, and not the institutional church, that has enabled the Southern gospel of fundamentalism to spread throughout the nation and to penetrate into the marrow of a people.

Another characteristic of Southern Protestantism closely related to its theological fundamentalism is its highly subjective character and exclusively individualistic orientation. Historically, the Protestant Christian has been more concerned with what God thinks of him than with what he thinks of God. Southern Protestantism, on the other hand, is precisely opposite in its orientation. In fact, one might say that Southern fundamentalism is not theology at all but anthropology, and therefore preaches a clearer social and political doctrine than does a doctrine of God. One reason for the national appeal of Billy Graham is that his message communicates something far less particular than the Christian doctrine of God: his subjectivism and radical individualism appeal to people over the country who struggle with the torment of littleness, with the insecurities that inevitably come to one seeking to locate himself in the vastness of a universe and a civilization over which he has no control. Graham's gospel was once a Southern gospel, which grew out of the sorrow and defeat of a region that remained rural while the world became urban; but this is no longer so, for the experience of cultural, even cosmic, littleness which was once the sole possession of the South is now familiar to all who struggle to know who they are in relation to what the world seems to be.

If the religious experience of the Southern Protestant is highly subjective, oriented almost exclusively to the individual and to his experience of salvation, the doctrine of the Church itself is similarly determined. Dr. E. T. Thompson has suggested that the distinctive doctrine of the Southern Presbyterian Church is that of its spirituality, and it might well be said for all Protestant denominations as they exist in the South. To understand the doctrine of the spirituality of the Church, one must consider the great ante-bellum issue in the South: slavery. The issue was complicated by sundry political and economic factors, and the story is well known. The point of mentioning it here is to show how the churches in the South, especially during the pre–Civil War period, took to the defense of their own region, baptized its institutions, and undergirded its life with a dubious brand of dogma. In 1850 James H. Thornwell, a Presbyterian and perhaps the most influential minister in the South at the time, defined slavery as an obligation to labor for another which had been determined by the will of God. The Reverend George D. Armstrong found in the Bible apostolic example, precept, and injunction for slavery, and declared it to be no less than God's appointment for the punishment and recovery of a people when they sink so totally in sin as to become incapable of safe and righteous self-government. A secularized version of this hideous logic is found in the South even today.

It was in this period, and in this atmosphere, that the Southern Church developed its peculiar doctrine of the "spirituality of the Church." John Calvin had sought to apply the Gospel to the total life of the human community, being concerned not only for the salvation of the individual but also for the salvation of Geneva. The inheritors of the Protestant tradition in the South, however, reasoned that the Gospel of Christ concerned "spiritual" things, not political, economic, or sociological things, and therefore the Church should stay out of the latter for the sake of the integrity and purity of the former. James H. Thornwell stated the doctrine clearly. As a spiritual body, he argued, the Church

> *has no right to interfere directly with the civil relations of society. Whether slavery shall be perpetuated or not, whether it conduces to the prosperity of States or hinders the progress of a refined civilization—these are questions not for the Church but for the State, not for Min-*

> *isters but statesmen. Christian men may discuss them as citizens and patriots, but not as members of the Church of Jesus Christ. . . . [The Church] is not a moral institute of universal good, whose business it is to wage war upon every form of human ill. . . . It has no commission to construct society. . . . The problems, which the anomalies of our fallen state are continuually forcing on philanthropy, the Church has no right directly to solve. She must leave them to the Providence of God, and to human wisdom sanctified and guided by the spiritual influences which it is her glory to foster and to cherish.*

This theory, born in the slavery controversies of the ante-bellum period, was strengthened by the Civil War, and cemented in the period of Reconstruction. It continues to haunt Southern churches to this day.

A fourth characteristic of the regional Church is its double mind in relation to the world. Many have criticized the Southern Church and its fundamentalist theology as being so other-worldly as to be unrelated to this world. This is simply not the case. There is a sense in which the Southern Church has been deeply concerned with its environment.

For one thing, its individualistic ethics have sought to inform the believer about what constitutes acceptable and unacceptable behavior. It is true that this is a moralistic ethic, defining "immorality" in terms of sexual promiscuity, drinking, gambling, dancing, and the misuse of the Sabbath—but it is not a lack of concern with the world. Often, one of the most effective lobbies in Southern legislatures is the conservative church lobby, and the maintenance of "blue laws" in many a Southern town is attributable directly to pressure from this source. To assess the Southern Church as unconcerned with the world is simply to make a bad political judgment.

Indeed, the problem is quite the opposite. The Southern Church, until recently, has been at one with the culture; in fact, it has felt very much at home there and has used its political muscle to keep it intact. There are exceptions to this rule, as we shall see. But when Martin Luther King, Jr., called the 11:00 A.M. worship hour the most segregated hour of the entire week in this country, he knew precisely what he was saying. As a rule, the Southern Church has shown little interest in social change and little compassion for the black and the poor in its midst. Southern religion has not been escapist, however; it has been adaptive, and that is a far more dangerous thing for social change than escapism. Harry Lefever has illustrated the point in his recent *New South* article on "The Church and Poor Whites." Lefever shows how religious influence in a small mill village in Georgia serves to socialize the poor in the dominant values of the society in which they live. He notes that

> *the reason the poor appear to be desirous to escape and withdraw from the larger society is that in their condition of deprivation, insecurity, and powerlessness they tend to develop an adaptive ideology of withdrawal as a rationalization for possible failure.*

This observation may be accurate not only for the influence of religion in the lives of the poor in the South, but also of religious influence in the South generally. Southern religion has offered neither a way out of the world nor a critical perspective on the world; rather it has concealed the issues of God and man so successfully as to enable men to live in the midst of injustice and oppression without thought of revolution.

IV

The year 1954 marks the beginning of the end of that regional expression of Protestant Christianity we have called the Southern Church. Had it not been for the impact of the civil rights movement, the unrest in the lives of students and campuses, and the broadening effect of its ecumenical involvements, the Southern Church might have gone on for years untouched by the movements of the twentieth century. And yet, this being said, there existed long before 1954 a tradition of ferment in the life of the Southern Church.

One of the most violent expressions ever of political disharmony in the South was the Populist movement of the 1890s. Born of poverty and economic frustration, it challenged the racial, economic and political shibboleths of the conservative South. Though not racially egalitarian, the Populists often advocated a biracial political alliance based on mutual self-interest. By advocating a third party, they challenged Democratic hegemony over the "solid South." Their economic proposals departed from the *laissez-faire* approach of the Bourbon conservatives, demanding government regulation, and, in some cases, flirting with socialism. Yet the movement drew support from among fundamentalist sects.

Part of the interest of fundamentalists in Populism may have resulted from social stratification. While Methodists and Baptists could claim the majority of the church population in most instances, they did not exercise a proportionate political influence. Conservatives from the planter classes who had run most Southern governments before 1865 tended to represent minority religious sects, particularly the Episcopal Church. Of 63 different South Carolinians who held the office of governor and United States senator between 1778 and 1865, only 5 belonged to Baptist and Methodist Churches, and this trend continued among Bourbon leaders in the 1870s. Populism was a movement of the lower-class white farmers, most of whom were Baptist and Methodist.

Religious influence helps to explain that part of the Populist ideology which sought to establish a new order of society, replacing unfettered competition with brotherly concern. Their leaders often took their inspiration directly from the imagery of Christ's concern for suffering, exploited humanity. The upland parishes of Louisiana, which numbered the largest proportion of

Baptist whites, also elected the most vehemently antimachine representatives to the Louisiana legislature, and the Farmers' Union in that state was born in a church, largely from among Primitive Baptist farmers. Furthermore, much of the political leadership of the Louisiana Populist Party came from the Baptist Church, including organizer L. A. Traylor, an ordained Baptist minister, and Bryant W. Bailey, Baptist layman and Populist candidate for Congress.

Turning from agriculture to manufacturing, one finds there too a protest movement which drew heavily on religious values. Since the South has been the most agricultural region of America, industrial workers have received minimal sympathy from the Southern Church. Moreover, Southern religion generally has been opposed to concepts of class conflict, while emphasizing individual responsibility. This has led some historians of Southern labor conflict to conclude that Southern religion always played a major part in undermining unionism; but this is reckoning on the basis of only partial evidence. Research into American religious thought before the Civil War has demonstrated that the doctrines of "perfectionism" (the belief that man can move toward social and moral perfection in his earthly life) and millennialism (a thousand-year reign of peace and justice) sometimes made Southern Protestantism a contributing force to social reform between 1830 and 1860. Professor Herbert Gutman, exploring proletarian thought between 1865 and 1900, has discovered significant Christian influence. This influence differed from the later Social Gospel movement, which was middle class in origin and born of interest in the unfortunate worker. The labor groups drew from the same Christian doctrine and tradition as the advocates of the Social Gospel, but they spoke to a different audience (workers), and their protest grew from their own experience with suffering and exploitation.

Focusing his theory on black coal miners in Alabama, Gutman emphasizes the influence of Protestant rhetoric and the black church on labor organizations. Union meetings abounded with biblical quotations, hymns, and demands for Christian justice. Gutman concludes: "Thus we notice the influence of evangelical, postmillennial Protestantism in the form of labor organization and in the rhetoric of both white and black trade unionists and labor radicals." The same influence was still present in Alabama in 1900 when labor organizers often held their meetings in black churches sometimes with the active support of black ministers.

Nor is the Christian influence only to be found among black "radicals." Indigenous Southern socialism often had its roots in the Christian notions of cooperatives and ethical justice, as can be seen in one fascinating case study. During the Depression of 1908, Pensacola, Florida, experienced several violent strikes with an attendant increase in the influence of the Socialist party. Far from a violent, anarchistic program, local Socialists defined their objectives in ethical terms. They protested that even if one could find a job, excessive hours of labor left no time for ethical pursuits or for working out one's spiritual salvation. God had made all men the same, but wealth had corrupted and brutalized those who possessed it and "dulled their sense of equity in their dealings with their workers." One worker advocated socialism after thus describing the plight of a father who could not find work and had to face a hungry, sick family: "A Christian country we call ours—the word is a mockery." Another Socialist worker called for "a complete revolution of our social system along economic lines," adding that socialism meant not anarchism or atheism, but the "practical Christianity of Christ; it aims at the universal observance of the Golden Rule."

When a laborer wrote a letter asking ministers what a man should do when he could not find work and his family faced starvation, he received two replies. Rabbi Jacob D. Schwarz condemned the prevailing economic system as wrong and unjust and called on his fellow ministers to support worker demands. The Reverend Thomas D. Calloway, pastor of Pensacola's First Baptist Church, preached a sermon on "The Problem of the Unemployed," in which he praised Christian socialism which was "earnestly seeking after the right solution of the problem of the unemployed and the oppressed." To be sure, such comments do not reflect the conclusions reached by a vast majority of Southern Protestants; but they do indicate that there has been a tradition of ferment in the Southern Church which could serve very liberal as well as very conservative traditions.

Radical Southern Protestantism usually met the same fate as radical Southern politics: it was buried beneath a conservative avalanche. More influential in practical results was the Social Gospel movement in the South. Until recently, this movement has rarely been acknowledged, much less analyzed. When one examines Southern fundamentalism after 1940, with its emphasis on individual salvation and its repudiation of social justice, one tends to reach the facile generalization that Southern religion as a whole has always lacked social consciousness. It appears, however, that as denominations became more highly organized and middle-class (conservative "church-type" rather than more radical "sect-type"), they actually retrogressed in their social awareness. The more firmly they established themselves in the social order, the more Southern churches tended to become defenders of the *status quo* in economic and political matters.

Kenneth K. Bailey, a careful scholar of Southern Protestantism in the twentieth century, has noted that the years from 1900 to 1917 were years of intensive social concern. Despite the anti-intellectualism and conservatism of many Southern Baptists and Methodists, these denominations in certain instances spoke out forcefully on social issues. Religious thought provided progressivism with much of its philosophical basis and greatly influenced many of its most effective leaders. From the battle over Prohibition, some Southern Protestants conceived the idea that sin could manifest itself in the form of a social evil which could be removed only by collective political action. Applying this premise to the entire plethora of social ills, segments of various denominations came to advocate the abolition of child labor and the convict lease system, better health and sanitation facilities, more equitable treatment of workers, and government regulation of corporate wealth. Editors of denominational newspapers in Alabama directed constant fire at the state legislature for its failure to restrict child labor, and advised ministers to become involved in the crusade and laymen to vote against representatives who failed to support such legislation. After an emotional recitation of adolescent casualties in Alabama mines and factories, Frank W. Barnett, editor of the *Alabama Baptist* from 1901 until 1919, wrote: "Let us call it by its right name—murder. But if the death comes quickly enough, it is less cruel than the life to which such boys and girls are condemned." The Episcopalian minister Edgar Gardner Murphy organized the Alabama Child Labor Committee, and, with the aid of other clergymen and laymen, was instrumental in obtaining remedial legislation in 1903 and further reforms in 1908. The same story can be found elsewhere in the South, as many Protestant ministers and laymen joined actively in reform movements.

A recent study by Hugh C. Bailey of leading Southern liberals during the Progressive era leaves little doubt about religious influence on them. Of the six liberals fully analyzed in the study, three —George W. Cable, Alexander J. McKelway, and Edgar Gardner Murphy—were either clergymen or prominent laymen. Furthermore, Southern liberalism was often expressed through religiously created or dominated reform groups, such as the Conference for Christian Education, the General Education Board, the Alabama Child Labor Committee, and the Southern Sociological Congress.

Some Southern Protestants found even more direct ways to express their developing social consciousness. One prominent example in the urban South was the settlement house ministry. Alabama, generally considered among the most backward and fundamentalist of the Southern states, offers an intriguing example of what a creative minority of activist Protestants could accomplish to ameliorate individual human suffering.

Beginning in 1903 a group of Methodist women from St. John's and First Methodist Churches in Birmingham organized the City Board of Missions, and the Board opened a settlement house in June 1903. The home included an "industrial school" for girls aged five to sixteen, a day school for children of working parents at a cost of only one dollar per month, a night literacy school for working boys, a free kindergarten, and a boys' military club. Between 1900 and 1905 over 3,000 children attended church-sponsored kindergartens in Birmingham, most of them workers' children supported by the Methodist Christmas offering. In 1908 a Wesley House with a kindergarten, a model home, and other social services was opened in another industrial section of Birmingham. A similar Wesley House was built in 1912 behind Avondale Mills, furnishing free a kindergarten, child care, a night school, a children's chorus, and other facilities. These ministries were extended to five thousand Italian immigrants at the Ensley works of Tennessee Coal and Iron Company in 1912. Staffed by fully trained social workers, this Wesley House offered all the services available at the other Wesley Houses in Birmingham, plus boarding facilities for women.

Methodists were not alone in this ministry. The Reverend A. C. Davidson of Southside Baptist Church in Birmingham adopted the motto, "An open church for every day and night of the year." His parish was organized as an "institutional" church, with an industrial school for children, a night literacy school for men and boys, a library, reading room, and gymnasium. Parker Memorial Baptist Church in Anniston, the fifth largest Baptist Church in Alabama, supported interdenominational social services in the industrial area of town, subsidized free beds in the public hospital, and employed a social worker to supervise a home built at the local net and twine mill which furnished a school, a library, and a reading room to workers.

Although it is difficult to evaluate the impact of such ministries, it is certain that they reduced the suffering of many workers and their families, and gave educational opportunities to thousands of people who would not otherwise have received them. Lack of research precludes any estimate of the extent of such programs throughout the South, but they did exist in many urban areas of the region, offering a new dimension to the social consciousness of Southern evangelicals.

Concern for the ills of society did not terminate with the coming of the First World War. Two studies which treat Southern Protestantism between 1919 and 1940 conclude that while the South's churches were less liberal than institutions in other parts of America, many of them maintained a keen interest in social action through a prophetic minority. Undeniably, Southern Protestant churches often showed sympathy for the Ku Klux Klan and led the antievolutionist crusade. But it should also be noted that numerous Southern Protestants participated in local interracial committees dedicated to improving race relations during the 1920s. A historian of the antievolutionist crusade in North Carolina, Willard B. Gatewood, Jr., focuses on William Louis Poteat, a Baptist minister, biologist, and president of Baptist-affiliated Wake Forest College. Poteat became the most prominent state defender of free thought and evolution. Though a majority of Protestants in the state disagreed with him, they divided sharply over tactics. One group of Protestant antievolutionists were militants, concludes Gatewood, constituting a minority of "embattled, panic-stricken warriors making a last-ditch effort to preserve their historic faith from the onslaughts of the evolutionists . . ." But their un-Christian tactics alienated less militant fundamentalists who wanted to come to terms with modern concepts, even those they opposed. It was this split in fundamentalist ranks, and not modernism, which led to the defeat of two antievolution bills in the North Carolina legislature. A similar division among Baptists was a prominent factor in the failure of the antievolution crusade in Kentucky.

L. L. Gwaltney, editor of the *Alabama Baptist* from 1919 to 1950, was the official voice of Southern Baptists in Alabama during that period. His social philosophy demonstrates the liberalism of thought among some Southern evangelicals during these years.

Gwaltney was an evolutionist, opposed capital punishment as anti-Christian, considered the Scottsboro trial which convicted nine Negro boys of raping two white girls to be a travesty of justice, applauded American diplomatic recognition of the Soviet Union, and in the 1930s questioned whether capitalism was a viable economic system or ought to be replaced by socialism.

Finally, the liberating influences coming from theological seminaries in the South should not be overlooked. The nineteenth and twentieth centuries witnessed the prophetic leadership of teachers in several theological seminaries in the life of the Southern Church. Numerous examples could be cited of the courageous teachers of Bible, theology, and church history who have stood against the Southern stream and given comfort to those local ministers willing to take controversial stands on sensitive issues. Dr. Ernest Trice Thompson taught church history for more than four decades at Union Theological Seminary in Virginia. Thompson was charged with heresy for his liberal beliefs, successfully survived the charges, and became professor to the entire Presbyterian denomination in the South for many years. Men like Dr. Thompson have been instrumental in leading their particular denominations, and the region as a whole, into a more serious consideration of Christian ethical responsibility to the society at large.

Thus, Southern Protestantism has been sufficiently complex to include within its history a courageous tradition of liberalism, dissent, and active social protest. It must be remembered, however, that social religion in the Southern Church, even when it was courageous and bold, always had its life in the context of the larger phenomenon of the cultural religion. Even today, liberal churchmen must struggle against the ancient foes of individualism and spirituality, for the emotions of evangelism can yet out-vote the passion for social concern. The most one can say, in summary, is that the future of the Church in the South as a viable instrument of social change is related to its historical past. The so-called "new breed" of Protestant clergy and laity, whose concern it is to shape a more human and just society for all people in the South, do in fact have a history. They are the newest generation of a small but significant minority of Southern Protestants, whose voices were raised in the wilderness of Southern Church history even when their respective denominations were mute.

V

Thus far we have concerned ourselves primarily with the white Southern Protestant Church, because it is this force which has helped shape the ethos of the South for good or ill. The Roman Catholic Church and the Jewish faith have rich traditions in the South, but they have constituted a minority, not mighty enough to influence significantly the Southern ethos.

The black Church in the South is something else again. The black Church was the one institution in the South not dominated by whites where a talented, ambitious Negro could rise in status. The black Church has been criticized for its lack of an educated clergy and its consequent conservatism and other-worldliness. But whether the black Church is to be assessed as a primary instrument of Southern oppression or the cradle of liberation for black people, its influence in shaping Negro thought is crucial. It fashioned among blacks the Christ-like image of the Negro. This image, a defense mechanism in a white man's society, portrayed the Negro as the real disciple of Christ because only he had known the suffering and exploitation which refined his soul. Martin Luther King's philosophy of the Negroes' redemptive function in American society reflects the influence of black ecclesiastical thought. The black Church has furnished much of the political leadership in the post-1945 civil rights movement, and even a glance at the most influential black leaders of this movement indicates the influence of black Southern evangelical Protestantism.

Religion in the Land of Cotton

The Southern Church has begun to stir, largely due to the civil rights movement. The Southern Church, now containing radical theological and ethical ferment, is threatened with deep division and ultimate dissolution. But it is this very ferment which is crucial—for the same institution that so effectively adapted a people to life in a dubious social order might also be capable of providing both the soil and the seeds of revolution that could finally tear that "order" asunder. First, let it be noted that, while churches in the more highly urbanized areas of the country have experienced the loss of both membership and participation, Southerners still go to church on Sunday. Second, a large percentage of people who belong to churches in the South still participate in the life and work of these churches. If this means nothing else, it certainly means that the minister of a local congregation speaks to a large audience each week and the possibilities for the Church acting as a vehicle of attitudinal change in the South are therefore still relatively unlimited.

Third, large numbers of Southern churchmen still read the Bible and are consciously involved in becoming theologically equipped to do their particular task in the world. Neil O. Davis, editor and publisher of the *Auburn* (Alabama) *Bulletin,* for example, is a literate Christian layman who has read widely in the theology of Reinhold Niebuhr and, from this perspective, has sought to shape the climate of opinion in his community. A man who reads the Bible with a measure of resonance is a dangerous man indeed to a society bent on remaining as it is.

Finally, there is a "new breed" of Southern clergy on the scene. They are theologically able, ethically sensitive to an unjust social system, astute in the ways of power politics, and committed to the task of bringing about social change in the region. There is, perhaps, no other region of the country in which so large a group of young clergymen have committed themselves and their professional lives to being agents of social change.

The fact that the Church is a voluntary association means many things, not the least of which is that it will not be coerced into anything. When the membership of a voluntary association ceases to be convinced of the justice of its ways, that membership will simply withdraw its support. It means that the Church, if it is to be a viable instrument of social change and social justice, must attract people who are skilled in the politics of effective leadership. But the fact is that the Church, given good leadership, might be able to accomplish some very radical things that other institutions, such as business or government, by definition simply cannot do. The Church is free, for example, to live on the frontiers of social organization, to experiment with new forms of human associations, to test new and radical structures for human community, and generally to be the harbinger of the future for society as a whole.

The United Campus Ministry at Duke University is currently experimenting with a coeducational living community in which students live and work together in the context of common responsibility. The First Presbyterian Church of Auburn, Alabama, finding no program in effect to meet the housing needs of the rural poor, has undertaken to establish a community ministry to build houses for poor people of Lee County, and to undergird this project with money. An ecumenical, nonprofit corporation has been formed in Atlanta for the purpose of building low-income housing in the urban area. Robert D. Miller of St. Petersburg, Florida, has sought to structure an interracial Christian community as an experiment in what it takes to make and to keep human life human there. The First Presbyterian Church of Durham, North Carolina, sensing the poor community's need for preschool education, including day care and health care, subsidizes a Children's Center for poor children at the rate of over $10,000 each year.

Finally, the Church can provide the region with a locus of radicalism and dissent. There are many communities in the South that are in fact "closed societies" and the local churches have often been the only places in which advocacy groups organized for strategy and action could meet.

The Southern Church, therefore, still has a place in the life of the region. It has people, property and financial resources that may be used at the will of the membership. More significantly, it has a tradition of belief that originates in a "man for others." These factors give the Church in the South the potential for providing that kind of critical perspective which can enable us to rediscover, if not (in the words of James McBride Dabbs) "to substantiate our soul."

Southern politics

GLORY HALLELUJAH, WHILE THEY'RE TRYING TO SOCK IT TO YOU

Maynard Jackson

[ABOUT one hundred and ten years ago, of course, I was selling for around twelve hundred dollars. If I were living today in any one of hundreds of thousands of ghettos, rural and urban, in this nation of ours, more likely than not I would find my life not only not worth twelve hundred dollars, but maybe not even worth a dime.

I think we are obliged to ask ourselves how that could happen. How is it possible that this nation can afford to ignore the lives of tens of millions of her citizens? How is it possible that, after spending millions of dollars and millions of hours of manpower on studies, conferences, research, seminars, and analyses of every kind, we still live in an era of more hate than love, more war than peace, more discord than unity, more ignorance than enlightenment, more poverty than wealth, more despair than hope, more neglect than attention, more problems than solutions? How can this be? The more we think we know about us—and I mean all of us, black and white alike—the more we think we know about *human* behavior, the higher the divorce rate goes, the higher the spiral in the illicit use of narcotics. The more we think we know about bridging the generation gap, the more the college campus, and even the high schools and elementary schools, explode. The more we have brotherhood Sundays, brotherhood weeks, and brotherhood months, the more this nation becomes an armed camp. What's wrong? How could it have happened?

I don't believe that anyone can say positively what the answer is. I certainly cannot. But I want to suggest what I believe is an answer. I think it was best expressed in the words of a rock and roll song recorded in Atlanta by a man whose name is, appropriately, Joe South. The song is called "The Games People Play," and these are the lines which, I believe, answer the questions we are raising:

People walkin' up to you,
Singin' Glory Hallelujah!
And they're try'n' to sock it to you,
In the name of the Lord . . .

—or in the name of "progress," or even in the name of "civic responsibility."

That song has a lot of truth to it. They've been socking it to us for over three and a half centuries, and during those years the tune has changed several times, but the message has always been the same. First, of course, there was slavery. I suppose we need not dwell on the brutalities and indignities suffered during those 250 years, a subject which, by this time, arouses horror and disgust in black and white alike. After slavery came the period of Reconstruction, when black political power suddenly appeared on the scene and black men had a chance to take their rightful places in government.

But the age of black politics was short-lived. To increase his chances of winning the Presidency after the disputed election of 1876, Rutherford B. Hayes let it be known that as President he would withdraw the federal troops from the South. The tactic was successful; Hayes was awarded the election and became President. The troops were withdrawn, as promised, and then began a reign of terror so insidious and so widespread it equals, I think, any evil in the history of mankind.

That is the past, and if hypocrisy and bigotry had died with

Reconstruction, the South would be in fine shape today. But think for a moment of the politics that was played in the wake of the rejection of President Nixon's nominations of Clement Haynsworth and G. Harrold Carswell to the United States Supreme Court. The Republican strategists told us Haynsworth and Carswell were rejected because they were Southerners, and they had *tried* to help us, when all the while they had intentionally nominated men who were simply not of the Supreme Court caliber. Consider, further, other "acceptable" hypocrisies—the commitment to send men 250,000 miles to the moon, and, again, the immoral waste of billions of dollars in Indochina while Americans starve to death at home. The perpetrators of these hypocrisies are the same ones we hear from when there is talk of welfare and human resources development. One of them is Senator Eastland of Mississippi, a man who can somehow reconcile taking thirteen thousand dollars a month not to plant food while there are kids running around within the shadow of his estate in Sunflower County with stomachs bulging from malnutrition and worms. "And they're trying to sock it to you . . ."

Our question, of course, is what do we do about this? As men and women, black and white, concerned about what happens in this country, and specifically in the South, how do we translate our concern into affirmative action? I believe that there are certain definite, practical steps which can be taken.

First, we must not tolerate a policy of neglect on the part of anyone, especially not on the part of a national administration. Any President who turns his back on the evils of physical and spiritual decay would have feet of clay extending above his neck. Let us not be deceived into believing that the New South is just over the crest. The task is far harder than we know even yet. There is no resting place down here. As James Baldwin reminds us, "Havens are high-priced. The price that a haven-dweller has exacted of him is to delude himself into believing that he has found a haven." As long as we have any leader who sacrifices anyone to his political ambitions, our task remains undone.

Second, we must understand that "black capitalism" is not a panacea. Although black Southerners must have the power of money and other forms of wealth to assist any strategy for freedom, economic power alone cannot save the day. That approach, as a sole strategy, has too many inherent weaknesses. Economic power alone carries with it no guarantee of safety or survival; and Augusta, Jackson, Kent State, Chicago, and Ghetto, U.S.A. ought to convince us that survival is now clearly a matter to worry about. History shows us that the Jews in Germany before the Second World War, through their creativity and innovativeness, had achieved a position of admirable economic strength—and we still don't know how many Jews the Nazis killed!

Furthermore, if the power brokers of America have not granted tens of millions of poverty-stricken white Americans the benefits of "white capitalism," you know what our chances are to have, in meaningful degree, any shade of economic power in the foreseeable future.

Finally, and most important, black capitalism is just not realistic. For a strategy of black capitalism to make a difference in our lives, it would have to have a significant and lasting corrective effect on the lives of the masses of black Americans, not just on the "talented tenth." That would necessitate massive and sustained infusions of money into the black community; but that is not likely to happen because those who hold power will not, in the nature of things, voluntarily give up enough of it to make a difference in what they have.

What, then, shall we do? Should we yell slogans unsupported by programs? Should we engage in violence as a means of social change? We have better sense than that. We should know by now that ballots, not bullets, are the answer to the problem of political oppression, just as soul power, not gunpowder, is the answer to the problem of cultural oppression. So what can we do?

If there *is* any one answer, the most promising, as I see it, is political power. The black vote is a powerful political force, as the resounding failure of Nixon's Southern strategy in the 1970 elections has proved. Albert Watson of South Carolina, the Republican candidate for governor, ran on a segregationist platform and lost roundly to John West. Two other Democratic gubernatorial candidates, Reubin Askew of Florida and Jimmy Carter of Georgia, owe much of their success to black voters. And the black vote was largely responsible for the senatorial victories of Democrats Lawton Chiles of Florida and Lloyd Bentsen of Texas.

In my opinion, however, there is another, even more powerful alternative open to us. Basically, politics is a fairly simple undertaking: the rules say that if we have two votes and they have one, we win.

But in order to win our share of a place in the American sun, we must redefine the word "we." "We" must come to mean a united black community acting in political concert with every available ally, including, and especially, poor and "working poor" whites. We should not turn down any ally, regardless of his motivation. As Julian Bond reminds us, "If your house is on fire and a man runs up with a bucket of water, don't ask him who he is or where he got it. Just make sure it's not gasoline, and then pour it on."

For example, when I ran against Herman Talmadge in 1968, I decided to run on the spur of the moment, on the last day to qualify. The assassination of Bobby Kennedy—the whole series of assassinations—was weighing on my mind, so I just decided to go in and run against Senator Talmadge. We started off three thousand dollars in debt, because I had to borrow the money to pay the qualifying fee. We had absolutely no campaign organization. I was thirty years old, I had never been in politics before in my life, and I was black. Talmadge said he would ignore the campaign.

About mid-July, he came home to campaign for the first time in his senatorial career. Why? To begin with, Talmadge is an astute politician, or he would not be where he is.

The UPI and AP had conducted secret statewide polls which indicated that if the election were held that day, about mid-July,

I might receive as much as 40 percent of the vote. Within two days, Herman Talmadge and Lester Maddox began to say that if there were a 60–40 split, it would still be an overwhelming victory, considering the number of blacks in Georgia. The next day, however, we packed the Carroll County courthouse in Carrollton with a rally that was 50 percent white and 50 percent black. (We had never campaigned in the shadows anyhow, and this time we went straight into the middle of town.) Within two days, Senator Talmadge opened an office in Carrollton, and during the following ten days he opened several offices in towns where we had successfully integrated rallies.

I suspect that deep within his heart, Herman Talmadge believed that even if he had not come home, he still would have won. What was it, then, that brought him home? I suggest that it was his realization of a new definition of "we" in Georgia.

A white man called me up one Sunday morning and said, "You don't know me, but I'm a cracker from below Macon and I represent a group of small farmers. We have to go out and beg for our small subsidies, and there is a guy down in X county who is receiving $88,000 yearly in farm payments. I ain't never lost no love on colored people but I have to admire somebody that can rise above their background."

Before I had a chance to inform him that he had just offended me, and apparently without his even realizing that he had, he went on to say, "Now we are going to vote for you and we don't have much money, but we are going to send you what we can." I received a check for about $39 dollars two days later.

Now the point of that story, and the result of that campaign, was, I think, the realization that we had at least the beginnings of a rethinking in the minds of low-income Southern whites. The white guy who lives down in Ludowici or in Cairo or even in the white ghetto of Atlanta is beginning to tell himself that it is not enough just to be white. When he feeds his children grits and grease for breakfast and sends them in rags and shoeless to an inferior school; when he gets up to go look for the job that has evaded him for five years; when he looks at his thirty-year-old wife and sees an old woman, you know he's telling himself it's not enough just to be white. He sees, through TV and other media, an America more affluent than ever before. And between that affluence and his own miserable life lies a chasm of despair, where hope has surrendered to frustration, and frustration threatens to become the womb of anger, the wellspring of violence. "All the while they're trying to sock it to you . . ." And so it was the realization that common problems are afflicting *people*—people who incidentally are white and incidentally are black—that brought Herman Talmadge back home to Georgia.

How can we make coalition politics effective? First, we must open up the lines of communication between blacks and poor whites. We must destroy the animosity and distrust which have been permitted to grow up between the races. The L.Q.C. Lamar Society is one vehicle for the accomplishment of this task.

Second, we must convince poor whites, through a massive educational and organizational effort, that we are afflicted, not only in common, but mutually as well. The man with a broken arm should feel sympathy for the man with a broken leg. True, this is not so easy when the evidence shows that the man broke his arm with an unneighborly stroke which broke the other man's leg. But cooperation for our mutual benefit and protection is a must if one man is to avoid keeping another man's wound from healing.

My grandpappy, the late Reverend Dr. Alexander S. Jackson, in a monograph he wrote in 1920, said, "The blight fell on master and man equally, different only in phase." I believe that poor whites are beginning to realize that they, too, have been denied and deceived by the exploiters of our land, and that Appalachia will not fade away with a wish and a prayer.

So I think the call now is to do what can be done, to use the vehicle that, although imperfect, provides the best possibility of helping us do what we know must be done in the South.

There are many who decry our strategy of coalition politics, who say the "Alliance of Poor Americans" can never come to be. There are also some Americans who disagree, who so fear the potential power of a coalition like this that they eliminate its more successful advocates when they begin to get results. As long as Malcolm X was a separatist, he was safe. But when he began to encourage such a coalition, he was murdered. And when Martin Luther King, Jr., began to organize and support white as well as black garbage workers around an economic issue that could shake our complacent society, he, too, was gone. But the strategy can work.

I happen to love the South. I do not love the South of the old days, when men lived with pellagra and starved-out lands and exploitation. I do not love the dehumanizing South of lynchings, castrations, and racial and religious discrimination. I do not love the South where black men are called "nigger." I reject that South. But I believe there is another South, a South of courage and dignity, of people like the late Martin Luther King, Jr., and the late Ralph McGill, men of compassion and concern.

Very often, when Southerners decide to do something, the decision is more than just a notion, for there is among Southerners a collective will, which means that we can do things that others can't or don't. It is the will to keep on keeping on, the kind of will Ella Wilcox wrote about when she said, "That there is no chance and no destiny is certain, for Will determines souls. . . . It is well known that great things fall before it sooner or later, and even Death will stand still and wait an hour and sometimes more on a will."

I believe we have that will; I hope we can make the decision to exert it. We in the South have an exciting opportunity to prove that, ultimately, black and white have only one enemy: not each other, but those economic, social, educational, and political conditions which cause and maintain hunger, neglect, bigotry, and disease. Too long have politicians made their money and power by separating black and white Southerners. We are one South, by blood and suffering, by horror and triumph. If we can prove here, in the old stubble-ground of hate and prejudice, slavery and segregation, that men and women of foresight and good will can create a new way out of the old, a multiracial society of democracy and opportunity, then we shall offer to our nation a model of possibility and hope in the midst of violence, fear, and conflict. Together, we can insure that history will someday record that the New South was a region of people who were too compassionate to ignore, too concerned not to fight, too great to turn away.

BEYOND RACE POLITICS: ELECTING SOUTHERN POPULISTS IN THE 1970S*

James Clotfelter
and
William R. Hamilton

[RACE politics is the politics of division and polarization between groups of people that may share a "community of need" on nonracial matters. It is the politics of diversion from the issues of how these needs can be met, of how people will work and educate their children and live fuller lives. Since the 1876 renegotiation of Appomattox, race politics has been the norm in most Southern states. The migrations stimulated by two world wars and the national political turmoil since the Brown decision have made the South's "peculiar problem" no longer peculiar—but it remains the "central fact" of Southern politics.

During the past century, most Southern political leaders have come from two social groups, both of which have used the race issue. The first group has been the lanterns-on-the-levee crowd, the blue-blood Redeemers and their successors, who usually whispered "nigra, nigra" when it looked as if poor whites would ally

* A complete list of references, tables, and data sources for this paper may be obtained from the L.Q.C. Lamar Society, P.O. Box 4774, Duke Station, Durham, North Carolina, 27706.

themselves with blacks against their "natural leaders." The second group has been the men who sweat and called it sweat, the Tillmans, Vardamans, Bilbos, and their successors, who used the black as something to step on on their way up. The Redeemers used the race issue with more subtlety and less obscenity, but without it they might have faced a lower-class rebellion. The Bilboites made a virtue of necessity, yelling "nigger" to the sound of "The Old Rugged Cross"; without the race issue, they might have been unable, in Vardaman's words, to get "the bottom rail on top."

Out of these two groups, on rare occasions, have come white political leaders who win elections with the support of biracial coalitions and perform their duties even-handedly. Biracial alliances have been formed from the first group by combining higher-income whites with blacks in a Limousine Majority. In Atlanta city politics, for example, the basis of this kind of majority was the notion that "the white woman who is driven to the polls in a Cadillac votes the same way her black chauffeur does." Such a coalition can work as long as blacks are content to play "chauffeur" roles—but the time for that has passed in Atlanta. The strategy is most adaptable to settings in which there are substantial white and black upper middle classes and to nonpartisan municipal elections where the emphasis is on clean government and "businesslike" leadership.

We are interested here in the possibilities for a black-white coalition of the second, or populist, type, because if it lives up to its billing, it could permit progressive, nonracist politics in almost any area of the South, urban or rural.

In the past, biracial political alliances have been formed by the second group of political leaders by combining lower-income whites with blacks in a populist majority. Tom Watson's Southern Farmers Alliance and the Colored Farmers Alliance tried such a coalition of the poor, but it was destroyed by the Redeemers' successful appeals to poor whites' racial fears. Huey Long practiced a modified Robin Hood policy of soaking the rich, or some of them building schools, hospitals, and highways for rural and low-income whites and blacks, and talking about race no more than was necessary. Earl Long became known as the "liberal Long" for similar reasons. Southern Populism was resuscitated by the New Deal in the 1930s, and this period influenced many progressive politicians now in their sixties. But most of the "colorful" Southern demagogues of the twentieth century have had little claim to be called populists: they sipped cocktails, very dry, with executives of power companies, insurance companies, and banks, and imposed consumer taxes with greater alacrity than income taxes.

Before we discuss the bases for populist-flavored, biracial alliances, we need to clarify what populism is, or could be. What does it mean to be a populist in the 1970s, especially in the South? Can populism be urban, rural, or both? Is it distinguishable from "liberalism," "racism," and "conservatism"?

WHAT IS POPULISM?

In the 1890s, Populism, concentrated in the less affluent rural areas of the South and Midwest, was part of the farmers' rebellion against the dominant economic and political interests of the day. In recent years, the term "New Populism" has been applied to the movement supporting George Wallace for President in 1968 and to the 1969 support for "reactionary," "people's" mayoralty candidates in several non-Southern cities. But this populism is not unambiguously of the Right or Left. In 1968 some ultra-conservatives criticized Wallace for being soft on the federal government because he favored continued farm price supports and Social Security, and the Young Americans for Freedom objected to Georgia Governor Lester Maddox's presence at a 1970 conservative rally because "we can't have the YAF associated with racist—or populist—viewpoints."

The "New Populists" were the lower economic and social half of "the unblack and the unpoor." They pointed to two enemies that hemmed in "Middle America": on the bottom the black underclass, seen as getting an unfair break in better jobs, education, and housing, and on the top their allies, the liberal, white have-mores, who already had the best jobs, education, and housing. Resentment was directed at the "pointy-headed intellectuals," the long-haired radicals and their comfortable upper-middle-class parents, the interfering foundations, the mass media, the Eastern financial establishment, the universities and educators, the liberal clergy, and the government bureaucrats whose briefcases Wallace vowed to "throw into the Potomac." (Great concern was shown about those briefcases, the mark of elitism and intellectual snobbery—what *papers* were lurking inside?) According to Peter Schrag:

> *. . . "law and order" (a major theme of the Wallace and Nixon campaigns) also means something like normality—the demand that everybody play it by the book . . . that things shouldn't be as they are but as they were supposed to be. . . . Stability is what counts, stability in job and home and neighborhood, stability in the church and in friends. . . . Black kids mean a change in the rules, a double standard in grades and discipline, and—vaguely—a challenge to all you believed right. . . . Everything is vulnerable. . . .* [*The working man*] *cannot imagine any major change for the better; but he can imagine change for the worse. And yet for a decade he is the one who has been asked to carry the burden of social reform, to integrate his schools and his neighborhood, has been asked by comfortable people to pay the social debts due to the poor and the black.*

The Wallace campaign benefited from this sense of vulnerability, and Wallace offered answers about who was responsible for the threats to hard-won prosperity and place in society, who were the conspirators against stability.

These "New Populists" usually characterize themselves as taxpayers, consumers, and family men, not as white supremacists, social reformers, or the proletariat. In fact, what kind of populists are they?

The contemporary vagueness of the populist notion stems partly from the inconsistencies of historical Populism. Just as many 1968 voters indicated support for George Wallace *and* Robert Kennedy or Eugene McCarthy, the Populist movement of the 1890s was simultaneously reformist and reactionary. The late Ralph McGill wrote of Populist-turned-racist-demagogue Watson:

> *Contradictions made the onetime flaming mind, bent on social and political justice, paradoxical in the extreme. In one issue of his magazine he defended the Russian revolution, attacked monopolists, the railroads, and Wall Street, and bitterly assailed Booker T. Washington, the Negro race, Jews, and Roman Catholics.*

The crushing of the Southern "Pops" effort to form a biracial coalition led Watson and his white followers to a racist stance. Similarly, although populism was primarily a rural phenomenon, and many populists thought the city was the origin of evil and oppression, the party attempted (with little success) to form an alliance with urban workingmen.

The Populist Party, in brief, was characterized by support for many reform measures, particularly those relating to agriculture and the railroads; resentment of cities and powerful economic groups; a general alienation from the political system; and a predisposition to use minority groups, such as Jews and immigrants, as "scapegoats." Populism today seems best conceived of as a political movement of people who feel threatened by rapid social or economic change. Populists tend to favor social welfare measures, unless these measures are thought to benefit hostile groups; to be alienated from some or all of the dominant institutions or "Establishment"; and to engage in scapegoatism of some kind, depending on the nature of their leadership and the vocabulary with which dominant groups characterize them. (In the 1890s many industrialists felt the Populists were reactionary, since they tried to hold back the introduction of new business methods.)

HENRY HOWELL IN VIRGINIA: ALMOST

Before we proceed, let us make clear that we believe that the election of race-baiters to political office is a bad thing. We believe —and hope—that it is possible in the 1970s, in most Southern states, for men to be elected and to govern effectively without coming down hard on the race issue; in most cases, an otherwise strong candidate will lose few votes on the race issue alone. This assumes that blacks will continue to be willing to support white progressives, as well as black candidates. (Black candidates can also speak of biracial, blue-collar alliances, but in that case it is more difficult to repress the race issue.)

Using public opinion survey data for eight Southern states from 1968 to 1970,* we will examine political alliances, both biracial and predominantly white, and political attitudes which are in some sense populist. With these data we will seek answers to the following questions: Have biracial coalitions worked where they have been tried? How can populistically inclined moderates be elected in the South? What are the groups they can hope to attract, and what are the issues and campaign approaches which

* The polls from which these data were taken were conducted by William R. Hamilton and Staff, a division of Independent Research Associates, Inc., a Washington-based public opinion research firm, and were commissioned by various candidates. The states surveyed were Florida, North Carolina, Georgia, Kentucky, and Maryland in 1968 (with a combined sample of 3309 white voters, later referred to as our Southern and border five-state study); Florida in 1969 and 1970; Maryland in 1969; Georgia in 1969 and 1970; Virginia in 1969 and 1970; and Tennessee and Texas in 1970. The manuscript was completed before the November 1970 elections.

might be used? Finally, would populist politics be any better than race politics?

One of the closest modern parallels to the Watson coalition of the 1890s can be found in Henry Howell's campaign for the Democratic gubernatorial nomination in Virginia in 1969. Howell lost the nomination in a runoff, but ran far more strongly than had been expected, moving from 23 percent of the decided voters in January (with three major candidates) to 38 percent in June, to 47 percent in the election. Howell, a state senator, had established himself as a champion of the little man by opposing increases in automobile insurance premiums and by suing to prevent power company rate increases. On the other hand, he was seen as a strong "liberal" by the press and the public, in a state where Democratic voters thought of themselves as moderate conservatives, and he had more than his share of personal political enemies. It was a period of relative racial calm, and Howell sought to keep the race issue out of the campaign. And his supporters were less interested in race than in taxes. Howell talked about measures to relieve the state tax pressure: exemption of food and patent medicine from the sales tax, and encouragement of the federal government to take over state welfare payments. Since Howell's strongest support came from those with annual incomes of $6,000 to $10,000, taxes were much more likely to concern his supporters than the need for "jobs and better wages." He was identified with unions, and received strong union support; between January and June, as he stressed "pocketbook" campaign issues, his support doubled among blue-collar workers and union members, and almost quadrupled among white retirees.

Howell's supporters were the most alienated and cynical about government. His campaign theme of "Keep the Big Boys Honest" underlined his past efforts and appealed to this widespread distrust of the men who controlled the dominant institutions. When asked why they supported him, 24 percent said Howell "understands the people, fights for the average people," while only 2 to 4 percent of the other candidates' supporters chose similar terms to explain their support. Specific issues were mentioned much less frequently by Howell supporters, and his governmental experience was mentioned even less.

What is most striking about Howell supporters was their racial and residential composition. He was strongest among urban blacks, followed by white, urban, blue-collar workers; he was weakest among white, rural, professional, and white-collar workers (rural conservatives), and among farmers. Although he received well over 50 percent of the black vote, he also was supported by nearly 50 percent of George Wallace's Virginia supporters who voted in the primary. In all class and racial groups, Howell was stronger in urban areas than in rural areas. Like Wallace, Howell attacked the "big boys," but unlike Wallace, he avoided race (and the code words for race) and talked about economic issues. Unlike Wallace's Southern support, Howell's following could best be characterized as urban populism, with its core of support among young white and black workers.

Support patterns in other 1970 campaigns reflect similar factors of class, race, issues, and style. Ralph Yarborough of Texas and Albert Gore of Tennessee, the last major holdovers from New Deal Southern populism, both were strong among blue-collar and union members, racial minority groups, and the retired—but not as strong as they had been previously. Gore was especially strong among farmers. The support pattern for Georgia "populist" Lester Maddox was similar to Gore's and Yarborough's except for the absence of black support and Maddox's far greater strength among rural whites.

In Georgia, former Governor Carl Sanders, unsuccessful candidate for the Democratic gubernatorial nomination, was strongest among blacks, the young, and urbanites; as with Leroy Collins and Robert King High in Florida, his most vulnerable point was his liberal, city-slicker image. Opponents characterized Sanders as an Atlanta lawyer, too rich and sophisticated ("Cufflinks Carl") to understand the common people, and somehow tied in to the immorality of the big city. Sanders was linked with the purportedly power-hungry Atlanta newspapers, banking interests, and country club set. Even some of Sanders' supporters came to believe that his opponent, Jimmy Carter, would be more likely to "give the average man a voice in government." Carter sought to fashion a predominantly white "rural populist" coalition by adding urban blue-collar whites to rural whites, with "average man" themes and a factory-and-gas-station hand-shaking campaign. In the primary, he succeeded in putting together the Wallace-Maddox coalition without an explicit antiblack appeal, and in the general election, he sought black votes. Carter's victory over Sanders was duplicated in Florida, where Lawton Chiles, "walking and talking with the people," defeated former Governor Farris Bryant for the Democratic Senatorial nomination.

To understand what these campaigns can tell us about the possibilities for populism, we need to look at the context of Southern politics in the 1970s.

AGE, RACE, AND CLASS

The Southerners who would be aligned with blacks in a populist coalition are urban and rural blue-collar whites and perhaps white retirees. Populist coalitions might include many of the young, since the young usually are attracted by aggressive rhetoric. Yet several troublesome facts need to be pointed out about these groups, about which much loose talk has been generated.

First, hard political choices cannot be avoided by the habitual refrain of Southern moderates: "Ah, there's a younger generation coming up, better-educated, more moderate, more tolerant, more aware of the issues . . ." The young are *not* predominantly liberal or progressive; never mind the campus militants and the minority involved in the McCarthy and Kennedy campaigns. In 1968 voters in their twenties supported Wallace more strongly than any other age group, in and out of the South. With eighteen- to twenty-one-year-olds voting in future elections, the youth vote will be even more important. The "New Politics" of mass participation and young, new faces can mean reactionary politics as well as bright-day-dawning politics. Some candidates whose primary appeal was on economic issues—Humphrey in the South in 1968, Ralph Yarborough and Albert Gore in 1970—had an older support base than their opponents. In five Southern and border states in 1968 Humphrey had three white voters over sixty-five for every two white Wallace voters of that age. Yarborough and Gore were strongest in age groups over fifty, with Gore particularly strong among retirees, and both were weakest among voters in their twenties. Their weakness among blue-collar workers in particular was among the young. It is the voting group that supported Humphrey, Yarborough, and Gore that is in danger of "dying off," not the Wallaceites.

Second, middle-to-lower-income whites in the South, as in the rest of the country, may be *more* alienated from politicians and the political system than are blacks. Increasingly, whites have been found to be suspicious of the institutions that were seen as benevolent during the New Deal and that were supposed to mediate, not accelerate, social change. Nineteenth-century Populism, according to Richard Hofstadter, was the first major movement "to insist that the federal government has some responsibility for the common weal"; to be a populist, one should not only feel alienated from established institutions, but should conceive of the possibility of doing something about his dilemma. Remedial action, however, usually involves the government, now a more pervasive institution than in 1892 and itself a target of alienation.

The modern yeoman "does all the right things," Schrag says, "obeys the law, goes to church, and insists—usually—that his kids get a better education than he had. But the right things don't seem to be paying off. . . ." A confidential 1970 study of blue-collar workers, made by the Labor Department for President Nixon, found that there was a "dead-end" quality to such work: salary scales level off toward middle age, as spending requirements increase. Added to the economic squeeze is a "social squeeze" said to be caused by pressure from "subsidized minorities" and by the worker's low social status. For many of these people, the future is counted in terms of years and dollars, not hopes.

Third, many lower-middle- and working-class whites do *not* want vast government spending programs which purport to help "the people" unless it is clear that taxes will not be increased significantly (or at least not noticeably), and that the programs are not geared specifically for blacks. Only 28 percent of Texas Democrats, for example, disagreed that "spending money on big federal programs cannot solve the most difficult problems facing Texas and the nation." The 1930s revival of Southern populism was associated with infusions of New Deal money; the South had not been prosperous even before the Depression, and there was widespread willingness to support government projects to promote economic development and create jobs. Men such as Yarborough, Gore, and Claude Pepper—as well as the prewar Lyndon Johnson—were nurtured by this revived populism which temporarily found support in the cities, the hill country, and beyond. But in 1970 Yarborough and Gore both lost some of their traditional strength among blue-collar workers, as labor partially confirmed Richard Scammon's epigram that workers have become more concerned about crabgrass than about Taft-Hartley. The issues of "full employment and economic growth" are most appealing when large numbers are unemployed or underemployed, but few of us would want to depend upon a permanent recession for political unity.

It is no longer dangerous for Southern candidates to associate themselves with the problems of workingmen: less than a quarter of Virginians agreed that "I almost never vote for a candidate who has the support of organized labor." Neither, however, can the working class be depended upon to be attracted by issues developed purely for "labor's" sake. Southern blue-collar workers, unionized or not, need to be appealed to as workers and as "Middle Americans," using the broad populist themes we will discuss later.

How widespread in the South are attitudes that might be characterized as populist? First, support for social welfare programs (without mention of taxation as a corollary to government spending) is moderately high, although uneven, among whites, and very high among blacks. Support is highest for the New Deal measures that enjoy widespread support throughout the country. In most states whites and blacks tend to support increased spending for "health," "education," and "more jobs for this area"; few want lower spending for "low- and middle-income housing," "transportation and roads," and "conservation and pollution." The national program most commonly opposed in Southern (and non-Southern) states are "nondomestic" programs: space exploration, military spending, and foreign aid.

Clearly, anyone running against a candidate talking race must hit hard on economic issues to overcome the still-powerful salience of anti-integration attitudes. Economic reform programs directed at lower-middle-income whites must include a palatable tax program. For the class groups to which a populist campaign would be directed, taxes and other economic issues usually are volunteered as "major problems" by more voters than volunteer education or racial problems. Overall, education is most frequently mentioned as the number-one problem; however, support for public education in the South is more of a "style" than a substantive issue. Any candidate must favor quality education, but it does not appear to be an issue that wins or loses votes.

Most potential populist voters oppose new taxes for *any* purpose, including education. "Ask a poor white what he wants for his young ones," black gubernatorial candidate C. B. King said, "and the black parent and the white parent want the same cotton-picking things." One of the things cited by King, Jimmy Carter, and other Georgia candidates was statewide kindergarten, to help children from lower-income families get better early educational opportunities. But many lower-income voters are hostile to taxes to support such programs even when it is the other fellow's ox being gored. For example, in Virginia, 81 percent agreed that "the average man is getting taxed to death while the rich people and big business get away with paying very little." Adequately graduated income taxes would draw more tax money from "the rich people and big business," while sales taxes hurt the poor and moderate income groups. Several state surveys show, however, that voters are less hostile to increased sales taxes than to increased income or property taxes, perhaps because the income and property taxes appear all at once and are more noticeable burdens. Education of the lower-middle class to the graduated nature of the income tax, as a means to insure that the "big boys" pay their proper share, would be wise strategy for any populist candidate. Several gubernatorial candidates in 1970 called for tax reforms and shifting of tax burdens from property, sales, and small business taxes to corporate and other income taxes.

What are the other issues that could fit into a populist campaign? Support for quality *public* education might become a real issue in the states faced with proliferating segregation academies seeking state aid. Health care (hospitals) is rarely an issue in Southern state politics, but it is one of real concern to middle- and lower-middle-income groups which believe that they are not being cared for properly.

If the "average man" sees himself as taxpayer, consumer, and family man, he must be talked to in those terms. In the consumer protection area, Henry Howell showed that standing up for the people who pay the electricity bills and insurance premiums pays off in electoral support. Creation of an ombudsman or a "citizens' action line" could also be an appropriate populist pledge. States regulate many consumer industries—banking, utilities, and communications, for example. Increasing numbers of comptrollers, attorneys general, treasurers, and insurance and public service commissioners (and candidates for those offices) are finding that "keeping the big boys honest" wins public support—although it may get them little financial support from the "clients" who will be regulated. Even the middle-class environmental issue can be approached from a populist perspective, since many large industrial polluters ("big boys") operate without fear of strict enforcement of pollution controls. Environmental protection should be discussed in its relation to maintaining a healthy setting for families and providing adequate recreational facilities, rather than to the more intellectual, upper-income goal of "conservation."

On the family dimension, a populist candidate must convince people that he shares their uneasiness about a possible "moral decline" in the nation. Reactionaries should not be permitted to preempt the Southerner's attachment to traditions, to his people, and to his land. Small-town and rural residents tend to be especially concerned about declining moral standards and rapid change (as manifested, for example, by student unrest), and liberal candidates often are blamed. "There must be something wrong," 68 percent of Texas Democrats agreed, "about a man who votes against morning prayers in the public schools." The 1968 Wallace campaign, with its "preservatist moralism," appealed to those concerned about rapid social change, including changes in religious morality. Although Wallace himself rarely attacked the liberal clergy, his national supporters were more upset about the clergy than about students and professors, two of Wallace's frequent targets. Anxiety about the long-hairs was not restricted to Wallace supporters; all voting groups were disturbed about the new "life styles" evangelized by the young and the "liberated." Populists might try not only to shore up the self-confidence of the workingman but, through reassurance about traditional life styles, to do the same for the old and those approaching old age. The creative old should be honored as often as the creative young, and development of more livable nursing homes should have the same priority as kindergartens and child-care programs.

Newsweek hypothesized that unhappiness with progressive politicians stems "far more from their permissiveness than from their programs." "Permissiveness" involves *style,* and populism has as much to do with political style as it does with issues. Just as historical Populism appealed (according to Hofstadter) to those who saw themselves "shut out from access to the centers of power," the "New Populism" has been called "a quest for recognition."

Charles Stenvig, elected mayor of Minneapolis after a "law-and-order" campaign, said, "People felt that nobody was representing them and nobody was listening." Every visible interest group was winning something from the system except those who were not a group, the "silent majority," the residuals.

Southern whites and blacks endorse populist-flavored alienation statements. On the statement, "It's still hard for the average man to get a fair shake," 88 percent of Florida Democrats, 72 percent of Tennesseans, 57 percent of Virginians, and 54 percent of Texas Democrats agreed. The statement, "There aren't many politicians or public officials today who'll speak up for the average man" was agreed with by majorities of 63 to 77 percent in those four states.

Populist campaigns are built on "average man" themes, although not all "average man" candidates, of course, are populists. Voters must believe that the candidate is responsive, that he "understands the problem of people like us," and is not preoccupied with the rich and the poor to the point of ignoring the middle. Respondents frequently comment that representatives should "get back and talk" and "pay attention to the people." Lawton Chiles's thousand-mile walk through Florida symbolized his attentiveness. Candidates as diverse as Sam Massell (in the 1969 Atlanta mayoralty campaign—voter base liberal, black, urban) and Jimmy Carter (in the 1970 Georgia Democratic gubernatorial primary—voter base white, rural) said that the issue was "who will control the government—the people or a small band of men?" (Frequently the meaning of the "small band of men" or "power structure" is left up to the individual voter.)

THE DARK SIDE OF POPULISM

Populism has a dark side, too: the tendency to seek out scapegoats to blame for problems. The "fear and suspicion of the stranger that haunted . . . the nativist American mind," Hofstadter says, "was exhibited by [the Populists] in a particularly virulent form. Everyone remote and alien was distrusted and hated—even Americans, if they happened to be city people." Most white Populists apparently were firm believers in Anglo-Saxon superiority and opponents of "ethnic mixture," notwithstanding their leaders' attempts to create a biracial alliance. Kevin Phillips believes the upcountry South's economic progressivism has never extended to race, because of the subregion's traditional fear of blacks as job competitors and resentment of them as "favored pawns of the plantation system."

Many lower-middle- and working-class whites see the government, the schools, and the media as increasingly preoccupied with helping blacks, while the hard-working Middle American is ignored. Especially in the South, of course, the black man has been the scapegoat for whites. Vocal antiblack feelings still are most likely to be found there, particularly in rural areas. Class and urban-rural differences among whites affect the manner in which race surfaces as an important concern, but race-*related* issues remain important to all groups.

The dark side of populism is reflected in the election of a Maddox or a Wallace. "George ain't nothing but an old Populist," former Alabama Governor Jim Folsom said of Wallace. "We just disagreed on one thing: I never did want to take any credit for hangin' niggers."

The 1968 Wallace Presidential voter is the key to the South's political future: neither Nixon nor Humphrey received more than his national share (43 percent) of the vote in any of the eleven Southern states, and Wallace received at least 29 percent in nine states. Phillips believes the Wallace voter is race-conscious, and that in the future he will support conservative (Republican) candidates. In 1966–68 he notes "a sharp conservative trend among hitherto populist Southern poor whites" who had shunned the conservatism of past Dixiecrat and Republican candidates. (Nationally, however, Phillips speaks of "a populist conservatism" attacked by the now-liberal Eastern Establishment which had attacked the New Deal from a conservative perspective in the 1930s.) On the other hand former Democratic National Chairman Fred Harris believes that some Wallace voters supported him "as much because of his progressive populist positions as for racist reasons."

Were the Wallace voters populists, racists, conservatives, or what? Certainly, the assertive "little man" rhetoric of the movement suggests that Wallace may have been trying to capitalize on populist feelings. They had nothing to be ashamed of, Wallace told his audience, there is nothing wrong with wanting to protect your home and job. So they were rednecks, what of it? They were the backbone of America. They were being taken advantage of by the liberal establishment, a conspiracy of the affluent and the well-educated—the enemies of turn-of-the-century Populism, the Money Power and the Eastern Seaboard. In September 1970 Wallace told a segregationist Citizens' Council meeting, "The affluent super-rich in this country are more dangerous than the militants." But, he said, "citizens' power will right the wrongs perpetrated against the middle class and lower class in the United States. . . . No government is administered according to the objective and intent of the Founding Fathers . . . unless it is administered for the weak, the poor, and the humble as well as for the powerful." In terms of specific national policy proposals, however, Wallace has been far from radical. Although he has proposed revising the tax system to make the rich pay more, once supported an excess war profits tax, and supports Social Security and collective bargaining, his populist suggestions have been restrained compared, for example, to Huey Long's "Share the Wealth" proposals.

Wallace supporters, on most surveys, showed "right-wing" opinions; in a Harris poll, they were found to be even more conservative on issues than voters who supported Barry Goldwater in 1964. We do not believe, however, that the Wallace movement is *best* interpreted as ultra-conservative. Several studies document the willingness of Wallace voters to support liberal anti-Establishment candidates in 1968. Also, Wallaceites disagreed about what kind of a man they were supporting—even in the South, where he was known best. In Florida in 1969, for example, twelve other state and national political figures were judged to be liberal, moderate, or conservative in a consistent fashion—meaning that if the largest number of voters believed a man was a conservative or a liberal, the second largest would judge him to be a moderate. However, while 53 percent of Florida Democrats with opinions judged Wallace conservative, 31 percent believed he was a liberal, and only 16 percent said he was a moderate. Furthermore, many of Wallace's supporters said they did not believe he had the qualities to be President; that they supported him anyway indicates the depth of their dissatisfaction with the political system.

In terms of party identification and state election voting habits, Wallace supporters surveyed in our Southern and border five-state 1968 study of white voters fell between Humphrey and Nixon supporters. On Social Security and Medicare—New Deal–Fair Deal measures on which traditional party allegiances continued to be important—Wallace supporters were more liberal than Nixon supporters and less liberal than Humphrey supporters. Wallace supporters took moderately conservative positions on food-for-the-needy and unemployment. On a majority of issues, however, Wallace supporters took the most conservative positions: on housing and slum clearance (probably seen as "urban," "black" welfare programs), and on all integration issues. On foreign policy and on law-and-order "style" questions (how should riots be handled, should the Chicago police have employed more force), Wallace supporters were overwhelmingly hard-line.

Wallace supporters were more likely to be male and young—groups which traditionally have provided support for "extremist" movements in Europe and the United States. The young are less firmly anchored to traditional political groupings, and could be more easily mobilized in a third-party campaign. Wallace's Southern supporters were much more likely to be rural or small-town residents, in contrast to his strong urban, blue-collar "hard-hat" support outside the South. Southern Wallace supporters also were more likely to be found in the Black Belt counties in the states surveyed. Overall, they ranked lower than supporters of other candidates on a social-class index (education, occupation, income), although there were fewer Wallace supporters than white Humphrey supporters in the very lowest class groups. Wallace supporters were heavily concentrated at the lower-middle-class point; they also were more homogeneous than other candidates' supporters in terms of religion (Baptist and other fundamentalist Protestants).

On the criterion of support for social welfare measures, Southern Wallace supporters as a whole do not seem to qualify meaningfully as populists. Only on Social Security and Medicare were their views on issues discernible from "conservative" positions. Subgroups within the Wallace movement, however, might qualify. For example, Wallace supporters who identified themselves as Democrats (63 percent in our sample) were more likely to support expansion of those two programs than were Wallace Independents or Wallace Republicans. On the alienation criterion for populism, Wallace supporters certainly qualify. They were most likely to agee that "it's all too true that the rich are getting richer and the poor are getting poorer."

We find that the populist criteria of class, alienation, and scapegoatism fall on different dimensions. In our five-state study, there are no significant relationships between social class and attitudes toward integration (meaning that persons of higher social class are almost as likely to be hostile to integration as persons of lower social class), and between alienation and attitudes toward integration (meaning that people do not have to be alienated to be hostile to integration). Alienation, of course, is more strongly related to social class, the lower strata being most cynical and alienated. Because segregation is not the position of a lonely minority in the South, people do not have to be social outcasts or alienated to support it. This means that no moderate candidate can escape having to appeal to people who are hostile to integration, regardless of the classes to which he appeals.

Whether Phillips or Harris or neither will be correct in his evaluation of the party that will be the eventual home of the Wallaceites is beyond the scope of this paper. But certainly the Wallace movement exacerbated an instability in Southern political alignments that could be used by different types of candidates of both parties. The substantive distance separating Wallace and Humphrey supporters on issues makes a tight reconstruction of the old Democratic alliances unlikely. At the same time, the substantial *social distance* (class and alienation) separating Wallace and Nixon supporters in the South undermines the view that Wallace voters necessarily will follow the more "conservative" candidate. Republicans and Wallaceites are different kinds of people—they belong to different kinds of clubs and churches, go different places on Saturday night and Sunday morning, and respond differently to "bigness."

While the salience of antiblack issues has declined to the point where few men can be elected on those alone, neither is it possible for candidates to be elected solely on the basis of liberal attitudes toward racial problems. Many of the 1968 Southern white supporters of Nixon and Humphrey, for example, were opposed to integration. In Southern states, no majority can be created that does not include some white voters hostile to integration. More optimistically, what disturbs many whites is not that blacks are benefiting from government programs, but that the federal government and the Establishment generally are seen as having broken the normal "rules of the game" to help blacks. While 63 percent of Florida Democrats favored spending more to help "senior citizens and retirees," for example, and 55 percent would spend more to help "poor people in general," only 22 percent wanted to spend more to aid Negroes and other minorities. Three times as many Floridians wanted lower spending on programs for Negroes than wanted lower spending on poor people in general, although many of the latter would be blacks. Therefore, candidates should emphasize the general benefits of social programs, trying to avoid the code words that say "blacks only." White Southerners who oppose outright "gifts" of welfare earmarked for the blacks, but who are not hostile to aid for those who are "in need," are essential to a populist majority.

To meet his constituents' need for scapegoats, a nonracist candidate might identify *new* targets for attack, more rationally chosen, to replace the blacks. The most appropriate targets would be powerful economic groups, perhaps local businesses that pay low wages, take advantage of the poor in loans and contracts, charge excessive prices, sell faulty products, or use their financial resources to oppose progressive measures. Another target could be groups that embody sharply contrasting class styles, such as managements of defense corporations that use the public's money for management perquisites and white-collar featherbedding.

"Populist thinking has survived in our time," Hofstadter says, "as an undercurrent of provincial resentments, popular and 'democratic' suspiciousness, and nativism." Hostility to federal programs is partly a reflection of those provincial—that is, rural and regional—resentments. Popular suspiciousness is reflected in the cynicism toward established political ways which characterized the majority in many Southern states. Hostility to racial minorities, contemporary nativism, can be supplanted as white Southerners' primary concern, but it is not likely to be eradicated.

* * *

Southern politics involves both national phenomena, such as the partial alienation of the workingman from progressive politicians, and regional trends, such as the erosion of traditional political loyalists.

We believe that populist candidates could be the beneficiaries of the kind of Southern disquiet cited by Kevin Phillips. We do not believe that progressivism is another of the hopeless causes which periodically enthrall the region. We are not saying that populism is the only way for progressives to be elected, but we do believe that "blue-blood" progressives and ideological liberals who become known as such will have a difficult time in most Southern states in the foreseeable future. Let us restate several points:

First, just as racial tension was the dominant theme of the 1960s, the "revolt of the common man" may be the dominant theme of political conflict in the 1970s. We believe that more political leaders, white and black, should appeal to both the hard hats (and their rural counterparts) and the blacks. The region needs local versions of Robert Kennedy who can pull together a majority coalition of working-class whites, blacks, and perhaps a few progressive upper-income whites—what Virginia's Howell partly succeeded in doing. A hard hat–black alliance is necessary not just to win elections, but to govern effectively after elections. Blue-collar workers (with $5,000–10,000 annual income) and their families number seventy million people nationally; they cannot be abandoned to the racists. To say that they are suffering from a sense of "neglected decline" may be becoming a cliché, but responding to that malaise would not be a cliché.

Second, the young cannot be counted upon to rally automatically behind progressive candidates. There is a long-term trend among the young, nationally and especially in the South, toward identifying themselves as political "independents." Many can be mobilized by either party, and by either reformist or reactionary candidates, depending on the style and mood of campaigns and candidates.

Third, romantic rhetoric of the type long familiar to discussions of "poor whites and poor blacks" has been applied to populist coalitions—with the term "populist" often used loosely to mean "rednecks" of whom the speaker approves. We believe populism offers hope for majority progressive politics in the 1970s, but it will be neither romantic nor easy. Government, the populist tool for righting wrongs and defending the common man, is widely seen as an Establishment villain, and sometimes with good reason. Although Wallace may have been a big spender in Alabama, some of his regional supporters are race-minded, uninterested in social welfare programs, and hostile to the very concept of change.

A new populism might not appear as a set of distinct (that is, recognizably "populist") issue positions. Instead, it might be a style of political conflict, a mood or a stance, characterized by "common man" rhetoric and fueled by widespread cynicism about the system and those who hold powerful positions in it. Being elected to office might become easier than being reelected. Some of the populists elected by the majorities discussed here might be less "respectable"—perhaps tinged with Longism—and less explicitly issue-oriented than some would wish.

Populism seems both reformist and reactionary because it involves *both* acceleration and slowing of change:

(a) An essentially *status quo,* though not fundamentalist, attitude toward life style. A populist candidate does not need to hate kids to make the point that the rules of the game do not change daily, and that the way people have been living for years makes sense—at least for them. To keep the confidence of a majority, a leader can be tolerant, but not permissive.

(b) A momentum toward economic reform. To his black constituents, a populist talks fair government employment practices and, more generally, jobs and prices and taxes, not race. To his white constituents, he says similar things: We will revise the tax structure (moving away from dependence on property taxes while increasing corporate taxes) and see that you get a fair share of government benefits—hard work *does* pay off, there is justice for whites as well as for blacks. Any candidate who takes this part of populism seriously will have to use personal campaigning and the mass media to direct his campaign over the heads of existing (usually conservative) political organizations to the voters. Campaign issues such as subsidized health care are not likely to win conservative support. Populism was destroyed in the 1890s because it threatened entrenched economic interests; the contemporary Redeemers are unlikely to look upon populism any more benevolently. Candidates should not become so concerned about what Richard Scammon calls the "Social Issue" that they forget that economic well-being is a part of life style, too—and remains vitally important to people.

Earlier we asked if populism would be any better than race politics. If elected, a populist would have a mixed mandate to initiate economic change and to abstain from massive "social engineering"; this is a precarious balance, but we believe it is preferable to any of the alternatives. Populism has the potential of moving people into the future in the name of the ideals of the past. Its attraction derives from its Janus-like feature: it seems to look backward, as a politics of traditionalism, but also can look forward, as a politics of progress and reconciliation between peoples. It should be recognized, however, that neopopulism at its worst (cynical Wallace-style power politics) is just another of the cruel hoaxes periodically played upon the South and upon working people throughout the country, dressed up only with the tangy rhetoric of Southern rural politics.

We have dealt here usually with short-term tactics. In a longer time perspective, we are hopeful that populism can be a vehicle for the reaffirmation of personal worth and dignity in the face of increasing social, economic, and political structural complexity, found even in the nation's least-developed region. Populism can focus on the basic problems of a healthy and satisfying life which too often are assumed to be curious anachronisms in this "Technological Age of Affluence." Maldistributed taxation and services remain serious problems in some areas, for example, and the quality of work for much of our population is decreasingly creative. Populism can provide the exhilaration that comes from a "people's movement" (with its Jacksonian disdain for the "experts"), the self-respect that comes from participation in forming one's own political destiny. It might work gradually to reduce the very alienation from government which now is a prerequisite for the development of populist attitudes. Although it is a delicate blend, populism has the potential of improving the lot of the people without destroying their links to the past and their conceptions of who they are.

SOUTHERN GOVERNORS AND THE NEW STATE POLITICS

Edwin M. Yoder, Jr.

[NOT so long ago a sandy-haired young man who occasionally called himself "a boy from the cotton patches" won the governorship of a Southern state. His inaugural address, promising concerted attack on poverty and illiteracy, low teacher salaries, and low per capita income and racial strife, shocked a few of the dinosaurs who regarded Dixie governors as caretakers. But to many of us who listened that crisp January day it seemed a hopeful—certainly it was a novel—overture to a new decade.

I am, of course, describing Terry Sanford, and the year was 1961. But everything above might be written again of the new governors of the 1970s: Linwood Holton of Virginia, John West of South Carolina, Jimmy Carter of Georgia, Reubin Askew of Florida, Dale Bumpers of Arkansas. A decade ago Sanford's blueprint found no imitators to the immediate north or west. Harry Byrd still dominated Virginia; Arkansas still nursed the Faubus hangover. But southward there were and would be other young chief executives, more or less of the Sanford ilk: a Collins of Florida, a Hollings of South Carolina, a Sanders of Georgia. All were "liberal" by Southern measures of the 1950s; all were obviously uneasy with the gloomy defensiveness and negativism into which the civil rights question had plunged the South.

I cite this history only because the cynic might observe, ten years later, that only the faces had changed, that after all the sixties did not belong in spirit to the Sanfords as much as to the Wallaces and Maddoxes, mouthing the South's oldest fears. Splendid as Sanford's own accomplishments were, the chrysalis of racial fear had not been decisively broken, and perhaps indeed the ancient history is worth citing by way of caution as at the outset of another decade another new crop of Southern governors catches the nation's eye and brings the television cameras scurrying South. As the new governors sounded their brave clarions from the porticos in Richmond and Tallahassee, Little Rock and Atlanta, Raleigh and Richmond, the circumspect would recall Professor George Tindall's recent counsel: "The prudent prophet [of Southern politics] must take a cue from J. P. Morgan who, when once asked what the market would do, responded, 'It will fluctuate.' "

Nonetheless, beginning at Richmond in the early winter of 1970 and continuing elsewhere a year later, there did seem to be a new market in Southern governors—all young, all anxious to install a vision of Southern possibilities, all anxious to put the slogans, the fears, the divisions, the despairs of the sixties behind them. Holton, the first Republican governor of Virginia in this century, struck the keynote:

> *... At the dawn of the 1970s it is clear that problem-solving, and not philosophical principles, has become the focal point of politics. ... The common belief is that state government must act, that the future of states' rights rests upon the success of state efforts. No more must the slogan of states' rights sound a recalcitrant and defensive note for the people of the South. For the era of defiance is behind us.... Here in Virginia we must see that no citizen of the Commonwealth is excluded from full participation in both the blessings and responsibilities of our society because of his race.... As Virginia has been a model for so much else in America in the past, let us now endeavor to make today's Virginia a model in*

> *race relations.... Let our goal in Virginia be an aristocracy of ability, regardless of race, color, or creed.*

Allowing for differences of style and emphasis, the inaugurals of a year later resembled Holton's. In Columbia, John West promised:

> *We can, and we shall, in the next four years eliminate from our government any vestige of discrimination because of race, creed, sex, religion, or any other barrier to fairness.... We pledge to minority groups no special status other than full-fledged responsibility in a government that is totally color-blind.*

In Little Rock, Dale Bumpers spoke of "open minds and open doors," and said:

> *The future we envision must be shaped and shared by all Arkansans: old and young, black and white, rich and poor.... This administration will be one of concern, compassion, and reality. Our mandate is to correct those things which are wrong and build on those things which are right.*

Reubin Askew, January 5, in Tallahassee:

> *It is not enough merely to ... give pious lip service to the justifiably urgent needs of our black citizens ...*

A week later in Atlanta, a "peanut farmer" named Jimmy Carter (his Navy career, including command of a nuclear submarine, discreetly soft-pedaled) told an inauguration-day audience that included Lester Maddox:

> *At the end of a long campaign, I believe I know our people as well as anyone. Based on this knowledge of Georgians ... I say to you quite frankly that the time for racial discrim-*

*ination is over. Our people have already made this major and difficult decision.**

Brave words; good sentiments. And for some Southerners, at least, novel words as well. To outside ears they may have sounded easy and somewhat tardy. But to those on the inside who had listened for them for what seemed an age, they were remarkable. Not for a very long time, if ever, had the South heard from its governors so many such pledges so straightforwardly stated.

And considering how remarkably the sentiments and themes coincided, it was striking how different was the political provenance of the men who voiced them. The Honorable Linwood Holton had shaped his well-tailored Jeffersonian creed after a victory for which the White House was said to claim considerable credit, Mr. Nixon having flown to Roanoke on election eve to speak for Mr. Holton. Those who believed in the alleged "Southern strategy" (absorbing the Wallace vote into new Southern majorities for Republican candidates) apparently represented Holton's victory to the President as its first fruits. But the flaws of that theory were made clear by a careful study of the Virginia election by Ralph Eisenberg of the University of Virginia's Institute of Government. Eisenberg cited the changes that had transformed Virginia from Byrdland to Holtonland in the twinkling of an eye: a 62.7 percent expansion of the gubernatorial electorate in four years, the removal of the poll tax, the passage of the 1965 Voting Rights Act—so that the decisive statewide vote, once so closely tied to the Byrd citadels of the county courthouses, is now "metropolitan," urban, and suburban. The key to Holton's victory, wrote Eisenberg, was "clearly his ability to win urban votes, both in the state's largest cities and in its developing suburban complexes." Forty-one predominantly Negro precincts in Virginia cities, while preferring Holton's Democratic opponent, gave Holton 37 percent of their votes—as against 7 percent and 5 percent for his fellow Republican candidates for statewide office. In South Carolina a year later, John West defeated Republican candi-

* Excerpts from the inaugural addresses of Governors Holton, Askew, Bumpers, Carter, and West will be found in the Appendix, page 360.

date Albert Watson in a hard-fought campaign, colored by the incident at Darlington in which a mob of white men had protested "busing" by attacking busloads of small Negro children. West's victory could be seen, perhaps, as an explicit repudiation of such White House influence as was identified with Watson and his chief tout, Senator Strom Thurmond. In the cases of Bumpers, Carter, and Askew national politics seemed less important. It was pretty obvious, for instance, that the President had declined to try to rescue Governor Claude Kirk from his buffooneries. The point was, then, that the new governors had reached office in a variety of settings, but then seemed to reach all but identical conclusions about their mandates.

One who had watched the curiously inconclusive struggle of the South in the sixties—the Sanfords, Collinses, and Sanderses grappling for its soul with the Maddoxes and Wallaces—might feel that at last a constructive impulse had won out. It seemed to have little enough to do with party alignments. In fact, one could serve himself at a smorgasbord of theories: Were these victories a debacle for the "Southern strategy"? It seemed so, especially in South Carolina. Were Carter and Askew resurgent Southern "populists"? Certainly amid the statesmanlike phrases, the occasional snap of the demagogue's gallus could be heard. Carter had rabble-roused a bit against former Governor Sanders, identifying him with the silk-stocking crowd in Atlanta. Askew, in his severely Calvinist way, had summoned Floridians to penance for overloading the poor man with taxes.

All the theories had some merit, no doubt. But if an upbeat line on race and economics now suddenly seemed the vogue, the major cause might be dazzlingly simple. Politicians respond to election returns; and those returns, from the passage of the Voting Rights Act onward, reflected the growing potency of the Negro vote, which has suddenly cast a long shadow over lily-white parties and candidacies. Southern politicians may be slow learners in some respects, but they are no slouches at political arithmetic. And the arithmetic was clear. Southern Regional Council figures showed that between 1968 and 1970 alone, Negro registration jumped by

212,000 to a regional total of 3,357,000. The impact was clear in Holton's case, and decisive in West's, where his estimated Negro vote had far exceeded his victory margin. Unless Congress condones a second disfranchisement—a prospect that dimmed when Attorney General John Mitchell failed to weaken the 1965 act—the Negro voter would be heard, and new governors would be deaf at their peril.

But it was more than mere arithmetic, of course. It could be said that state government in the South was beginning to hear what the Southern cities had heard a decade earlier. Throughout the sixties, as "Never, no never!" rang from the statehouse steps and lines were drawn in the dust, the city halls of the South had to face real problems. Defiant rhetoric offered no help. While at the state level Negro voters could brandish neither economic nor political power in most states, in the cities it was another story. In Birmingham, Nashville, Atlanta, Greensboro, the determined use of voting and buying power had been a spur to conscience—and good sense. Whatever accommodating tone had crept into the language of governors by 1970 was long since familiar in the speeches of Southern mayors of the better sort—mayors like Ivan Allen of Atlanta or the late David Schenck of Greensboro, two city officials I have watched. And the lesson the Southern cities had learned, often to their astonishment, was that the skies didn't fall with the making of a racial *modus vivendi.* In many ways, then, the cities were at least five years, even a decade, ahead of the states in dealing with black demands.

And that brings us to what must be called the great irony of the scene: that a conservative Republican administration to which many a Southerner had looked to slow racial change had presided willy-nilly over its greatest acceleration since Reconstruction. That school desegregation was all the Nixon administration claimed when addressing its liberal clientele could be doubted. That the change flowed from deliberate policy could be doubted even more, given the pleas for judicial delay, the "Southern strict constructionist" nominees to the Supreme Court, and the rhetoric that attended both. But it had happened; that could not be doubted.

More, it didn't hurt as much as the prophets of doom had said it would; and suddenly many a diehard who'd been riding the horse of Apocalypse found himself rudely unsaddled. Just as the Southern city halls had moved on from the sit-ins to more complicated problems, leaving the old posturing behind, it now seemed that a similar course lay ahead for the states. Room had accordingly been created for new men in the governor's mansions. And it happened, uncannily, just as the nation suddenly found itself tired of federal good works, and was gripped with a sense that many a high-minded program had failed to ring in the New Jerusalem and that government at all levels was slipping farther from personal control.

It was obvious to Southerners—especially to Southerners, one might say—that after decades of hollow rhetoric about states' rights the South suddenly might have ample opportunity to do a few things for itself, if it would. The seventies, it seemed, might be a statehouse show as no decade had been since the 1920s, or the Progressive Era, and what would be achieved could come only under energetic problem-solving leadership. If that were so, then, the new governors would have to be pragmatic, even-tempered men of conscience, men with a sense that old problems would not yield to old slogans—men with names like Holton, Scott, West, Carter, Askew, Bumpers, and others who cared to enlist.* The market might fluctuate again, of course. As far as the South's old quarrel with itself was concerned, the seventies might end as indecisively as the sixties. But it would not be for want of a few brave words from its elected leaders. As for the acts, they would have to be awaited and judged on their merits.

* Others, in fact, did choose to enlist. William Waller, Governor of Mississippi, was elected in a run-off with another racial moderate. The superstar of segregation in the state, Jimmy Swann, placed a poor third. Congressman Edwin Edwards barely edged out another moderate in the Louisiana Democratic gubernatorial primary, which saw the segregationist former Governor, Jimmie Davis, far behind in fourth place. By 1972 the score in favor of racial moderation in the eleven states of the Old Confederacy was ten to one. Only Alabama's George Wallace promised protection from "black dominance" as a means of capturing the statehouse, and even he won by a hair-line majority.

The southern sense of place

THE SOUTHERN CITY: NORTHERN MISTAKES IN SOUTHERN SETTINGS

Joel L. Fleishman

[THERE was a time not so long ago, before urban conditions became the urban crisis, when Southern leaders exhorted the South to join the American mainstream. We were given the vision of a "New South" which would be urban, industrial, and affluent. We were the poorest among a rich nation's regions, and in our eagerness for a richer and fuller life for all our people we zealously recruited industry and commerce to our states. Inevitably, the new jobs clustered in our cities, and, as with all other cities throughout history, the promise of greater economic opportunity proved irresistible to the young in the small towns and on the farms. Pushed off the land by its poverty, faster and faster they came to the metropolis, changing the cities to which they moved, and in the process changing the South as a whole. We have listened well to Henry Grady, and are winning this

A complete list of references, tables, and data sources for this paper may be obtained from the L.Q.C. Lamar Society, P.O. Box 4774, Duke Station, Durham, North Carolina, 27706.

second War Between the States hands down—a war not only more moral but more lucrative than the first. Not only has urbanization now caught on in the South, but in the fashion of all late converts, the South is zealously leading the nation into the last third of this urbanizing century. This war has been won, but it will take more ingenuity to enjoy our victory than it took grace and humility to accept our defeat. As we are coming to realize in so many different respects, there is no growth without some costs, no gains, as Adlai Stevenson used to say, without pains.

I do not regret the passing of the Old South, nor will I take my stand with those who would compel us to choose between gracious agrarian poverty on the one hand and economic well-being on the other. Cities, because of the concentration of transactions within them, are the generators and multipliers of wealth in any society. A landscape without cities is a region without wealth. Indeed, because we are part of a national economy which seeks wealth-generating opportunities wherever they can be found, we *will* have cities whether we want them or not. The choice for the South is not whether it will have cities, but what kind of cities it wants to have. The choice for the South is whether to remain agrarian in values while becoming urban in form, or to take hold of the energy of urbanization and shape it into more graceful, more humane, and more livable cities than those in other regions.

We can still choose; most other parts of the country cannot. There is still time for the South—precious little, but time enough. If we allow Greensboro to become a Pittsburgh, or Atlanta a Baltimore, we will have only ourselves to blame.

The argument is very simple. It consists of three steps:

1. Southern cities are still different from Northeastern and North Central cities in ways advantageous to the South. 2. But the forces which have depressed the quality of urban life in other parts of the country are starting to erode the Southern advantage, threatening to make our metropolitan areas Southern replicas of

Northern disasters. 3. We have only a short time to design and implement policies which can prevent our similarities to Northern cities from overwhelming our saving differences from them.

HOW DO SOUTHERN CITIES DIFFER FROM THOSE IN OTHER PARTS OF THE COUNTRY?

1. The South is still less metropolitan than other regions. A smaller share of its population lives in metropolitan areas. In 1970, barely half of the South's population, as opposed to more than two thirds of the nation's population, lived in metropolitan areas. Population and economic projections make clear that our time of greatest urban growth—and therefore the period of greatest peril to the quality of life in our cities—is still before us.

2. Southern cities are smaller than cities outside the South. As of the 1970 census, the South had nearly 10.5 million people living in metropolitan areas with populations between 250,000 and 1,000,000. That sum is more than the number of persons living in metropolitan areas that size in both the Northeast and the North Central regions combined. Furthermore, more Southerners lived in cities with populations between 50,000 and 250,000 than in any other region of the country, and more lived in small cities of populations between 10,000 and 25,000. Eighty percent of all urban Southerners live in cities between 50,000 and 1,000,000; in the Northeast, the proportion is the reverse—75 percent live in cities of more than 1,000,000. Even in the North Central states, the largest cities contain 60 percent of the urban population.

The fact that Southern city dwellers live in smaller cities is a great advantage. According to virtually all opinion and research on city size, cities start to get unlivable at populations of about 1 to 1 1/2 million. The quality of life for the residents of smaller cities is higher, and the economic projections for small cities are much more favorable.

3. Heavy manufacturing provides a smaller proportion of jobs in Southern central cities than in any other part of the country. Consequently, our cities have less congestion, noise, pollution, and, most important, less investment in unsightly and intractable manufacturing facilities than do Northern cities. Having little heavy manufacturing in the first place, our central cities do not suffer job and tax base losses when manufacturing firms seeking the greater and cheaper horizontal space they increasingly require locate their facilities in rural or suburban areas.

4. Southern central cities have suffered less decline in population and employment than central cities outside the South. Growth in United States metropolitan areas disproportionately favors *non*central city areas. In some parts of the country, especially in the Northeast, there has been an absolute decline in central city population and in employment, especially in manufacturing and retailing. Most Southern central cities, however, have not declined absolutely in either of these respects. Indeed, in contrast with many cities in the Northeast and North Central regions, some Southern central cities even continue to grow. (Compared with their own suburbs their growth is at an increasingly slower rate, but they are growing nonetheless.) Because our central cities have not begun to decline, there is still the possibility that they can remain viable centers of both residence and economic activity long after those in the Northeastern and North Central areas have completely stagnated.

5. Whereas cities in many other parts of the country are smothered by proliferating governmental units, Southern metropolitan areas have a much thinner bureaucratic overlay. Of the 29 Standard Metropolitan Statistical Areas with fewest governmental units, 22 were in the South; of the 51 SMSAs with fewest governmental units, 31 were in the South. Only 3 Southern SMSAs were in that half of the SMSAs with the largest number of governmental units. In grappling with the myriad of metropoli-

tan problems, the fewer the governmental units, the more flexible, imaginative, and effective can be the solutions.

6. Southern metropolitan areas are less densely settled than metropolitan areas in other parts of the country. Twenty-five of the Southern SMSAs are below the median density of all the SMSAs—449 persons per square mile. No Southern city has a population density greater than 1000 persons per square mile, which means that none of the Southern cities is among the top 16 in the country in population density. Perhaps lower density explains the feelings of greater ease, relaxed pace, and lingering graciousness which both Southerners and Northerners experience even in the South's busiest metropolitan areas.

7. The favorable position of Southern central cities is not likely to prevail unaided for very long, however, because of a seventh double-edged difference between Southern and Northern metropolitan areas. Taking metropolitan areas as a whole, Southern metropolitan populations are now increasing at a faster rate than are those of any other region in the country. Indeed, the South's rate of metropolitanization is nearly *double* the average annual rate for the United States as a whole, and has been all during the forties, the fifties, and the sixties. Furthermore, the largest population increases are expected to occur in metropolitan areas of the size of which the South has a disproportionately large share.

Although this difference poses a threat to Southern central cities, it also offers Southern cities a precious chance to reshape themselves by means of the immense growth ahead. Consider the advantage of having that opportunity before us at a time when the mistakes of other cities stare us in the face—mistakes which they can no longer correct but that we may be able to avoid.

These are not the only respects in which Southern cities differ from those in the North, nor indeed may they be the most important. A highly favorable climate may be for us, as for California, the most powerful influence on our growth. Whether or not this is so, the differences which do exist, whether through the grace of nature or the wit of man, are temporary assets which give Southern cities an immense advantage as they begin their period of greatest growth. Seizing these advantages *and* instructing ourselves by the negative examples of Northern cities, we still have the power to make Southern cities the qualitative benchmarks of urban America. It is not too late to establish a framework for controlled and orderly growth. When we despair of the vast intellectual and political tasks required, we need only remember our opportunity for creation: *most* of what will comprise Southern metropolitan areas in the year 2000 has not been bulldozed yet. Such a scope for action means that there is very little we cannot do if we begin now. If we will properly govern our cities today, we can be sure that they are unlikely to overcome us tomorrow.

COUNTERVAILING NATIONAL TRENDS

Unfortunately, two major forces are working against us. One is the thrust of our own momentum, which makes it difficult to change direction under any circumstances; the other is the power of several national trends.

It should be unnecessary to mention these trends, because they weave insistently in and out of every public issue. Because they are increasingly shaping Southern cities, however, and therefore constitute one of the major threats to Southern urban promise, they must be considered explicitly.

1. There is the national trend toward suburbanization of residence. Between 1960 and 1969, the national population increased by 22 million people, of whom 16 million—75 percent of the total—lived in metropolitan areas. Within the metropolitan areas, noncentral city areas received almost the entire increase, with little change in the central city population. Indeed, the rates of suburban population increase were so great that by 1969 more than half of the metropolitan population in the United States lived in *non*-central city areas.

Exactly the same pattern held true in the South. The total

metropolitan population increase from 1960 to 1969 was 4.7 million people, of whom only 600,000 were added to central cities—a net gain of less than 4 percent over our 1960 Southern central city population. (Most of the gain probably reflects considerable annexation activity in 1967–68, which has the effect of expanding the city limits to include more people, who would otherwise be in suburbs and exurbs. The adjusted central city gain from 1960 to 1968 was estimated at only 100,000—less than 1 percent. That was exactly the same percentage gain registered by the nation's central cities as a whole.)

The South's suburban population in 1969 was 37 percent larger than in 1960. This rate of growth was second only to the West. Because the South had a much smaller number of suburbanites in 1960, its percentage increase in 1969 would be expected to be large as a function of a small starting base. And not only was there a greater *percentage* increase than in any other region except the West, but in absolute numbers 4.2 million people were added to the suburban population in the South in comparison with 4.6 million in the West, 4.5 million in the North Central states, and 2.9 million in the Northeast. By 1969, half of the South's metropolitan population lived outside her central cities—15.5 million in the central cities and 15.5 million in the suburbs. (Again, note the effect of annexation. The suburban growth from 1960 to 1968 was 40 percent, the number added to suburban population was 4.5 million, and the split between central city and suburb was 15 million and 15.8 million respectively.)

2. There is also a national trend toward suburbanization of jobs within metropolitan areas. In an excellent study, professors John Meyer, John Kain, and Martin Wohl discovered that, over the decade from 1948 to 1958, there was a mean annual decline of 9.6 percent in manufacturing jobs in central cities, while during the same period there was a mean annual increase of 15 percent in such jobs in metropolitan rings. In wholesaling, central cities increased 0.7 percent, while metropolitan rings increased 29.4 percent; in retailing, central cities declined 0.4 percent, while

suburbs increased 16 percent. In service jobs, the increase was 2.7 percent annually, while the metropolitan ring increased 24.4 percent annually. (These figures are corrected for annexation.) Of the 39 central cities which they examined, Meyer, Kain, and Wohl found that 24 had experienced a decline in manufacturing jobs, 13 in wholesaling jobs, 30 in retailing jobs, and 3 in service jobs during the decade. On the other hand, only 4 metropolitan rings experienced a manufacturing decline, only one experienced a wholesaling decline, and none experienced retailing and services declines.

If one examines employment changes in the light of the population growth rate for the same decade, one finds, not surprisingly, that the metropolitan areas with the highest growth rates had the greatest differential in the mean annual changes between suburbs and cities. In other words, metropolitan areas that grew the fastest had the greatest annual gap between numbers of new central city jobs and numbers of new suburban jobs.

The same trend is evident in Southern metropolitan areas. Of the 13 cities of greatest growth surveyed by Meyer, Kain, and Wohl, 8 are in the South. Of the 13 cities in the medium growth group, 5 were in the South. There were no Southern cities in the group of lowest growth. In short, Southern employment differentials are even wider than those in other cities.

A later survey, utilizing data from the 1963 Census of Manufactures and the 1963 Census of Business, and covering a different group of cities, found that while there was some increase from 1958 to 1963 in Southern central city employment, the increase in employment outside the central city was nearly two and a half times greater.

3. There is the movement of blacks to metropolitan areas. From 1950 to 1969, the percentage of the nation's blacks living in metropolitan areas across the country increased from 56 percent to 71 percent, while the percentage of whites increased only from 60 percent to 63.7 percent. Looked at from another perspective, from 1950 to 1969, the black proportion of the nation's metro-

politan areas increased from 8 percent to 12 percent, while the white proportion declined from 88.3 percent to 86.7 percent.

4. Within metropolitan areas across the country as a whole, there is a continuing migration of blacks to the city core and an exodus of whites to the urban fringes. From 1950 to 1969, the percentage of the nation's blacks living in central cities increased from 43 percent to 55.2 percent—12 percentage points—while during the same period the percentage of the nation's whites living in central cities declined from 34 percent to 25.8 percent—10 percentage points. By 1969, more than one half of all blacks in the nation lived in central cities.

These changes are reflected in the black and white *proportions* of central city population. From 1950 to 1969, the black proportion of the nation's central cities increased from 12 percent to 21 percent. Thus the entire black *metropolitan* increase landed in the central cities. In the same period the white proportion of central cities declined from nearly 87 percent to 77 percent.

While there were rises in the black proportion of central cities of all sizes, the largest increases were recorded in central cities with populations of one million or more, which grew from 13 percent black in 1950 to 26 percent black in 1969, an increase of 100 percent. Central cities between 250,000 and one million increased from 12 percent black to 18 percent black, a gain of 50 percent. Despite the large migration of the last twenty years, the percentage of blacks living in the noncentral city areas of SMSAs has remained constant at 5 percent.

What about the South?

From 1960 to 1969, the black percentage of the nation's central cities increased from 17 percent to 21 percent, a gain of 4 percentage points, while the gain in the South during this decade was only 3 percentage points; but note that it was an increase from 25 percent in 1960 to 28 percent in 1969, which means that the black percentage of the total population of Southern central cities is the highest in the country.

The extent of the magnetism of Southern central cities for

black migration is underscored if one recalls that, during the same time that the black proportion of the Southern central cities was increasing, although by only 3 percentage points, the South was losing one million blacks—mainly to central cities in other parts of the country. Despite the enormous outflow of blacks—so enormous that the 1969 Southern black population was only 300,000 more than it was in 1960, owing entirely to natural increase—the black proportion of the population in the South's central cities still managed to follow the national trend and increase.

That it rose at all is surprising, because there were at least three factors which should have held it stable. In the first place, Southern central cities started with a higher proportion of blacks than any other cities in the country, and, statistically, the larger the base the more difficult it is for a percentage increase to occur. While the black proportion of Southern central cities went up only from 25 percent to 28 percent, that small percentage increase meant an addition of 700,000 blacks. Because of the difference in base size, the Northeastern percentage increases, while 2 1/2 times larger, represented a numerical increase of only 200,000 more than the Southern increase. In the second place, the black percentage increase occurred while the total populations of the Southern central cities, and of Southern metropolitan areas as a whole, were growing. That alone makes the black increase in Southern central cities more significant than in Northeastern central cities, where the total population has been declining. In the third place, black percentage gains in Southern central cities occurred despite the lack of a significant exodus of whites. The outflow of whites from Southern central cities was a bare 100,000 people, less than 1 percent of the total white population of Southern central cities, while the white population decline in Northeastern central cities was 1.4 million, or 10 percent of their white population.

At least one major force is beginning to weaken, however, and that weakening is bound to result in an increase in black central city populations in the South. Over the past thirty years the rate of black migration from the South has been declining steadily. In the

1940s an average of 159,000 blacks left the South each year; in the 1950s an average of 145,000 left each year; and in the 1960s the rate had dropped to 88,000 blacks each year.

During the late sixties, the Census Bureau found and then lost signs of a sharp slowing in black migration from the South. Whether or not a decline occurred, the general slowing of black out-migration from the South can result only in increasing the black proportions of our central cities.

As economic activity increases in the South's metropolitan areas, it seems likely that not only will black emigration be entirely stopped, but that there may even be a reversal of the flow with some of the more recent black migrants to Northern cities returning home. As Charles Tilly has pointed out, "The net migration to an area corresponds very closely to its income level and its production of new jobs as compared with other potential destinations." The gap between median black family income in Southern and Northeastern cities had narrowed from $1,300 in 1959 to only $700 in 1968, in 1968 dollars, and is probably even smaller now.

To bring all this down to earth, keep in mind that the black proportion of New Orleans is 41 percent, Memphis 50 percent, Atlanta 44 percent, and Houston and Dallas 22 percent, despite extensive annexations in the latter two cities in recent years. The trends indicate that these proportions will increase in the future.

It need hardly be added that the increasing number of blacks in Southern central cities has added to the concentration of poverty there, and has been accompanied by a corresponding increase of affluence in the suburbs. This, of course, is also a national trend. Between 1959 and 1967 the gap in median family income between Southern central cities and suburbs increased from $760 to over $1,300, an increase of nearly 100 percent, while the gap for the nation as a whole grew from a little over $900 to $1,500, an increase of 67 percent.

Although these population and employment trends will generally lead to an increase in the overall standard of living in

Southern metropolitan areas, they will also exacerbate the geographical distribution of income within metropolitan areas, tending to make our suburbs rich and white and our central cities poor and black.

Southerners living in metropolitan areas are already considerably less affluent than those in metropolitan areas in any other part of the country. In 1969 the median family income of metropolitan area residents for the nation as a whole was $8,673, while in the South it was $7,881—$800 less. It is true that from 1959 to 1967 the South registered the greatest percentage gain in urban family income of any region in the country (27 percent as opposed to 21 percent in the nation as a whole), but our urban families are still poorer than those of all other regions of the country.

The differences in median family income reflect the lower average hourly earnings in Southern cities compared with cities in other parts of the country. In a rigorous study based on 1959 earnings figures, Victor Fuchs determined that average hourly earnings outside the South—not just in cities, but across the board—are about 25 percent higher than in the South. We know that hourly earnings are higher in large cities than in small cities, and we have seen that the South has mostly smaller cities, but after controlling for city size, it is clear that Southern workers receive substantially less per hour than workers in the same size cities in other regions of the country. Fuchs's most interesting finding was that, even after compensating for the fact that there are more smaller cities in the South than in other parts of the country and the fact that the labor force has different age and educational characteristics in the South than in other parts of the country, there is still a wage differential which can be explained only by reference to the fact that the cities are in the South.

It is no great surprise to any of us that there is considerably more black poverty in Southern metropolitan areas than in Northern ones. Fuchs breaks down his income statistics by race, enabling us to see clearly the extent to which Southern blacks remain severely disadvantaged simply because they are in the South. While the white earnings differential between Northern and Southern SMSAs below 250,000 is $.22 an hour, the black differential is $.77 an hour; in cities between 250,000 and 500,000, the white differential is $.06 an hour, while the black differential is $.85 an hour; in cities between 500,000 and 1,000,000 the white differential is only $.17 an hour, while the black differential is $.81 an hour; even in cities of more than 1,000,000, where the white differential is only $.10 an hour, the black differential is still $.42 an hour. Fuchs points out that for white males the regional differential is 18 percent, for white females it is 17 percent, but for blacks it is 60 percent. Even after adjusting for age and educational differences, blacks show a net regional differential of 35 percent, in contrast with adjusted white differentials of about 6 percent for males and 9 percent for females.

These combined national trends of suburbanization of population and jobs, migration of blacks to metropolitan areas, concentration of blacks in central cities, and the exodus of whites to urban fringes are beginning to shape Southern metropolitan areas decisively. Insistently and with increasing speed they are wearing away our assets and diminishing the time which we have left to take advantage of them. If, while substantial Southern metropolitan land is still vacant, we do not bring it within central city zoning and taxing power, we might as well abandon forever our hopes for orderly growth of suburban areas, and forget about any possibility of tapping suburban property for tax revenue to support services to the entire metropolitan area. Now is our last chance to stem the erosion of the central city tax base which has prevented central cities in the Northeast and North Central regions from grappling successfully with their problems. If we fail to move now, we will soon be watching powerlessly as our need for central city services goes up and our capacity to pay for them goes down.

If, while annual rates of suburbanization of population and employment are at their peaks, we do not take imaginative and persistent action to stem and reverse residential racial polarization, we may as well abandon all hope of achieving such changes in the next half century, and with that hope the possibility of a peaceful and equitable society.

WHY ARE SOUTHERN CITIES DIFFERENT?

We have seen that in some very important and potentially beneficial respects Southern cities are significantly different from Northern cities.

Why? The main reason is age.

At root, the advantage of Southern cities stems from the fact that they are younger than Northeastern and North Central cities. While 64 percent of Northeastern cities and 10 percent of North Central cities had attained one half of their 1960 population prior to 1900, only 8 percent of Southern cities had done so. Furthermore, while 32 percent of Northeastern cities and 71 percent of North Central cities attained one half of their 1960 population between 1905 and 1920, only 18 percent of Southern cities did. Thirty-eight percent of Southern central cities attained one half of their 1960 population between 1925 and 1960, and another 36 percent attained it between 1945 and 1960. Between 1925 and 1960, therefore, 74 percent of Southern cities reached this level, in contrast to only 19 percent of North Central cities and only 4 percent of Northeastern cities.

Because we started urbanizing later, Southern cities are smaller than Northern cities, not having had as long a period of time to grow. Because we started urbanizing later, Southern cities are less densely settled than Northern cities, having experienced 75 percent of their growth during the ascendancy of the automobile. Because we started industrializing later, Southern cities have little heavy manufacturing, having fortuitously begun the quest for industry at the precise moment when the location of industry ceased to be determined by convenience to rail and water transport for its raw materials and finished products, and to easy walking distances—or public transport—for its employees.

Because we started later, and because we were poorer than our fellow city dwellers in the North, we have had neither the time nor the money to immortalize—in concrete—quite as many of our mistakes as they did.

Because we started later.

To the extent that our cities are different from other cities in the country, and to the extent that those differences are potentially advantageous to us, the main reason for the difference is time, the most elusive of all assets. It is the only asset which, by its nature, consumes itself. What time has given us, time itself will take away.

The differences between our cities, and those in other regions, give the South some potential advantages. These assets are rooted in the *timing* of our original urbanization and our current interest in the urbanization future. The value of these assets will be determined soon by our use of the *time* which has been yielded to our corner of the nation and which refuses to wait for us.

The inorganic matter of a city lacks a precise genetic design for its future. Instead, it is a plastic social institution subject to the shaping hand of the present. The longer its past, the more determined its future.

Looking backward, we see that our cities are still young and pliable. Because of the timing of our regional development, and because of our present rationality, the "hand of the present" can do a great deal of shaping. As William H. Nicholls has pointed out, "The very lateness of the South's economic development offers a real opportunity to avoid some of the excesses of Northern industrial-urban growth; with proper foresight and planning, the South can still avoid them." Our period of greatest growth is just ahead; time, for the South, is reduced to *now.* We have the fortunate opportunity and the awesome challenge of doing it all ourselves—redirecting life in the South within our lifetimes. Unless we do something unusual with our cities, unless we make an extra effort to direct our urban growth, we will develop with the same patterns as most other American cities. We will be plunged into the same moral and physical discomfiture. Except that in the South it will all happen faster.

We began the century fifty years behind the nation in urbanization, and by 1954 we were still fifty years behind. Leonard Reissman, in 1965, said that "the results of those changes were to explode the South into the urban era within the short space of twenty years, or about *three times* faster than it took for most other regions in the nation to accomplish a similar urban transformation [emphasis mine]."

The figures which are presently available suggest that Reissman is correct. We have seen that from 1900 to 1940 the South gained approximately ten years. In 1940, 55.1 percent of the population of the United States resided in SMSAs while only 34.5 percent of the Southern population did—a gap of 21 percent. In 1950, the figures were 59 percent national and 41 percent Southern, a gain of 4 percent for the nation and 7 percent for the South, but still a gap of 17.8 percent. The same relative gains were recorded between 1950 and 1960, by which time the United States metropolitan population had increased to 63 percent and the South's to 48 percent, but the gap had narrowed to 15 percent. While metropolitan rates for the country as a whole, including the South, seem to be slowing down, the Census Bureau projections would have the South 50 percent metropolitan by 1975, and the gap would be only 13 percent.

The nation as a whole achieved the 50 percent level of metropolitanization in 1940, which suggests that by 1975 the South will have reduced its forty-year lag by another five years. As the estimated national growth rates for the next five to ten years are expected to be highest for the size of cities of which the South has more than any other region of the country, we can expect a mere thirty-year lag by the time the 1980 census is taken.

If at the same time this extraordinary urbanization is taking place the distribution of that growth continues in the patterns of the 1960s, we stand to lose most of our present benefits and all of our future advantages. Unless we arouse ourselves to shape the growth that is going to occur, it will shape us, and to our disadvantage. Not only will it depress the general quality of life for all in our cities and wreak havoc on our governmental structures, but it will also kill whatever chance we have to solve our race problem: the concentrations of blacks in the central parts and of whites in the peripheries of our metropolitan areas, already greater than in any other section of the country, will continue to increase. The rich peripheries will get richer and the poor centers will get poorer. Unless we bear the responsibility for our impending growth, we will be inflicted with the malformations which form the common urban scene.

How much time do we have?

We have about one generation. Twenty years. If somehow we and our contemporaries do not use the time before us to shape the processes of growth and change in the cities of our region in accordance with the values of human dignity, health, and well-being, by the time we die whatever advantage the South may have had during our lifetime wil be no more.

ARE WE USING TIME TO OUR ADVANTAGE?

From all that I have been able to observe, it is clear that we are neglecting the advantages we have over cities in other parts of the country, and ignoring our differences. We seem determined to let our unique opportunities dissipate, blind to the despair of Northeastern and North Central cities which lack our freedom to choose.

An example of a valuable lost opportunity can be seen in housing patterns. Perhaps the most disturbing respect in which Southern metropolitan areas differ from those in other parts of the country is the extent to which racial segregation in housing has been increasing in the South, both within the central city and between central city and suburbs.

You Can't Eat Magnolias

There is an extensive literature which suggests that in the past residential segregation by race was not as prevalent in Southern cities, especially the older ones, as in cities outside the South. An excellent recent study by Karl and Alma Taeuber undercuts any optimism one may have about a Southern edge in housing desegregation. It documents what many of us have feared—that not only has the South grown more segregated *residentially* than the rest of the country in recent years, having by now caught up with and surpassed the rest of the country in racial segregation in housing, but it has been doing so while the rest of the country has either remained static or actually declined in residential segregation. All but 1 city in the Northeast (Pittsburgh) out of the 25 for which time series data were available, all but 6 cities out of 29 in the North Central region, and all 10 in the West registered net declines in the index from 1940 to 1960. Among Southern cities, only Norfolk, Virginia (minus 1.4), and Roanoke, Virginia (minus 0.9) registered declines. All other Southern cities had a net increase from 1940 to 1960 in the extent to which their populations were racially segregated in housing.

Most of the increases did not occur, as might have been expected, after the Brown decisions in 1954 and 1955, but between 1940 and 1950. Memphis increased its degree of housing segregation from 79.9 percent in 1940 to 86.4 percent in 1950 and to 92 percent in 1960, for a net increase of over 12 percent. Charleston, South Carolina, remains the least segregated city in the South, as we all know, but even Charleston went from 60 percent in 1940 to 80 percent in 1960, a rise of 20 percentage points.

It is clear that the trends which the Taeubers detected between 1940 and 1960 have continued through the 1960s as well. Each of the special censuses conducted between 1960 and 1968 has revealed a substantial increase in residential segregation by race in Southern cities. In Memphis, according to the special census of 1967, 78 percent of all blacks are living in census tracts which are 75 percent or more black.

As to segregation between central city and suburbs, I regret that so astute an observer of the Southern landscape as my colleague Leonard Reissman was misled by census figures into believing that "a feature of the urban migration by the Negro within the South has been the absence of any clear segregation of the Negro to the central city and the whites to the urban fringe, as has become generally typical for the rest of the nation." Professor Reissman fails to take into account the fact that blacks show up in census figures for suburban areas of Southern SMSAs because the SMSAs are expanding into former rural areas, largely populated by black sharecroppers, who are in no sense members of the metropolitan economy. They are remnants of the agricultural hinterland, not suburban participants in a metropolitan culture. The only reason they are included is that they happen to be living in the same county as parts of the SMSA's central city.

It is also clear that increasing housing segregation is not, as some have contended, either merely or mainly caused by people of similar education, income, or occupation wishing to live together, or by the natural operation of market processes. On the contrary, it is the result of conscious intent and persistent action. Every new study confirms that federal officials and local government officials have used the increasing new amounts of federal urban renewal funds consciously and persistently to increase, and increasingly cement, the racial segregation of Southern cities. In addition, Federal Housing Administration and Veterans Administration mortgage insurance programs have been explicitly used by federal officials, real estate interests, and the financial community to perpetuate segregation all over the country. Eunice and George Grier reported as follows:

> *From 1935 to 1950—a period in which about 15 million new dwellings were constructed—the power of the national government was explicitly used to prevent integrated housing. Federal policies were based upon the premise that economic and social stability would best be achieved through keeping neighborhood*

> *populations as homogeneous as posible. Thus, the Underwriting Manual of the Federal Housing Administration (oldest and largest of the federal housing agencies, established by the Housing Act of 1934) warned that "if a neighborhood is to retain stability, it is necessary that properties shall continue to be occupied by the same social and racial group." It advised appraisers to lower their valuation of properties in mixed neighborhoods, "often to the point of rejection." The FHA actually drove out of business some developers who insisted upon open policies.*

There is little evidence that the FHA's explicit abandonment of its deliberately segregated policies has had any effect in changing the momentum or direction of the trend which it established. What occurred by explicit directive in the North during its period of housing boom, both in the central city and in the suburbs, seems to be continuing in both North and South as a result of real estate practices tacitly encouraged by federal housing programs. Until such programs are used actively to counter prevailing housing patterns and trends in our metropolitan areas, separation by race will continue and even increase.

Barely sixteen years ago Henry Alan Bullock projected what seemed to him to be the current trend.

> *The story of Negro housing in the South shows the impact that urban growth is making on the traditional pattern of Southern race relations. Although the expansion of Southern cities creates a Negro housing problem, it also lays the foundation for its solution. City growth renders traditional Negro areas inadequate. The pressure of population shows up; it captures public interest; and it offers a fertile market for urban capital. Capital becomes available to Negroes who seek to buy or build,*

> *and the members of this group become somewhat relieved of the residential chains which tradition has forged about them.*

This passage must now make us want to weep.

WITH WHAT LITTLE TIME WE HAVE LEFT, WHAT SHOULD WE DO?

Keeping one eye on our present advantages, and the other on the trends which are affecting them, what should the South do about its cities?

CONTROL AND ORDER GROWTH

First, states and cities need to join together in developing immediately an urban growth policy and a mechanism for its phased implementation. Given the dominance which metropolitan areas will have in all of the states, it is in the self-interest of all the citizens of each state to see that a rational metropolitan growth policy is established. Already some Southern states are beginning to exert considerable effort to deploy new jobs so as to minimize congestion and achieve orderly growth. But as yet it is only a beginning. Planning is not enough. We need combined decision-making and planning entities which can orchestrate all state, federal, and local actions which bear on the use of land.

One of the most important things which states can do is to make state funds available for advance land acquisition. Given the nature of the real estate market, only government can move quickly, decisively, and with enough assets to assemble, plan, and zone the remaining land around populated metropolitan areas. Insofar as states and cities wish to prevent the concentration of the poor and the black in inner cities, they can do so only by guiding the development of vacant land near cities so as to insure, over time, a racial and economic redistribution of the population over the metropolitan area as a whole.

Without such a design, we shall inevitably have land pollution through what has come to be called urban sprawl. If, on the other hand, growth is channeled by a carefully developed plan, the South will have an urban civilization more humane than that of the North—less dense and chaotic, and more open.

Even if I believed in the superior quality of Jane Jacobs' high-density urban living, it would seem futile to urge such a policy on the people of the United States since it is clearly contrary to our strong preferences. A few such high-density cities did grow up in the United States, but they were mainly port cities—New Orleans, Charleston, Boston, Philadelphia, and New York—and they grew when water transportation was the dominant "means" of connecting commerce. More recently, however, Americans have made clear over and over again their preference for low density and high mobility, and I am not convinced that, given the alternatives, that choice is wrong. Whether wrong or not, there is no evidence to suggest that it is politically or economically possible to shape the development of younger cities, as are most of those in the South, so as to increase their density. Consequently, if you want to know what Southern metropolitan areas will look like in 1990 or the year 2000, look at Los Angeles and not at New York or Chicago.

We tend to scoff at Los Angeles for its pollution, sprawl, and general philistinism, but it is important to remember that Los Angeles has, perhaps, the best city services of any large city in the country. Furthermore, it continues to be attractive to the thousands of Americans who continue to move there. Whatever one may think about the style of Los Angeles, its growth pattern *has* been orderly—chiefly as a result of the zoning and planning which was done for the county as a whole, long in advance of actual growth. When people started moving in and building houses, they were acting within the context of an established matrix.

This is not the way that most suburban growth has occurred around American cities. Generally, developers buy unzoned land outside the city limits and build as they wish, regardless of the effects on surrounding communities and on transportation patterns, and totally oblivious to the larger economic and racial patterns of the community. If Southern cities want the growth on their fringes to be more like that of Los Angeles than that of the cities in the Northeast corridor, then they had best follow the examples of Oklahoma City, Dallas, and Houston, and annex as much land as they can as fast as they can within existing law so they will be able to impose some kind of rational framework within which the coming growth can occur.

Metropolitan consolidation—as in Nashville-Davidson County and Miami-Dade County—is another strategy for coping with metropolitan problems. Where central cities are already surrounded by incorporated municipalities, it is the only feasible one. Although annexation is by far the preferable strategy, quick action is required to utilize it. Where both voluntary consolidation and annexation are impossible, it may be desirable for the state legislature to impose consolidation as the Indiana legislature did, at least with respect to certain services, in Indianapolis.

FINANCE EDUCATION EQUALLY THROUGHOUT EACH STATE

As the Advisory Commission on Intergovernmental Relations has recommended, the states should take over support of education as a whole in order to equalize educational quality throughout entire metropolitan areas. The fractionalization of governmental authority in metropolitan areas has led to sizable differentials in the amounts of per pupil expenditures between central cities and their suburbs, as well as sizable differentials in a whole host of other service sectors. Part of the problems of the cities in this respect can be solved if they annex quickly and shrewdly, but the Southern cities which are already surrounded by suburbs are precluded from taking the route of annexation, and will require some kind of state assistance.

BLACK ECONOMIC DEVELOPMENT

As a specific and central objective of our urban policy, we must foster the economic development of the black community. As James McBride Dabbs pointed out, "as he [the black] gains economic power he moves toward equality in economic relations. He is already equal in a detail of our financial life: at the bank counter he is plain John Doe. He is rapidly becoming an equal in the world of merchandising: all folding money is green." For the black community to be able to mesh politically with the larger community—which must occur if democracy is to survive—there has to be a critical mass of economic resources supporting and powering the sociopolitical structure of the black community. This requires white assistance in the establishment of black businesses, with priority to the kinds of institutions which can accumulate, mobilize, and deploy capital.

DESEGREGATE

Finally, and most urgently of all, we have got to attend directly to the matter at the heart of all our socioeconomic problems: racism. Strong, positive action is required to prevent past and current patterns of racial distribution in our metropolitan areas from perpetuating themselves. We need to take immediate steps in housing integration, including the sponsorship of urban and suburban housing developments which are actively integrationist, which establish minimum racial quotas, and which actively recruit white and black families to fill them. With the rapid rate of suburbanization, it will be much easier to effect this kind of fundamental change now by riding piggyback on the large numbers of housing units which will be built in the immediate future than it would be to try to effect a significant change in racial patterns in housing already occupied. Unless we can integrate existing suburbs or build new suburbs where blacks can in fact live, more and more blacks are going to be cut off from jobs and, as Kenneth Clark aptly described it, they will be "embalmed" in our central cities, as they are in those of the North. So long as our cities are growing rapidly, it will be relatively easy to diminish housing segregation. When our rates of growth begin to slow to the pace of those in the North, it will be too late.

Until we can have an open housing system within central cities and across the metropolitan areas as a whole, without racial restrictions and racial patterns determining a family's neighborhood, we had best do all that can possibly be done to integrate our educational systems, either through the construction of integrated educational parks for pie slices of the metropolitan areas as a whole, or, perish the word, through busing.

Schools are important to society not only for the intellectual and job training they provide, but also in their roles as the nurseries of social attitudes—as the incubators of citizens' feelings about one another. Schools are absolutely crucial in creating those bonds which build a community out of many separate individuals.

Whether or not one accepts the thesis that integrated classrooms are better for learning, it is impossible to overemphasize the harmful role played by segregated schools in cultivating racial biases in our children. If some schools remain 90 percent black and others remain 90 percent white for very much longer, a peaceful multiracial society may not be possible for another hundred years. Racism built separate schools, and separate schools—whether *de jure* or *de facto*—nourish racism, both in blacks and in whites. We shall never rid the society of either variety so long as our schools are separate.

Even if housing patterns remain segregated for some time, as it appears likely they will, the integration of schools can begin to foster social attitudes which tend to counteract racism. Without fully integrated schools, there is nothing to offset the perniciousness of race hatred.

Instead of relying on the North's difficulty in overcoming the obstacle of overwhelming housing segregation as an excuse to stop the integration of Southern schools, we should say instead, "Let us show you how it can be done."

* * *

In most respects, Southern cities *are* like other American cities. There remain significant differences, yet how remarkably similar our present condition is to that of their past. Are we satisfied to let our cities follow the path of the Northern metropolis? Are we content to imagine our Atlantas, Greensboros, Columbias, Huntsvilles, Houstons, and Nashvilles with the pollution, congestion, racial chaos, and governmental paralysis of New York, Chicago, and Cleveland? If so, we can relax, take it easy, and be absolutely confident that shortly after the turn of the century we will be brothers with Northerners in their bonds.

If we have a better vision of our future, we must use all of our imagination and more than all of our energy to bring it to pass.

We have all heard it said that the South will solve its racial and urban problems before the North. I have said so myself, very smugly, especially to Northerners, but now I am in the kitchen with the family and must confess that while we have the margin required to solve our problems more easily, more quickly, and with less cost than the North, there is absolutely no evidence that we have been or are now using that margin constructively. What data we have suggest that we are blindly following the North down the path which has led it to its present disaster.

C. Vann Woodward tells us that, for the first time since the Civil War, the South's distinctiveness gives it a unique position in the nation to provide leadership equal to the present American ordeal. The South, he observes, is poverty stricken in a land of plenty, has the only defeated people in a nation which has always won, and has the only guilt-stricken population in the country which believes in its innocence; now that the nation has had to face defeat, the truth of its sins, a pocketbook too slim to buy all that it wishes, the South's special qualifications for leadership have become relevant once again to America's needs.

The best way to prove our capacity to lead the nation is by our deeds at home.

MAKING DIXIE'S LAND LIVABLE

Frank E. Smith

[THE South has not been much concerned about the excesses which threaten the quality of our environment, just as there has not been as much concern in our region as in some others about the excesses of an affluent society. What might seem at first glance to be indifference is actually a matter of economics, for both of these circumstances arise from the fact that we have not fully shared in either the affluence or the economic base which produced it. We are, therefore, still too much preoccupied with efforts to develop an adequate share of that affluence to be very much concerned about some of the questionable long-range effects of the technology upon which a vastly productive economy and an affluent society rest.

The Southeast today has a slightly greater part of its population employed in manufacturing enterprises than any other section of the country. Our continued comparative poverty results from our lower wage rates and from the lower percentage of our income devoted to and derived from service industries and those other aspects of the economy which provide and consume the material amenities of present-day life. Most of our major manufacturing industries are relatively new to the region—often they are new to the entire industrial scene. As a result, they are not usually among the worst polluters, for they have developed at a time when willful violations of pollution control standards can no longer be completely ignored.

This comparative position is not cause for satisfaction, however. Even though we have escaped the dubious blessings of some of the heavy industries which are major contributors to pollution in the established manufacturing centers of the East and Midwest, we have our fair share of pollution. Our principal river is the Mississippi, the great artery of life and commerce not only for the mid-South, but for all of mid-America. The Mississippi has abused us many times in the past, but we have also been abusing it for many years. It has been and still is mid-America's main garbage and sewage disposal unit, and each year it also carries into the Gulf hundreds of acres of topsoil, washed out from the alluvial plains. In addition to these long-standing pollutants, the Mississippi in recent years has picked up the burden of the petrochemical industry, concentrated from Baton Rouge south, and the agri-chemical industry, which stretches throughout the Mississippi Valley from Wisconsin and Minnesota to Louisiana. There is no way to measure accurately the total of all these pollutants, or the resulting compounds, carried each day into the Gulf of Mexico.

Competent students say that the Gulf is showing visible evidence of the impact of this vast tonnage of pollutants, more destructive than mere topsoil. Dr. James M. Sharp, president of Gulf Universities Research Corporation, has been quoted as saying that the Gulf "could become a dead sea," pointing out that "several of our estuaries and sounds are already losing their recreational value and biological productivity."

Dr. Sharp told a group of congressmen that studies costing $150 million are needed merely to pinpoint necessary pollution controls for the Gulf. I do not doubt that such studies are needed. But they must not be accepted as a substitute for action. We know already that the Mississippi must be vastly improved, to say nothing of putting an end to oil spills in the Gulf itself.

One of the problems we face in the South in dealing with pollution is that we have struggled so long and so hard for industrial development that it is easier to look the other way at industrial abuses, whether they be low wages or the abetment of pollution. New industries, like old ones, have learned to employ politically effective law firms and have not been hesitant to use them. I recall that ten or twelve years ago, while fighting on the floor of the House of Representatives against an amendment designed to weaken the federal antipollution law, I naïvely mentioned that paper companies were among the chief polluters of our streams as well as being among the leading opponents of a strong antipollution law. There were no paper companies in my district, but within a few days I had had letters and phone calls from a dozen or so of the most prominent law firms in Mississippi, all wanting to know what I had against the paper industry.

The same hunger for industrial jobs may condition us to accept too readily the easy rationalization of dubious practices instead of demanding a confrontation with the facts.

Nearly twenty years ago I asked the Public Health Service to look into the possible damage to human health caused by the widespread use of pesticides and defoliants in my Delta district. I am ashamed to say that I accepted too readily the PHS response that no serious threat was involved. A case that there is no serious threat can still be made, but today we have a more inclusive definition of what "threat" means.

Since this paper will point up the fact that I have serious reservations about some of the current prophets of doom about the ecology, let me point out that I, too, have several times been branded as such an irresponsible doomsday man. This began when I attempted unsuccessfully, back in 1954, to have recreation added to the benefits considered in evaluating Corps of Engineers water projects, and includes ridicule when I said just three years ago that the nation would have to spend at least $100 billion before the year 2000 on improving the quality of its water and maintaining an adequate supply. Today I think we can agree that $100 billion is a very conservative estimate, even without reading between the lines of the President's recent relatively modest proposals.

You Can't Eat Magnolias

Today we are told that the nation's entire life style must change if we are to avoid a disastrous upset in the ecological balance (assuming we accept the premise that the upset has not already occurred). I agree that we must reevaluate many priorities and some of our long-accepted standards of economic progress. But I do not accept for one minute the concept that we can turn our backs on economic expansion and development. We cannot achieve a satisfactory quality of life for all Americans, let alone the South, from our present inadequate economic base. To expand that base, we are going to have to continue to develop our natural resources. That, in turn, requires a completely candid appraisal of our environmental condition.

First, as much as I deplore it, we must recognize that there is no pristine wilderness left, and that we will sacrifice even more quality of life if we let our existing resources waste into a pseudo-wilderness.

Some of us must wake up to the fact that there was more pollution in a Cherokee or Choctaw wigwam than there is on the streets of Knoxville or Los Angeles, and that some of the Cherokee and Choctaw villages were as befouled with waste and water pollution as bad as some of the worst alleys in Memphis or Greenwood.

Some of the worst pollution, for me, is visual pollution, and I count as part of that the dirt and misery of rural and urban slums which still abound over the South. In my trips over southern Appalachia I see some of the most disheartening signs of rural poverty, degrading housing, and diseased water supply against a backdrop of beautiful rustic mountain greenery that, without the close-up, delights the soul of us environmentalists.

There is no possibility of providing the economic base for full opportunity for our black citizens without continued economic expansion. Whether they realize it or not, some of our best-intentioned people would maintain our black people in the bleakest of environments in the name of protecting the quality of our environment. Perhaps unconsciously they buy the "big house" premise that the Negro is better off in a blessed primitive state, dreaming from the cabin stoop of Saturday night in the by-and-by.

But continued economic expansion and development need not mean a continuing decline in the quality of our environment. Achieving the necessary environmental controls to bring about the quality will not, however, be cheap. They already cost large sums, but they will have to cost truly vast sums if they are to be effective. So far it has been easier to talk about the need to protect the environment than about the cost of protection, and we are losing valuable time every day because the talk is an excuse for further delay in putting up the money on a realistic scale.

Make no mistake about it—the added costs are going to be borne by individual citizens, both as taxpayers and as consumers. Much of the cost will come in the form of additional taxes, if the various levels of government undertake to meet their responsibilities in achieving environmental quality. If tax incentives are used on a large scale to encourage industry to adopt proper antipollution devices and processes, the result will not immediately appear in the consumer's bill, but it will appear in additional taxes to replace those which are, by this device, foregone. I think the tax incentive system has many inherent weaknesses, not the least of which is that the government may be lax in enforcement if severity means a loss of tax revenue. Pollution abatement should be a part of the basic cost of doing business—which is already deductible—not an added tax benefit.

If rigid pollution control is accepted as part of the cost of doing business, naturally the cost will be borne by the consumer who buys the products or services produced. The added costs of living which result are already noticeable, and they will become more so relatively soon. The real test of the public's willingness to pay for a quality environment will come within the next few years, in the form, for example, of added costs for automobiles and the fuels which propel them. We cannot afford selective nonpollution, however, and all automobiles and all fuels should have to meet the same standards.

I am personally involved in an on-going program to provide

adequate environmental controls for the TVA power-generating facilities. The capital costs here will total several hundred million dollars, and they will represent a substantial item which will have to be reflected in increased costs to the users of the electricity being generated. Fuel costs have been stepped up at a steadily increasing annual rate, as a result of environmental considerations. Low-sulphur-content coal is an example of added control, at added cost, that TVA and other utilities are attempting to obtain, with little success. There is a limited supply at best, and most of it is being sold at negotiated prices well above the current market to foreign metallurgical buyers, notably Japan. Another possible solution is low-sulphur oil. Here we are victims of the artificial price restraints of import quotas—if there were no import quotas, low-sulphur oil from other parts of the world could serve this area of the country at a price competitive with other fuels. There are processes already developed for reducing the sulphur content of oil which can be applied far more extensively.

TVA was an environmental delinquent in not establishing until 1965 a reclamation provision in its contracts with suppliers of strip-mine coal. Such a provision is now part of our standard form, however, even though, as far as I know, no private utility has adopted one. We are carefully following up the reclamation procedure required, and if it proves to have any defects or loopholes, they will be corrected. I have checked a number of the areas where reclamation procedures have been followed, and in some cases, after only three or four years, the land is actually in better shape than the scarred hillsides that existed before mining, from both the aesthetic and the economic viewpoints.

The chief emphasis of this paper is that we must continue to develop our natural resources and otherwise expand our economy to provide the jobs and the economic security necessary to give all of our people a share of our national abundance. At the same time, however, we must do whatever is necessary to make sure that every aspect of this development not only protects the quality of our environment but improves it.

Improvement can be made, even if we achieve few millennia. The smog expelled from London is the now oft-repeated example, but I want to cite an example of what has been done in one part of the South which demonstrates what can be done all over the nation.

The Tennessee River is the cleanest major river in the country. What is more important for the purposes of this discussion, it is the one river that is cleaner today than it was thirty years ago, in spite of the investment of some two billion dollars in new industrial plants along the shorelines of its lakes. It is cleaner because the TVA, with relatively little enforcement power, has been working to make it so. The only antipollution power which TVA has is built around the requirement that an easement to cross the TVA shoreline be obtained from TVA for discharges from any type of installation on the shore. We have, however, no control over discharge abuses which existed before TVA, or over the pollution of some of the tributary streams before they reach the TVA impoundments.

As a result, the Olin Mathieson Company, which now owns the historic salt lick at Saltville, Virginia, continues to pour so much salt into the north fork of the Holston River that special treatment of the water in the river as far southwest as Knoxville is necessary. Paper companies in western North Carolina continue to discharge both waste and discoloration into our tributaries there, so it has been generations since the once beautiful French Broad was clear. Farther south is the classic example of pollution, the Copper Basin of the Ocoee River east of Chattanooga, where the metallic water colors the entire stream bed, even though the sulphuric acid no longer escapes into the air.

Recently, with the help of newly developed laboratory devices, we discovered that fish in Pickwick Lake were contaminated with a potentially dangerous absorption of mercury. Our only remedy was to publicize the names of the offending chemical plants.

Despite these drawbacks, however, the Tennessee River system as a whole is clean enough to allow millions of people to swim in it each spring, summer, and fall, and to afford millions more the opportunity to fish in it during all twelve months.

We believe we have made some positive gains in air quality, and not only in relation to our steam plant plumes. The most obvious example is the improvement in the smoke emissions for our cities generally. The air quality may be worse because of greater numbers of automobiles, but there is no longer the black overhang of coal smoke where electricity has become the source of both heat and power. We have hopes that TVA can help demonstrate central effluent systems for industrial corridors as an example of how existing industries can cut down air pollution with minimum cost.

I have dwelt at considerable length on TVA's efforts to improve the environment because they are related to a broader effort to help improve the quality of life by advancing the quality of income, as well as the broader quality of the environment. The South is in the process of becoming industrialized, and consequently urbanized, but there is good reason to hope that it can escape some of the worst of urban blight while throwing off some of the worst of the rural blight which has been so prevalent for so long.

The dominant characteristic of the changing patterns of living has perhaps been the fading of independent living and working conditions based on the agrarian economy of a generation ago and the emergence of a far more complex pattern of urban living based on an industrialized economy. The many streams of economic and social life, once looked upon as separate and self-sufficient, have reached an interdependence at once both stimulating and depressing.

As we attempt to adjust the South to this new interdependence, we accept, without question, the necessity of physically cleaning up our environment, but we still need to give first priority to the cleansing of the human environment so that Southerners can be equally free to develop the skills necessary both to earn a livelihood and to pursue happiness in the kind of society where people can live and work together with decency and dignity.

What can we do to protect the Southern environment and improve its quality?

First of all, we can protect and improve the national environment. Very few environmental problems recognize state boundaries. Only national solutions and national standards will cure them. We must recognize that very few conservation programs have been established, in the South or anywhere else, without the carrot of federal money or the stick of federal standards.

There is legitimate reason for cooperative enforcement programs, but final enforcement should not be a matter for solely local determination. If for no other reason, dedicated local officials need the mainstay of federal standards as a backup for their own procedures. As in many other matters, states' rights in this field is usually a cover for states' wrongs.

More imaginative and aggressive local programs would, however, be adaptable to existing federal programs. Usually they would be heartily welcomed by federal agencies.

Sewage treatment is now accepted as a local responsibility, helped along by generous federal grants. Why could not state agencies take a more active role in management and supervision, not only better to protect the waters into which discharges are made, but to get more efficient systems and better trained personnel, and even to handle enforcement of standards?

Among the few sources of land reverting to state ownership in these relatively prosperous days are the "orphan" strip mines, abandoned by their owners without reclamation after all the economically extractable coal could be removed. The coal-producing states could organize reclamation projects for the orphan land as part of their wildlife and recreation programs. If the land could be restored to become healthy fishing and hunting sites, it would be put to a probably higher use than before mining. Coal mining, moreover, is not the only mineral industry which requires reclamation. Other extractive industries have left orphan lands over the South.

Too many Southern states have allowed regressive tax structure to prevent them from securing income from their nonrenewable resources like timber and coal. Good severance taxes on timber have been adopted in some states, but by no means enough. The failure to have an adequate severance tax on coal and other minerals is an example of the often disgraceful influence that mine operators have had at state capitals.

Thanks to many historic, geographic, and economic factors, we in the South have a better than average share of open space. We very much need, however, to improve its quality and make sure it is available for all citizens.

Among other goals, we need to protect it from visual pollution. The stretch of Interstate 40 that I drove from Knoxville to Memphis was one of the most beautiful in the entire country when first completed, but it is rapidly and thoroughly being polluted with endless roadside signs and billboards. The same observation applies to a dozen other new roads in the South.

Billboard control and rural zoning are examples of the local effort needed for quality local environment. Noise abatement is another, and there is long precedent in towns like Memphis. Organized efforts do not have to be confined to national campaigns to be productive.

The fact that landscape architecture has been so little developed in the South offers a potential for skipping over past mistakes. H. Grady Clay, editor of the *Landscape Architecture Quarterly,* has proposed a Southern Regional Center for environmental design, which I endorse enthusiastically. Such a center should exist through a communications network, however, not as a new bureaucracy to be housed.

Another vital need is the addition of more open-space recreation areas. We do not have enough now, and the shortage will be acute in a few years. Beyond the need for more federal, state, and local programs to acquire them, we need to step up local pressures to expand existing and developing federal projects to make recreational benefits available as a by-product. An aggressive state agency, for instance, is an ideal instrument for helping to establish open-space recreation areas as an adjunct to virtually every Corps of Engineers project.

The national trend toward decentralization of industry is a good one. We in the South have been trying to achieve this for a long time as part of our economic development, and for the first time there is today a general acceptance of the validity of our goals.

For a long time we were willing to accept any sort of industrial development or expansion, because it was better than nothing. We are becoming more selective, and we can become even more choosy if we selectively develop our resources on a more carefully planned basis. For instance, there is plenty of room for a Tennessee-Tombigbee project, just as there is room for more industrial site-harbor development on the Mississippi. But before we bring industries into any of these sites, developed wholly or partially at public expense, the design of their plants and operations should be rigidly examined to bar any pollution. Even the plant itself should meet requirements about harmonious blending with the landscape or the general environment. The participation of some type of public program in most of the major industrial locations in the South today provides basis enough for improved environmental standards.

Before we allow ourselves to be overcome by nostalgic recollections of the real or imagined qualities of small-town life in the South, let us remember some of the very real defects. Most obviously, small-town slums and small-town poverty have been equaled only by rural poverty, generating a situation that made even ghetto slums more inviting. The dirtiest big city street of half-abandoned houses, stores, and factories can be no more dismal and depressing than the streets of some of our small Southern towns.

Despite the defects of our traditional environment, we Southerners have a sense of identity with place that is only slightly less compelling than our identity with family. It is one of the distinctions which still separate our section from the rest of the country.

This sense of place is not likely to be nostalgia for the white-columned mansion, but it may be for the scent of magnolias, or honeysuckle in an alleyway, or for the shade of pine trees over a shotgun cabin, mellowed in season with the fragrance of apple or peach blossoms.

It is the reason for the annual trek of cars with Illinois and Michigan license plates to the Mississippi Delta and the Alabama Black Belt. These black folk are not returning for another exposure to Southern folkways, but for another day of fishing on the bank of the creek or the slough that was a part of childhood. These people do not want to pick more cotton, but they like to see the salt-and-pepper-colored fields again, and the green and brown leaves against the hillside.

It is the dreary ugliness of much of the Southern home place that has pushed so many of our young people away from home—not merely the lack of job opportunity. We need place as well as family to keep them in the South to make their reasonable contribution to improving the quality of life for another generation.

Elimination of visual pollution can be as important in keeping young people off the migrant trail as any other factor, assuming the all-important job opportunity is available. The people influenced by the small aesthetic qualities are likely to be the ones who contribute the most to achieving other environmental qualities.

There are other important goals we in the South can work for to achieve environmental quality without sacrificing the imperative need for continued but more intelligent overall economic development.

One of our most urgent problems in the field of human conservation is the necessity of reducing the birthrate. In much of the South we have, in the past decade, achieved for the first time a balance of in-migration, primarily as the result of increased job opportunities in the region. Even though migration has been greatly reduced, it is still a major influence on population trends, especially in parts of Appalachia and from the old plantation country of the Mississippi Valley.

There is no pat formula for reducing the birthrate. Some reduction is occurring naturally as people with higher economic and educational levels voluntarily reduce the size of their families. Essential success, however, will come only with an aggressive program of making birth-control and family-planning information a basic requirement, not only for welfare clients but for all young people as they reach the age level where they might become parents. In most areas of the South there is less organized resistance by religious groups to population-control procedures. There is no real reason why there should not be widespread liberalization of abortion laws, primarily to benefit low-income groups. There could also be large-scale information programs about sterilization procedures.

To sum it all up, let us in the South be in the forefront of every realistic move to protect the quality of environment. But let us not forget a lot of our environment needs its quality vastly improved before it is worth protecting. Our human resource still needs the benefit of much natural resource development before it will be in a position to use and enjoy the quality environment we all want. Because we have a better physical environment to start with, there is no reason why we should not seek the highest quality of life in our goals for the South.

Southern education

SOUTHERN EDUCATION: A NATIONAL PERSPECTIVE

Norton L. Beach

[ALL around the world today national governments are considering educational problems in revolutionary terms. Education is among the highest priorities of all developing nations. A growing number of influential citizens in every nation are convinced that their nation is suffering from a shortage of highly educated persons competent to assume leadership roles in society. There is also a widespread feeling that much creative talent has been lost because educational institutions have failed to recognize and develop the national potential. Southerners are beginning to feel this way, too.

These and other concerns about education suggest a worldwide educational revolution; but this phrase has different meanings in different countries. In some European nations, the revolution is concerned with using public education as an instrument for diminishing the degree of stratification of society. Another movement stresses the relationship between the material prosperity of a nation and the degree of education of the population. Other nations believe education can make a difference in the quality of human living.

There are signs in America that educational revolution means drastic changes for the public schools. For example, the experimental voucher system which gives parents the freedom to select their child's school may have far-reaching effects on methods of financing education. Accountability for educational quality may be transformed by the use of private corporations in school systems to guarantee specific learning results for the money spent. The comprehensive delivery of educational information through the extensive use of technology has the potential of turning even the home into an education center. In the South, as in the rest of the nation, there is a sense of the power of education; but the South has yet to realize fully the necessity of commitment.

What does the modern educational revolution mean for the South? Does it have the same meaning for the South as for the rest of the nation? Can the South move forward independently through the revolutionary period or must it follow the same pace as the rest of the nation? Can the South put the power of education to work? How will the South discover the strength of commitment to education? These and other critical questions can only be understood and answered by examining and understanding education in the nation and in the South.

A new climate is born in a revolution. Hope replaces discouragement. A renewed spirit of inquiry comes to life. People are eager to take on the responsibility of solving tough problems. It is a time when the strength of commitment can be discovered.

Ironically, because of its years of backwardness, the South now has the opportunity to move forward more rapidly than the rest of the nation in making educational changes. It can avoid the mistakes that have been made by the other, traditionally more "progressive," regions.

Ultimately, the power of education in the South will be determined by how fully education develops our human resources, so that the problems of Southern society will be solved today instead of at some future time in history.

As one tries to understand education in primary and secondary schools, colleges and universities, it is important to recognize that our educational system was set up to serve an America that has changed greatly in the intervening years. We need to begin our understanding with a look at history.

THE GREAT TASKS OF OUR SCHOOLS

"No other people ever demanded so much of education as have the Americans. None other was ever served so well by its schools and educators." This opening statement of an editorial by Henry Steele Commager, noted historian, sets the stage for his story of four great tasks which our faith in education imposed on our schools, three of which have particular relevance to Southern education.

The first and greatest task was to provide an enlightened citizenry in order that self-government might work. Has this experiment in democratic self-government worked? Was it a good investment? To a great extent the answer to both questions is yes. Americans have avoided military dictatorship and revolution. We have settled all major problems by compromise except the greatest one, slavery; and perhaps that could not have been settled by compromise. We have revealed at every moment of crisis an ability to find a great leader. Only a people taught self-government could record these achievements.

And yet, until Reconstruction, a substantial fraction of our population was denied the most basic right of democracy, that of citizenship. Furthermore, it was not until the last decade that equal educational opportunity for blacks was recognized as a legitimate demand and a pressing need. We have yet to record that our success in the first task is complete.

The second great task imposed upon the schools was the creation of unity, political and social. In Southern education, the lack of unity has been strikingly evident. The maintenance of a dual school system has reinforced racial division, and, to a large extent, accounts for the relative inferiority of Southern public education. It seems obvious that we have a long way to go toward achieving unity within our region and nation; and, further, that our country cannot fully realize its potential greatness until we do.

The third task imposed upon education and the schools was the responsibility for developing equality and democracy. Perhaps this is the area in which we have failed most decisively. The fact is that schools reflect the society they serve. If we as citizens expect the schools to meet this task in our time, we must first reform ourselves.

From the beginnings of our nation, America has had persistent concern for education, a faith in education so strong that education became the American religion. This faith was a strong driving force in educational achievement through the nineteenth and well into the twentieth century.

In late 1950 Commager said, "The American mind today seems deeply worried about its school system as it never has been before. In the vast literature on education there is more discontent than complacency, more blame than praise. There is an uneasy feeling that the schools have somehow failed to do their job." Now, two decades later, the concern is even greater; the murmur of discontent has turned to outcries of frustration and anger. The most critical question asked is, "What is the job of the schools *today?*"

The major educational goals of yesterday grew out of clearly defined tasks supported by a substantial majority of the citizenry, and, to a great extent, the public schools were successful in meeting its challenges through the mid-1920s. The Depression, World War II, and a mounting complexity of problems such as race, urban living, environment and population factors, peace, the impact of technology, and the impetus of rapid change have caused us to stop and redefine the goals of education in a changing society.

TODAY'S EDUCATIONAL PROGRAMS

One of the most difficult problems in assessing where we are in the decade of the seventies is the great range of school performance. We can find thrilling examples of enlightened educational practices as well as practices which are completely ineffective. A general characterization of the quality of educational programs in the South is not reassuring when compared to the needs both of individual students and of a growing, dynamic society.

A number of observations may be made to help us evaluate the effectiveness of education today. First, our society is increasingly dominated by concern with such major issues as peace, population and environmental control, equal opportunity, urban living, and race. The present school program gives little or no attention to these issues. Most teachers have limited backgrounds, understanding, or knowledge in these areas. Where will the students now in school and who will be in school during the rest of this century learn the meaning of these issues in their lives, the effect of these issues on society, the possible ways to manage these issues?

Second, the development of excellence in education demands that we define our objectives. A major shortcoming of today's schools is their inability to state the objectives of education for the school system, the individual schools, the classroom, and the student. We cannot know in which direction to travel unless we know where we want to go.

Third, most of the promising innovations that have been introduced in Southern schools during the last decade—team teaching, the open classroom, new grouping plans, and the ungraded class—are modifications of traditional administrative arrangements. These innovations can and do contribute to the improvement of instruction, but the evidence suggests that they have changed very little the quality of teaching and learning. To improve instruction requires that the teacher change her style of teaching as well as the learning styles of her students. In general, the quality of teaching has undergone little change in the last quarter of a century. The truly innovative approaches to education have made little impact in Southern schools.

Fourth, one promising development now in its beginning stages is "individualized instruction." For years educators have worked to make the educational system more responsive to individual differences among students, through recognizing the unique capabilities, needs, and interests of each student. Several Southern schools are currently experimenting with individualized instruction, and, in general, the results point to a higher level of academic achievement.

The opening of the decade of the seventies finds Southern schools trying out new patterns of organizing classes and personnel. In actual operation these practices have been less than successful. While many teachers and administrators have been enthusiastic about the promise of these innovations, inadequate training and the lack of appropriate technological assistance have seriously hampered their effectiveness.

The almost complete absence of specific goals and objectives for our schools and the present confusion and uncertainty about our curriculum priorities suggest that these two tasks, interlocked as they are, must become the major concerns in planning for a new education in the South.

ISSUES AND PROGRAMS FOR TOMORROW

For the last two decades, school leaders have intensified their efforts to emphasize and strengthen the separate-discipline approach which has long been the foundation of our educational program. Seldom have we asked ourselves whether or not this approach is equally appropriate for all levels of education; nor have we seriously considered the possibility of organizing part of the curriculum around the present problems of young people or the pressing problems of mankind.

During the last decade, a number of issues have emerged as the dominant concerns of our time. It is a sad fact, but true, that in most, perhaps all, public schools in the South these ten to fifteen major issues receive little or no attention the instructional program. Our young people are leaving school to spend their lives in a society dominated by these issues without any understanding of them.

John Gardner has defined some of these issues in his *Agenda for Americans.* A number of them are particularly relevant to Southern education.

The first is building an enduring peace. The South, because of its peculiar history, is in a position to demonstrate within the region, between competing states, between competing areas within a state, and between competing groups within a community, ways of building mutual understanding, trust, and tolerance. Tensions will not disappear, but they can be managed. Changes can be planned in the school program which will give students first-hand experiences in the community in resolving differences in a just and orderly way. The success of desegregation efforts in many parts of the South indicates that this goal is not an impossible one.

Second is the related issue of the developing nations. The South has faced in the past and is experiencing in the present many of the problems of developing nations: the growing gap between rich and poor, the threat of color as the basis for new divisions among peoples, the conflict of existing political ideologies, and the combination of poverty and rising expectations. This very personal and deep identification with what is happening in other lands provides an opportunity for Southerners to help their educational system build new programs to involve their students with people from other countries and cultures. Student exchanges, school adoptions between countries, teacher exchanges, study tours, and the extension of Peace Corps activities to wider age groupings would make a good beginning.

Third is the issue of equal opportunity. Gardner describes this:

> *Today, racial discrimination is the chief barrier to equality of opportunity, and is unquestionably our number one domestic problem. But the racial front is not the only one on which we are struggling to provide equality of opportunity, or equal access to the benefits*

of American life. There are other massive barriers to individual fulfillment—poverty, illness, ignorance, physical and mental handicaps.

Education offers the South its finest chance to meet the problem of equal opportunity. Strong beginnings are already under way in meeting this challenge. Consider some statistics from the April 18, 1971, *New York Times.* A comparison of governmental figures indicates that in two years the percentage of black pupils attending integrated schools in the South rose from 18 percent to 38 percent, while the percentages in the North and West remained essentially static at about 27 percent.

Fourth is the issue of economic growth. Although the rate of growth of per capita income in the South exceeded that of all other regions in the United States during the decade of the 1960s, the South is still the poorest region in the nation—a fact which is both cause and effect, to some extent, of our inability to educate our people effectively.

All the studies of the last twenty years show strong positive correlations between increased years of school and economic growth. The South verbally recognizes this fact but the support to date for education has not been sufficient to effect the economic growth that is possible for the region. Thoughtful study of Southern manpower needs and the planning of effective education to meet them is an immediate imperative.

The fifth relevant issue is the relationship of an individual to society. What happens to the individual in our educational system determines to a great extent his success or lack of success in later life. Again, we can be ironically grateful for our developmental lag in comparison with the rest of the nation. Many educational institutions in the South are new or still in the developing stage. It will be comparatively easy to redesign them to serve both the individual and the system.

Sixth is the issue of the role of intellectual institutions. During the last half century the business corporation has played the pre-eminent leadership role in American society. We are told that in the next fifty years, universities, research institutions, and related organizations may become the central innovation institutions in a postindustrial society. Today the South is witnessing an impressive growth not only in the number of its intellectual institutions but, more important, in the quality of these institutions and their ability to produce research and service. Communities, the public school systems, and these idea centers need to learn how to use their human resources in new, more creative ways.

Throughout our history our greatest statesmen have challenged us to educate for citizenship. One of the most effective ways to produce a lifelong good citizen is to provide practice in being a citizen in real situations during his school career. To try to solve, and to be successful in solving, these major issues of our time will provide some of the toughest tests of effective citizenship. It will help the South discover the strength of commitment to education.

CITIZENS AND SCHOOLS

I am persuaded that good schools are not made by teachers or by school superintendents or by school boards—at least, not by them alone. Good schools are patterns of human behavior in which the example of parents and other citizens plays an extremely significant part. It is important that the whole public realize what schools as an institution really are. Schools are a social instrument, the policies and practices of which merit the earnest consideration of every serious citizen. What the schools do now to individuals will help determine the kind of people and the kind of society we shall have in the next generation. Everyone has a stake in this outcome.

Public education, unlike any other profession, is the creature of the public. Schools were originally established at the instigation of laymen, and in the interests of public welfare. Schools are publicly financed. The schools reach all the public at some point—as students, as parents, or as employers of students.

Sometimes it is argued that the public should not try to influence the schools, that the public is too ignorant of the newer techniques in education to participate in school planning. But much of better school practice is common sense, once the basic principles are understood. Men and women whose vision has helped create modern technology and merchandising, modern science and collective social action can also be relied on to count heavily in creating a better educational system.

It is not necessary that the layman understand all the minutiae of modern educational technology. Those truly are the concern of the professional educator. The public needs to understand only enough to give them a sense of the potential power of education. Then, through what they expect the school to do for youngsters and for society, through the demands which they make on administrators, through the questions which they ask teachers, through the suggestions which they make in informal planning meetings, the influence of their interest will be felt in the schools.

Evidence shows that the best schools are those which have most fully involved the human resources of the community in planning for a better educational system. There are two key roles that every citizen can play in helping to improve schools. The first is to find ways as individuals to work with teachers and students in areas where they have a special interest or competence. Second, citizens can join with neighbors and members of the professional staff in committee work on school problems. In terms of practical achievement, citizen participation can mean the difference between the failure or success of such measures as school bonds and desegregation schemes.

THE FUTURE OF SOUTHERN HIGHER EDUCATION

The future of higher education will be determined in part by a number of factors which do not apply to elementary and secondary education, such as the diversity of institutions; the multiplicity of purposes; the age of students, somewhere between adolescence and adulthood; the power and the independence of the modern university and its growing social significance. A recent study by the Carnegie Commission on Higher Education reported the views on higher education of a number of legislative leaders. They took the following positions:

. . . a favorable attitude toward federal aid with a preference that it be spent through state governments.

. . . a favorable attitude toward long-range planning of higher education and centralized coordination as a means of making good use of resources and of expressing the will of state government.

. . . strong support for community colleges.

. . . a substantial degree of understanding of student dissent but a clear preference for a firm hand in dealing with it.

Partly for financial reasons, and in some instances for political and social reasons, the views expressed in this study may have undergone change since its completion. It is worth noting, however, that the legislators show strongest concern for issues of money and control.

In the concluding essay of this volume, Thomas Naylor expresses the following viewpoint: "Higher education in the South (and the nation) suffers from a lack of imagination and innovation, poor economic policies, antiquated management techniques, and a frantic competition for funds and prestige—realities that taxpayers, alumni, and students are beginning to recognize." He isolates those factors which have led to a massive loss of public confidence. His comments reflect a concern for stronger leadership and an emphasis on the need for quality in education.

Students in the last five years have expressed a multitude of viewpoints about college and university life. The constantly recurring theme is the lack of relevance of the educational program, and the increasing dissatisfaction leads to the most pressing question facing higher education today. How will American colleges and universities respond to the enormous strains and dislocations already visible within them?

You Can't Eat Magnolias

The university must respond with a new definition of its historical role to include the three R's of contemporary higher education: the relationships, rights, and responsibilities of students, faculty, administrators, trustees, and alumni. Traditionally, universities have been the seats of learning where the cultural heritage of man is valued, preserved, and passed on to later generations. Since the end of World War II, as the problems of our society have grown more complex and as universities have become the major research centers for studying many of these problems, another view of the role of the university has taken shape. According to this view, the university is primarily an institution concerned with social change, with helping society solve its problems. As Frank A. Rose, former President of the University of Alabama, notes: "Among the many directions the major state universities in the South must take in the coming decades, none is so urgent or essential as the development of the social sciences, particularly as these may be applied to the full development of this region's human and natural resources." Those who support this view believe that the university has the largest concentration of human resources and is in the best position to marshal them for the benefit of all the people in the state. Because of the closeness of its state universities to the people, this new role is particularly attractive to the South.

Leading scholars have cautioned us of the dangers inherent in this view. Carlyle Sitterson says, "If the university is to promote inquiry on the most difficult, complex and persistent problems of man, it cannot as an institution, at the same time, become the advocate of a monolithic view of truth." It is also clear that when an institutional position is established on any of the complex social issues of the day the university has entered the political arena as an active participant.

Much of the demand by Southern students for relevant programs of undergraduate education is a revolt against formal learning and a wish to be involved immediately and directly in society and its problems and opportunities. This realistic point of view suggests the possible creation of various forms of non-academic learning and service, organized by colleges and universities (frequently by students themselves) allowing students to fulfill their degree requirements in off-campus activities.

Today, the South is becoming an increasingly diverse region, encompassing larger numbers of people with different backgrounds and interests. Because the understandings, attitudes, and expectations for higher education of today's citizens, legislators, and corporations are complex and frequently in conflict with each other, universities are uncertain of their position on the purpose of the university and hesitate to modify their traditional role. Most Southern state colleges and universities depend for their funds and support on the good will of people, citizens and legislators alike. As a result there is an unwillingness to change unless the climate is right—and the climate has not been right for some time.

During the last decade a new trend has emerged in the state university systems of the South—multiple universities or the regional university. This trend has served to diffuse the allocation of already limited resources so that mediocrity instead of excellence in the quality of education threatens to result.

It is clear that the present arrangement of interinstitutional competition in Southern states is costing the taxpayer millions of dollars in funds unwisely spent. Duplication of programs, facilities, and staff are evident wherever one studies what colleges and universities are doing. What may be worse is that these duplicated programs are often so ineffective that their graduates, through no fault of their own, may not have the competence to perform their work effectively.

There is no single answer to this dilemma. States in each geographic area of the United States are trying different approaches to the problem.

One approach that has much merit is based on a view of the educational system as a unitary process from preschool through programs of adult education. This means that a single citizens' board of education would have the authority and responsibility to determine the continuing needs of citizens for educational programs from early childhood through adult life. This board would recommend plans, policies, and legislation, and would provide broad policy direction to the public schools, community colleges, four-year colleges, and the universities. An executive director would provide statewide educational leadership.

Two other areas of higher education are important to those concerned with its improvement in the South. Over the years, substantial numbers of persons in the South have elected to receive their education in private colleges and universities. These institutions continue to render important public service and are a valuable educational resource. Most Southern states have not established a public policy of direct aid to these institutions, many of which now face serious financial difficulties. A plan for state financial aid to private universities should occupy a top-priority position in planning the future of Southern higher education.

Second, the projections of manpower needs in the South for the rest of this century call for the provision of occupational education for middle-manpower needs, the basic first two years of a four-year degree program, and programs of continuing adult education. The community college is the best institution to meet these three needs. As the South continues to plan for higher education during the next three decades the community junior college should receive high priority.

A PLAN OF ACTION FOR SOUTHERN EDUCATION

The New South is an urban South; but urbanization is a relatively new phenomenon in the South, and therefore the character of Southern cities is different from that of cities in other parts of the nation. One distinct difference is especially pertinent to our discussion. In the big cities of the Northeast, Midwest, and Far West, public education is in trouble. It is reported, for example, that forty years ago the Newark school system paid the highest salaries in the nation to its teachers. It was one of the finest school systems in the country. Today, reports describing this once-fine school system say it is in a shambles; and much the same is true of the public schools in many large American cities. But this is not true of the South. In every Southern state, with few exceptions, the finest school systems are found in the largest cities. It is important to recognize, though, the emergence of the first signs of the disease which has all but destroyed the big-city school systems in other parts of the nation. The urban South can wait no longer to deal with the problem of education. We can be fairly sure that in two decades—twenty years—in a rapidly changing society, large Southern cities will be in the same condition as their counterparts in other regions if the present conditions of decay are allowed to go unchecked. This problem needs to be attacked both regionally and on a statewide basis, as one of the most important educational issues requiring immediate attention.

As citizens in the South search for a better education for their children they should know that the differences in both wealth and tax rate in local school districts are so great that the quality of education a child receives is largely a function of where he lives. The President's Commission on School Finance recently observed that educational spending among the states in 1970 ranged from $1,237 per pupil in New York to $438 in Alabama, and, among school districts in Texas, from $243 to $2,087. With the level of federal support down and only negligible increases in state support, it is obvious that it will take a major creative effort among Southern citizens to finance the kind of educational program they want for their children.

I would like to mention one more problem area where action can begin now. Throughout the last forty years I have heard scores of ideas proposed to improve education. Many of them I have seen tried in the classroom. Very few of these ideas have been concerned with changing the teaching styles of teachers and the learning styles of students. It is likely that concentration on these two aspects of helping students learn might turn out to be the most productive ideas we have tried in education.

As a basis for an initial plan of action for Southern communities and states I would like to make the following recommendations:

1. A Southern Educational Congress should be held immediately to plan a comprehensive, coordinated regional program to deal with the educational problems of the South. Those who attend should include governors, state representatives to the Interstate Commission, legislative conference members of the Southern Regional Education Board, selected citizens, and key educators.
2. Citizens' organizations, such as the L.Q.C. Lamar Society, might consider education among their highest priority problems for action in the decade of the 1970s. For example, the annual meeting of the Lamar Society might focus on this topic in such a way that model plans for state and city chapters could be developed.
3. State governments and independent organizations should develop a five-year plan for building a program of better public understanding of the problems of education. All mass media resources should be used.
4. Southern governors should be encouraged to hold special prelegislative workshop sessions for legislators to examine and better understand the educational problems of our times.
5. A survey should be undertaken in every Southern state to determine societal attitudes toward and expectations of education. As our society becomes more complex, so does the diversity of attitudes. One result is that the chances for educational reform are often blocked because of decision-makers' uncertainty about what would be accepted "out there."

It is clear that the time has come in our nation for an educational renaissance. What is the specific role of the South in bringing it about? In the words of Terry Sanford:

> *Southerners are veterans of the kinds of battles that American education must now*

undergo. We know how to struggle against a lack of support, against public apathy, and against such excuses as war. We know how to persevere against such odds, and finally how to prevail against them.... We must also move beyond sectionalism now to assume a role of leadership within the mainstream of American education.... This, frankly, is a call to service, not for any reasons of sectional prestige, but for the salvation of American education.

The southern economy

HUMAN RESOURCE DEVELOPMENT IN THE SOUTH

F. Ray Marshall
and
Virgil L. Christian, Jr.

[DEVELOPMENT of human resources is important for both economic and social reasons. Investments in education, training, and health services yield high returns to society in general as well as to the recipients. Further, it is clear that the scientific-technical-industrial revolution we are currently experiencing will cause knowledge, skill, and health to be increasingly important assets in the future. As the distinguished philosopher Alfred North Whitehead observed, "In conditions of modern life the rule is absolute, the race which does not value trained intelligence is doomed."

Unfortunately, the South's political, social, and economic institutions have not been of a nature to attract investments in the region's people. The greatest problems have been in agriculture, where the sharecropping system devised to replace slavery provided little incentive for improvements in either the people or the land. Indeed, deliberate undereducation of rural Negroes was

A complete list of references, tables, and data sources for this paper may be obtained from the L.Q.C. Lamar Society, P.O. Box 4774, Duke Station, Durham, North Carolina, 27706.

widely used as a device for keeping them effectively tied to the soil. Separate and inferior black schools, in line with Southern segregationist philosophy, served this purpose admirably, but resulted in the squandering of the region's meager educational resources on a dual system that left the people of the South—black and white, rural and urban—lagging far behind the rest of the country in education. Federal aid, as a remedy, was not sought, and would not have been welcomed. The region's one-party political tradition and negative states' rights position, combined with the dominance of the race issue, made it difficult for political processes to effect cooperation with the federal government on any question, even such a vital one as human resource development.

But industrialization is eroding the South's traditional institutions. The region cannot escape the scientific-technical revolution, one of the universal imperatives of our time; it can, however, by its action or inaction determine the extent to which the revolution is peaceful or disruptive. It can also influence the end result of the industrializing process. Segregation and caste systems are incompatible with the logic of industrialism, which is based on merit and technical competence, but deliberate human intervention can modify the most powerful trends, and only the foolhardy would fail to respect the tenacity of the South's resistance to change. If industrialization is to bring significant increases in real income to all Southern people, we must develop institutional flexibility to eliminate the region's traditional barriers to the development and utilization of skills.

Attention here will be concentrated on changes in the Southern economy during the 1950s and 1960s, with special emphasis on agricultural and racial employment patterns. Agriculture has been the source of many of the South's economic problems (for example, much displaced agricultural labor has become surplus labor in the region because the vocational and educational skill base of agricultural workers is lower than that required by the expanding industrial and service sectors); and it remains, despite dramatic displacement of the farm labor force, a more important source of black employment than any four of the region's manufacturing industries. Racial employment patterns will be stressed because race permeates the problems associated with the development of the South's human resources, white as well as black.

THE PROBLEM

Per capita income, the best indicator of economic welfare, remains lower in the South than in the rest of the United States despite a long-run tendency for regional income gaps to narrow. The average per capita income in the South in 1966 was 80 percent of that of United States as a whole—even lower in some of the poorer Southern states. Poverty in the South is heavily concentrated in rural areas and among nonwhites. Indeed, the region accounts for two thirds of the nation's poor nonwhites, though it has less than half the nonwhite population.

A relatively large proportion of Southern nonwhites are poor not because they are unemployed, but because they are underemployed. Southerners of both races have lower labor force participation rates than their counterparts in other regions, and the disparity for nonwhites is especially pronounced. Moreover, the fact that the amount of farm work actually performed is declining faster than the farm labor force suggests rising underemployment in agriculture. Finally, nonwhites have higher unemployment rates in the South than elsewhere. These factors add up to a substantial disadvantage in real incomes, because the South's lower cost of living is not sufficient to offset the discrepancy.

PROBLEMS OF SOUTHERN AGRICULTURE

According to the 1960 census, three fourths of nonwhite families and 39 percent of white families in the rural South earned less than $3,000 a year. In the deep South states of Alabama, Arkansas, Georgia, Louisiana, Mississippi, and South Carolina, the income level was even lower. U.S. Department of Agriculture data indicate that $10,000 of farm products are needed to provide the $2,500 net income regarded as the poverty line for farm operators. In 1964 only 1.3 percent of Negroes and 14.1 percent of white farm operators met this standard.

Even more disturbing was the tendency for the racial income gap to widen. The incomes of Negro male farm operators averaged half those of non-Negroes in 1960, but the average increased by almost 40 percent for non-Negroes and only 6.5 percent for Negroes between 1960 and 1965. Moreover, the increase in Negro farm operator incomes went up at about the same rate as the Consumer Price Index, so it appears that their real incomes did not improve at all between 1960 and 1965.

The Negro farmer's ability to adjust to technological and market changes has been markedly different from that of whites because of his limited education and vocational training, the small size of his farm, and his restricted access to credit. Consequently, Negroes operate farms only one fourth the average size of those operated by whites; they have less livestock, lower crop yields per acre, and less machinery per farm; and they are more dependent on cotton and tobacco, which have been hardest hit by technological changes and federal agricultural policies.

MIGRATION OUT OF SOUTHERN AGRICULTURE

The number of Southern Negro farmers peaked at 926,000 in 1920, but the attraction of urban jobs and the hardships of Southern agriculture—hardships made even worse during the 1920s by soil erosion and the ravages of the boll weevil—caused a steady decline thereafter. The migration of Southern Negroes was accelerated by federal agricultural policies during the 1930s, but the really significant declines came after World War II. The number of tenant farmers in the region declined by more than 70 percent from 1945 to 1959, and, by 1964, the number of farms of all types operated by Negroes was 184,000. Of these, more than half were on some form of share tenant basis, as compared with 19 percent for whites.

In spite of heavy out-migration of cotton and tobacco farmers for several decades, Negro labor has remained concentrated in those crops. Unfortunately, their involvement with these particular crops made them (as well as small white farmers) especially vulnerable to federal agricultural policies, since the cultivation of tobacco and cotton was controlled by acreage allotments and price controls. Under the New Deal agricultural programs, landowners clearly benefitted at the expense of their tenants despite the best intentions. Gunnar Myrdal, in *An American Dilemma* (1944), concluded:

> *Landlords have been made to reduce drastically the acreage for their main labor requiring crops. They have been given this large part of the power over the local administration of this program. They have strong enough economic incentive to reduce their tenant labor force, a large part of which consists of politically and legally impotent Negroes. Yet they have been asked not to make any such reduction. It would not be compatible with usual human behavior, if this request generally had been fulfilled. Under the circumstances, there is no reason at all to be surprised about the wholesale decline in tenancy. Indeed, it would be surprising if it had not happened.*

Moreover, the demand for labor in cotton farming was drastically reduced by the mechanical harvester and chemical and mechanical methods of weed control. In the South the proportion of cotton harvested by hand declined from 52 percent in 1962 to 20 percent in 1966—rapid mechanization in four years.

The production of tobacco has not been mechanized to the same extent as cotton, but the prospect is for greatly reduced labor requirements in the future. Before World War II this crop employed many black workers because it was labor-intensive and could utilize the work of entire families. Since then, however, the number has declined drastically, and technological advances in the harvesting and curing of tobacco promise still lower labor requirements in the future. Perhaps attention to the further displacement of tobacco farmers might avoid the tremendous social costs associated with the disruption of cotton farmers during the 1950s and 1960s.

The extent to which displacement of the total farm labor force in the South has run its course is problematical. The technological revolution in cotton production is nearly complete, but it is far from finished in tobacco, and U.S. Department of Agriculture (U.S.D.A.) data covering other crops suggest continuing displacement and rising underemployment. In the years from 1950 to 1969 the ratio of fulltime jobs per potential fulltime farm worker fell from 70 percent to less than 50 percent. Not surprisingly, nonwhites bore a disproportionate share of the pressure on farm operators and their families, in terms of both unemployment and underemployment.

FEDERAL AGRICULTURE POLICIES

As stated before, much of the Southern black farmers' difficulty has been due to their concentration on small farms, in particular on small farms falling under the aegis of U.S.D.A. programs. Myrdal's conclusion that the condition of small farmers in Southern agriculture was made even worse by federal agricultural policies seems as applicable now as it was in 1944. Although justified on the grounds of "parity," these programs continue to help most those who need help least. Southern white rural interests have been able to perpetuate their control over poor people in general and poor Negroes in particular through a constellation of political and economic powers extending from Congress to the local sheriff's office. As a consequence, the Agricultural Stabilization and Conservation Service (A.S.C.S.), which administers agricultural price supports, establishes acreage and crop quotas, and provides for "conservation" by taking land out of cultivation, has been controlled by whites. Indeed, it is incredible that as late as the end of 1968 no Negro was a regular member of a county A.S.C.S. committee. Since then, Negroes have had no more than token representation on either the state or community A.S.C.S. committees or the staffs which actually administer these programs. Except for employment in special places like the Data Processing Center and Commodity Office in Louisiana and the Eastern Photo Lab in North Carolina, very few Negroes were employed by A.S.C.S., and those were at low levels.

The Cooperative Extension Service (C.E.S.) was established to help farmers improve their productivity by providing advice on management and technical aspects of farming. But C.E.S. in the South was segregated until 1964 and did little to help the poorest farmers. Indeed, many of the poorest farmers have never been visited by a C.E.S. representative.

The Farmers Home Administration (F.H.A.) makes loans to enable small farmers to improve their homes, buy or expand farms, raise and market crops, buy machinery, or finance businesses which will improve their incomes. It also makes loans to farmers' cooperatives. Since the F.H.A. concentrated in the area of greatest rural poverty, a large proportion of the 48,000 Economic Opportunity Act (E.O.A.) loans made during the program's first four years were in the South. However, F.H.A. was required by law to help those who could benefit from the loans, and as a result it helped whites more than Negroes and the affluent more than their poorer neighbors. During the first four years, Negroes, who constitute about 20 percent of the rural poor, received about 29 percent of the loans—but loans to Negroes averaged some $300 less than those to whites. And Negro farmers, a third of all farmers in the South, received only a fourth of all loans between 1964 and 1967 and a seventh of the funds.

Although the characteristics of F.H.A.'s loan recipients might be a defense against "creaming," since loans obviously went to people who were disadvantaged by urban standards, most Negroes in the rural South fall below the average income and education levels of those who get loans. In March 1965, for example, the median level of education of Negro male agricultural workers was 6.1 years, as compared with 9.4 years for whites. Moreover, the average yearly income of Negro farmers in the South was a good bit less than the $1,891 earned by farmers who received opportunity loans. Finally, the smaller average loans to Negroes reflect, at least in part, F.H.A.'s procedure of gearing the amount of loans to the recipient's ability to use it. Since the more affluent, better educated borrowers could convince F.H.A. officials that they could make better use of the loans than their poorer, less educated neighbors, there obviously is an element of creaming in F.H.A.'s procedures, and F.H.A. officials are quick to defend the procedure as maximizing the use of limited resources.

There is conflicting evidence on the extent of racial discrimination in the administration of F.H.A. Some officials point out that in spite of nondiscriminatory pronouncements from Washington, local administrators in the South reflect the racial prejudices of local political and agricultural leaders. In 1961, for example, there was not a single Negro on any of the 7,000 county committees which determine the eligibility of loan applicants. In 1969 there were 385 Negro county committeemen in the South, presumably because of the 1965 F.H.A. directive that counties where 20 percent of the farmers are black must have at least one Negro committeeman. In Alabama, however, although there were 30 Negroes among 183 F.H.A. committeemen in 1968, none of the three-member committees had more than one Negro.

Moreover, the F.H.A. apparently has very few Negroes in staff positions. As of June 1969, the F.H.A. reported 170 Negro employees in the South, or only 6 percent of its total Southern employment, and a very large proportion of these were employed at grades GS-7 and below. Thus, while F.H.A. has improved its Negro employment picture since 1965, Negroes have penetrated key positions mainly on a token basis.

AGRICULTURE AND THE REGIONAL ECONOMY

The loss of 2.29 million agricultural jobs has put considerable pressure on rural people of both races, and also on the regional economy. The agricultural job loss amounted to 14 percent of total nonagricultural employment in 1967, and the percentage would have been higher if the number of people displaced from agriculture, rather than the number of full man-years lost, had been used in making the calculation. The nonagricultural sectors were therefore called upon to absorb 140,000 farm workers a year above the increment in the labor force associated with population growth. They could not do it. Bureau of Labor statistics data show that employment in the nonagricultural sectors of the South increased by 6.6 million between 1950 and 1967—but population jumped 12.2 million, involving a gain of 4.7 million in the labor force. Tragically, some of the gain in the labor force grew out of the necessity to import skills not available in displaced agricultural labor to fill the needs of the region's growth industries. Nevertheless, nonagricultural employment would have had to expand by at least half a million more than it did to accommodate both the growth in the labor force and the overflow from agriculture. Net out-migration served to hold the gap to this size by retarding somewhat the expansion of the population; even so, there was a steady pile-up of surplus low-skill labor in smaller urban centers and in rural nonfarm areas of the region, where it stands as a monument to the South's failure to prepare her rural people of either race for the unleashing of technological change in agriculture.

The Southern industries showing the largest amounts of growth in employment between 1940 and 1960 were: (1) wholesale and retail trade (1,453,100), (2) professional and related services (1,068,700), (3) construction (644,400), (4) government (417,600), (5) finance, insurance, and real estate (357,400), (6) business and repair services (234,500), (7) apparel products manufacturing (219,800), and (8) food and kindred products (213,200). These eight industries, taken together, expanded employment by 4,609 million between 1940 and 1960—107.6 percent of the total change in regional employment over that period. That is, all other industries aggregated to a net decline, agriculture, of course, being responsible for most of the loss. Clearly equilibrium in the regional labor market hinged on the extent to which displaced agricultural manpower was able to adjust to the needs of the expanding nonagricultural sectors. Unfortunately, the adjustment was far from ideal.

Rural Southerners of both races have less education than their urban counterparts, and both have less education than people outside the South. In short, rural Southerners trail the entire national population in years of schooling. Beyond that, at the bottom of the bottom, are Southern rural Negroes, who, traditionally, have been further disadvantaged by schools of inferior quality. Studies have disclosed that more than 80 percent of the black males who left Southern agriculture had less than an effective seventh-grade education, and well over half had less than four years. Whites were a little better off, but hardly more than half of them had reached high school. As a result, the supply side of the nonagricultural labor market was steadily swelled by rural males having far below average educational attainments.

Had the educational requirements of the region's growth industries been such as to accommodate larger numbers of uneducated and untrained workers, then the displaced farm workers would have had alternative job opportunities. This was not the case. Census data for 1960 show that the median years of schooling for males in the industries having the largest amounts of increase in employment over the last two decades ranged from 17.21 years for professional and related services to 9.48 years for food and kindred products industries. Clearly farm workers, given their educational levels, were sore pressed to penetrate these industries. And were they lucky enough to penetrate them, advancement very far up the occupational ladder was virtually impossible. So the regional pattern was set: importation of skilled labor to fill the needs of the South's growth industries; net out-migration, on balance, because employment in the nonagricultural sectors did not expand sufficiently to take care of the shift out of agriculture; and steady accumulation of a pool of low-skill labor because out-migration did not drain off all the labor surplus. Inevitably, the pattern created serious psychological effects for millions of the region's people and imposed heavy burdens on its restricted welfare budgets. The South's policy of deliberate underdevelopment of her human resources had come home to roost.

MIGRATION

Both the South and the non-South were called upon to bear the costs of the imbalance in the Southern labor market. The dynamics of the disequilibrium operated to push the upper layers of Negro labor into the industrialized urban areas outside the region, and nearly 1.5 million black people left the South in the fifties alone. Paradoxically, this movement affected median education and skill levels of blacks in both South and non-South adversely, as those who migrated were above average where they left but below average where they went. Thus the South suffered heavy losses of the most progressive of her black people, and the non-South picked up a larger quantity of "immigrant" low and semiskilled labor than it could readily absorb. Indeed, the Southern Negroes were received outside the region with much the same resentment and hostility as other ethnic groups before them, and with much the same consequences—except that in this case the consequences were more severe because the migrants were more numerous, and because, as American citizens, they had legal claim to rights and privileges that the receiving community was not willing to grant. Most major American cities can attest to the violence of the ensuing conflict.

The Southern migration pattern has changed since the stampede from the region in the fifties. In the early sixties there was a sharp reduction in net out-migration, followed by a shift to net in-migration. White migration turned round to net in-migration in the late fifties, and this trend gained strength in the sixties. Negro migration, always out, slowed somewhat, though preliminary reports from the 1970 census indicate that it continued fairly strong throughout the sixties. The two together—rapidly increasing white in-migration and slowing Negro out-migration—imply the end of the time when the South will be able to export its labor surplus. Beyond that, the history of Southern migration supports the proposition that there is no such thing as a purely regional manpower problem: market forces and labor mobility see to it that all share in the failure of any region to develop its people.

MANUFACTURING EMPLOYMENT

Racial factors are also important in the South's nonagricultural industries. Data from the Equal Employment Opportunity Commission make it possible to study the manufacturing industries in some detail. Three statistics are useful in this context: (1) a penetration rate which shows the percentage of Negroes in each industry; (2) an index of occupational position, IOP, which roughly estimates median income, by race, in each industry; and (3) the ratio of the Negro to the white index of occupational position, which measures the extent to which the Negro occupational profile in the industry parallels that of whites. It should be noted that the data which generate these statistics were collected in 1966, before the 1964 Civil Rights Act had time to take effect, and that they were collected for firms with 100 employees or more, thus missing the many small firms which in total have sizable concentrations of black employees. Nevertheless, they accurately reflect the occupational structure for the region's largest employers, and capture enough nonagricultural employment to be highly informative.

The data show that white and Negro males are concentrated in much the same industries, though there are some important differences—for example, the preponderance of Negroes in food and kindred products, tobacco manufacture, and lumber and wood products, and their underrepresentation in chemicals and allied products and petroleum refineries. Likewise, Negro and white females are concentrated in the same industries, although the tobacco, wood products, and furniture industries are relatively more significant for Negro females.

The indexes of occupational position (IOP) for Negro and white males demonstrate some noticeable similarities. The IOPs of Negro males in the South are consistently below those outside the South. Indeed, in all but three cases Negro males in the non-South were better off in the absolute than white males in the South. However, there is a strong similarity between the Negro's percentage of the white indexes in the South and in the non-South, indicating that the Negro male's relative position is about the same in both places.

Although the Negro male IOPs are strongly correlated with the white male indexes in the South and the non-South, showing strengths and weaknesses in the same industries, there is no significant relationship between the Negro and white female indexes in the South. In all cases, Negroes are apparently restricted to menial jobs while whites are in white-collar occupations. Outside the South, however, the situation is different; that is, the non-Southern industries which provide a large number of good jobs for white women also provide them for Negro women.

A South–non-South comparison of the IOPs of Negroes relative to whites in ten leading industries shows that the Negro's relative position is better in the non-South than the South in every case. The relative position of Negro males is highly correlated by industry; a similar but weaker relationship is present for Negro females. It is also noteworthy that, for these ten industries, the lowest relative position of Negro males in the non-South is higher than the highest relative position in the South, although this conclusion does not hold for females.

While Negroes constituted 14.2 percent of total employment in Southern industries, they accounted for less than 1 percent of the managerial and professional categories and only 1.9 percent of sales and technical employment. Negro females, too, were underrepresented in the professional, technical, sales, and clerical classifications in both the South and non-South, but they were in a relatively better position than Negro males. On the other hand, Negro females in the South were heavily concentrated in the labor and service classifications, but Negro females in the non-South have been far more successful in penetrating the clerical class.

Two questions dealing with work forces of growing as contrasted with diminishing industries were posed in the analysis: (1) Does the Negro comprise a larger proportion of the work force in the declining than in the expanding industry? (2) Does the Negro achieve a significantly different occupational status in the two cases? The answer to the first question is definitely yes; the answer to the second is that there seems to be very little difference. The seven Southern industries exhibiting the poorest growth characteristics are: (1) agriculture, (2) sawmills and planing mills, (3) tobacco products manufacturing, (4) mining, (5) personal services, (6) textile mills products manufacturing, and (7) forestries, fisheries, and logging. The seven most rapidly expanding industries are: (1) electrical machinery manufacturing, (2) transportation equipment manufacturing, (3) rubber products manufacturing, (4) apparel products manufacturing, (5) nonelectrical machinery manufacturing, (6) paper and allied products, and (7) metal industry manufacturing. In declining industries (1), (2), and (5) above, Negroes make up 34.13 percent, 42.23 percent, and 44.4 percent, respectively, of the industry work forces; the mean for the seven is 25.25 percent. On the other hand, the largest Negro representation in the expanding industries is 14.32 percent in paper and allied products; the mean for the seven is 10.18 percent. (Of course, it would be useful to know whether or not Negro employment is *increasing* or *decreasing* as a proportion of total employment in the growth industries, but this calculation cannot be made with data for one year.)

Several other tentative conclusions flow from the first year's E.E.O.C. data:

1. There is some evidence that the Negro's occupational status is moderately affected by the income level of the industry, but the evidence is not strong and the effect is not great. Apparently, Negroes who penetrate the higher income industries move up in the occupational structure about as well as those in the lower income industries.

2. There is no evidence that the Negro's occupational position relative to the white is adversely affected by his being a larger proportion of the industry work force.

3. There is considerable evidence that the Negro's relative educational attainment adversely affects his occupational status. Twenty-two percent of the occupational discrepancy between Negro and white males can be attributed to the failure of the Negro to achieve the same median years of schooling; adjustment for quality of education raises the figure to 53 percent. For females the figures indicate that 65 percent of the discrepancy is erased by equal schooling and virtually all of it following adjustment for quality.

These data on manufacturing, combined with those on agriculture, indicate that Negroes have been greatly underdeveloped and underutilized in the South. Similar data on government employment give further confirmation to this notion. Indeed, Negroes have not only been educationally deprived, but, beyond that, they have not been used in accordance with educational levels actually reached. Consequently, many of the better trained Negroes have responded to inadequate employment opportunities by moving out. Apparently Southern policies designed to export the region's race and welfare problems succeeded only in driving off the most productive elements in the black population. Moreover, such migration widened the racial education gap to the extent that better educated whites moved in as the better educated blacks moved out. Clearly this imbalance has serious implications for race relations in the region, particularly in view of the forces reducing job opportunities for Negroes in agriculture. Finally, the Negro–white technological gap has widened because Negroes tend to have a larger share of the jobs in declining industries than in growth industries. Should these trends continue—and they will unless measures are taken to counter them—serious trouble lies ahead for the South during the 1970s.

REMEDIAL PROGRAMS

ECONOMIC DEVELOPMENT

When economists talk about economic development they usually mean improvements in either aggregate or per capita personal incomes. And economists as well as politicians too often conceive of development in terms of *places* rather than of people. Actually, however, economic development of places, while in the interests of local politicians and businessmen, is much the less significant of the two. The development of places is not necessarily incompatible with the development of people, of course, but it may be. For example, it might not be in the best interest of the younger, more adaptable, and better educated people in a place with poor economic prospects to create marginal jobs for them there. Their best interest would be served by policies to improve mobility out, but such policies will rarely be condoned by either local politicians or local business interests. On the other hand, marginal jobs in rural areas might be in the best interest of *some* people in the South.

The policies required to make it possible for people in the South (or elsewhere) to upgrade themselves are fairly clear. The first is an adequate economic base to provide income-earning opportunities. In the national economy, this ordinarily means the adoption of measures to insure full employment. In a region like the South economic development requires an increase in job opportunities both sufficient in number to offset growth in the work force and suitable in kind to enable people to use and develop their skills according to their interests and abilities.

Although incomes in the South are improving in relation to the United States as a whole, there is considerable local variation. Moreover, to the extent that there has been economic development it has not produced adequate job opportunities for all the region's people. Racial discrimination is one cause; a second is that much of the region's industry has been labor-intensive and has provided very low-wage, dead-end jobs. Indeed, it is precisely this kind of industry that economic development programs are likely to produce. Higher-income-producing firms are less likely to be attracted by the blandishments of cheap labor, an antiunion climate, or tax incentives than they are by skilled workers, expanding markets, abundant resources, or external economies found in growing cities and towns.

Since industry adapts to the kinds of resources available, the South might lure higher-paying extramarginal industries if it upgraded its human resources through education and training. This has led many observers to the conclusion that the South should try to attract capital-intensive manufacturing industry and increase labor mobility from low- to higher-productivity areas in order to improve its per capita income. However, that is a place- rather than a people-oriented solution. For while there is little question about the desirability of capital-intensive industry and manpower upgrading programs over the long pull, the presence of a large pool of underutilized low-skill labor demands a strategy for the development of labor intensive activities, at least in the short run. For one thing, there is a serious need for labor-intensive industry in the rural areas to employ people whose education and experience have not prepared them for high-wage occupations.

These people are likely to work in marginal enterprises, or be welfare recipients, wherever they live. Indeed, the region's limited welfare resources might be much more effectively utilized by subsidizing marginal enterprises in the rural areas than by directing them entirely to income maintenance programs.

Further, it is abundantly clear that measures must be taken to improve the position of small farmers, and especially black farmers, by making it possible for those who wish to remain in agriculture to do so. Given adequate technical assistance and loan programs, many of these farmers might successfully make the switch from capital-intensive crops to such labor-intensive crops as vegetable and livestock production. It is also worth noting that the growth of large farms may have resulted more from federal agriculture policies, which favor large-scale activities, than from any demonstrated economies of scale or comparative economic advantage which large farmers enjoy. If that be true, a long overdue reform of American agricultural policies might slow the steady displacement of labor from small farms.

Although cooperatives and other labor-intensive activities might be marginal economic enterprises, they have significant noneconomic advantages which in the long run could have beneficial implications for human resource development. For example, there are not likely to be significant changes in those institutional arrangements—discrimination, poor education, unwise agricultural policies, and inadequate health and welfare programs—without strong political pressures for these changes. Marginal economic enterprises might form bases to generate those pressures. They might also slow the deterioration of rural communities by improving the productivity of the rural poor and providing them with minimum income bases.

ANTIDISCRIMINATION PROGRAMS

Economic development programs alone will not solve all the economic problems facing the people of the South. This is true, in the first place, because discrimination has made it difficult for

Negroes to benefit from general economic development. Indeed, as noted earlier, black employment is failing to keep pace with white employment in those nonagricultural activities which are expanding. Moreover, the displacement of workers from Southern agriculture is not being offset by either out-migration or employment of black workers in nontraditional jobs outside agriculture. Strengthening antidiscrimination laws can help with this process, but legal remedies must be supplemented by other measures. Antidiscrimination laws are limited because economic discrimination is difficult to prove; because legal action is expensive and slow and the outcome is uncertain; and because measures to combat specific overt acts of discrimination operate only on the demand side of the labor market and do not guarantee that blacks will be able to take advantage of the lowering of racial barriers. In spite of these limitations, however, state and local antidiscrimination laws create a moral climate for eliminating discrimination, establish agencies to study problems of minority employment, give those who want to adopt fair practices an excuse to do so, and eliminate the most obvious areas of overt discrimination. Agencies created by these laws, cooperating with federal antidiscrimination activities, could adopt equal employment opportunity programs geared to the realities of the South.

EDUCATION

While it is possible to exaggerate the importance of education as a means of upgrading people and overcoming poverty, few can argue with the need to attain general literacy. And whether or not education leads to greater productivity, American institutions are such that both the quantity and quality of education are extremely important in the competition for jobs. There is a particularly urgent need to upgrade the level of education available in the rural South if the technological gap between whites and blacks, and between the South and the non-South, is not to grow larger. In 1960, the median education of Negro males in agriculture, almost all of whom were in the South, was only 5.4 years, as compared with 8.6 years for whites. Since Negro educational achievement in the rural South lags behind that of whites by at least one year for every three years taken, the average Negro male in Southern agriculture did not have the five years of effective education required for functional literacy.

The level of education for Southern Negroes has been very low relative to whites everywhere and to nonwhites outside the South. The greatest disparity between Southern white and nonwhite education levels was in Mississippi, where the white median was 11.0 years and the nonwhite 6.0 years. Strikingly, the Mississippi nonwhite median was over two years behind the national average, but the white median was slightly above. For the whole region, 33.5 percent of nonwhites and 10.5 percent of whites had less than five years of schooling.

The Southern states are making vigorous efforts to improve their educational systems, as indicated by the fact that the only Southern states to spend smaller proportions of their personal income on education in 1967–68 than the United States average were Texas and Kentucky. Beyond that, Southern states have supplemented their own resources by heavy reliance on federal funds. The average state in the United States as a whole received 7.7 percent of its revenues for public secondary and elementary schools from the federal government, but no Southern state received a percentage that low, and Mississippi's 18.29 percent was higher than any other state's but Alaska.

But these efforts, impressive as they are, fall far short of what is required to close the educational gaps between Negroes and whites, between rural and urban areas, and between the South and non-South. The problem is the low per capita incomes of the Southern states, which result in a smaller expenditure per pupil than the national average. In 1967–68, only Louisiana's $754 per pupil exceeded the United States figure of $750, and Mississippi's $413 was the lowest in the nation. While expenditures per pupil do not necessarily measure the quality of education, they, along with the high proportion of the South's young men who fail to meet the mental requirements for induction into the armed forces, and the Negro–white, South–non-South, and rural–urban gaps, add up to a serious need for massive improvement. It is fairly clear, however, that a large share of the funds will have to come from the federal government. The South probably lacks the will to finance a quality educational system for blacks as well as whites even if it had the resources to do so.

Despite the importance of education, it is easy to misconstrue its role in explaining the Negroes' plight in the rural South or, indeed, anywhere else. It is true that educational differences appear, on the surface, to explain a large part of the Negro's inferior occupational position in industry. However, this is not surprising because education, more than any single variable, captures discrimination in all forms—schools, housing, incomes, and social activities which influence aspirations and attitudes—and it is therefore highly associated with statistical measures of Negro disadvantage. Moreover, the fact that a variety of discriminatory forces are concentrated in the educational system makes it unlikely that improvement can be accomplished through the schools alone.

MANPOWER PROGRAMS

The state employment services, which are supposed to provide job information and to refer workers to jobs, are among the most important potential Southern manpower agencies. Unfortunately, the state services have done little in the past to counteract the traditional discriminatory patterns of training and employment in the region. Apparently some promising beginnings were made during the early 1960s, but there is little current information to show that employment agencies in the various states are operating effectively as nondiscriminating manpower agencies. Indeed, even if the state employment services were to cease their discriminatory practices, serious impediments to nondiscrimination would continue to exist so long as the present federal-state system makes it difficult to have a coordinated national labor information and exchange system. It is only fair to note, however, that the state employment services have been handicapped by staff salaries geared to low state employee levels and have accordingly been handicapped in the search for high-quality personnel.

Another traditional manpower program that could be beneficial to the South is an effective vocational education system operated on a nondiscriminatory basis. Vocational education in the South, as in the rest of the country, traditionally stressed agriculture and homemaking. But even this was on a racially segregated basis and inferior Negro schools offered a very limited range of courses. The prevailing theory of preparing Negroes (or whites) for existing job opportunities has meant that courses in Negro schools were geared to Negro jobs and they therefore reinforced rather than changed existing employment patterns. However, the passage of the Manpower Development and Training Act (M.D.T.A.) of 1962, the Vocational Education Act of 1963, the Economic Opportunity Act (E.O.A.) of 1964, and the Civil Rights Act of 1964 caused some changes in manpower programs.

There is now evidence that every Southern state considers quality technical education to be an important attraction to high-wage industries. This conviction was backed up with an effort to use limited educational resources as effectively as possible, and hundreds of technical training institutes, community colleges, and junior colleges have been established throughout the South. These schools have been able to utilize funds from M.D.T.A. and E.O.A. for specialized training programs for young people and adults. Some of these programs, especially those in the Carolinas, seem to be playing a significant role in attracting extramarginal economic enterprises. As manpower skills are upgraded, enterprises are coming in to take advantage of them. Indeed, the best skill-training programs are those which are coordinated with existing jobs or jobs which will come into being with the completion of training.

The South's experience with apprenticeship training varied only in degree from that of the rest of the nation. Until the 1960s Negroes were restricted mainly to the trowel trades or to programs operated by Negro contractors. There were almost no Negroes in the better-paying programs. However, specialized apprenticeship programs and tightening labor markets began to offer some prospect of significantly changing this traditional picture in the sixties. Between 1966 and 1969, for example, the number of Negro apprentices in the South more than doubled and there is evidence of continued momentum since that time.

The South's experience with the manpower programs established in the 1960s resembles that of other areas. Although there has been considerable variation among the states, the South has participated in various Office of Economic Opportunity (O.E.O.) training programs, especially the Job Corps, Neighborhood Youth, and Community Work and Training programs. Southern O.E.O. training programs had a large welfare component, and frequently had very limited training and work experience features. As is true elsewhere, Negroes had much better representation in institutional programs than in on-the-job training. Because of the significance of the rural farm and nonfarm Negro population in the South, it would seem to be highly desirable to concentrate additional resources on training programs in rural areas. While existing programs have provided rural participants limited income maintenance, they have not provided adequate training to permit many of them to obtain steady nonagricultural jobs.

It is, however, impossible with the limited data available to give an overall evaluation of the new manpower programs. That would be difficult at best, and experience in the South, as in the nation, has been too limited to permit more than the most general appraisals. Nevertheless, it is safe to say that they have had a very limited impact on the universe of need in the region.

Greater efforts must be made to promote the mobility of those who want either training or jobs in the most rapidly growing areas of the region. Mobility programs offer much better promise than efforts to locate industry in rural areas. But these programs should be supplemented with those leading to marginal industry in rural areas because, as pointed out before, there are many rural Southerners who are not likely to benefit from manpower programs aimed at urban employment.

Whether or not training programs, like the work incentive and Neighborhood Youth programs, should have large welfare components is debatable. Training should be serious business designed to lead to better jobs, and the reputation of training is damaged when it fails to do this. On the other hand, the need for income maintenance is undeniable, and welfare programs which cannot be adopted except under the hypocritical guise of "training" are better than nothing.

Manpower, education, and training activities have been very limited in rural areas in spite of their potential. Rural manpower training has been limited by small size, inadequate staffs, and poor equipment, and has faced very limited opportunities for effective work on the job. However, area vocational schools and new programs for the disadvantaged established under the Vocational Education Acts of 1963 and 1968 seem to promise more meaningful rural job training.

Manpower programs also seem to have considerable promise when they are correlated with growth center strategy, though as presently designed they have placed too little emphasis on developing people and too much emphasis on developing places. Further, current manpower, education, and growth center programs will have very little significance for older, relatively uneducated workers. Unless these workers can be made somewhat productive through marginal enterprises, they will be forced to rely entirely on welfare, or, at best, on some combination of the two.

HEALTH, WELFARE, AND HOUSING

A last general recommendation regarding human resources in the South is for an adequate program to support people who cannot, or should not, work, and to provide the necessary remedial activities for those who need help to improve their productivity. Health and welfare programs are particularly important in the

South because poverty, inadequate diets, and poor health facilities make it very difficult for many people to develop themselves. Hunger and disease are constant threats to thousands of Southerners, black and white, because of the very concentration of poor people in the region. In December 1966, for instance, eight of the ten states with the highest old age assistance recipients per 1000 aged persons were in the South. Welfare programs, especially aid to children and the aged, are particularly important in rural areas where many children live in poverty and where the residual population, following decades of migration, is saturated with the elderly.

In 1968, the average monthly Aid for Dependent Children (A.F.D.C.) payment per recipient in the United States was $42.35; the New York average was $69.70. No Southern state came close to the national average, and seven of the thirteen states paid less than $25.00 per recipient.

Benefits in other welfare programs in the South lag behind those of the rest of the United States. In August 1968, the average old age assistance payment in the United States was $68.35. The only Southern state exceeding this average was Louisiana ($69.35); Mississippi had the lowest in the nation ($35.90). At the same time, average aid to the permanently and totally disabled for the United States was $81.70; the range in the South was from $44.40 in Mississippi to $72.65 in North Carolina. Unemployment insurance payments, which average $41.25 in the United States, range from $26.44 in Mississippi to $36.68 in Louisiana.

The South also led the way in adopting such degrading and self-defeating restrictions on aid to children as the "substitute father" rule, under which children lost aid if welfare authorities caught a man in the house. The effect of the ruling is to give incentives to fathers to abandon their children in order to get them on welfare. Of nineteen states with this rule when it was invalidated by the United States Supreme Court in June 1968, thirteen were in the South.

Poor health facilities in the South result in particularly high child-mortality rates. Although only six of the thirteen Southern states had overall death rates higher than the national average in 1966, every Southern state had higher mortality rates for children under five years of age. Not surprisingly, maternal mortality rates for nonwhites in the Southern states were two to four times as high as those for whites.

There were 156 physicians per 100,000 people in the United States in 1966. The only Southern state to equal this average was Florida; the others ranged downward to Mississippi with 75. Florida also was the only Southern state with as many nurses per 100,000 people as the national average of 298; Mississippi had 142. No Southern state had as many dentists as the national average of 45 per 100,000 people; the range was from 20 in South Carolina to 40 in Florida.

The average figures for the South conceal local conditions which are much worse than the state averages, particularly in areas with high proportions of Negroes. For instance, a 1968 survey of sixteen counties in the Alabama Black Belt found 95 percent of Negro housing to be dilapidated. Some indication of the state of health of black children in the rural South was provided by an investigation conducted in 1966 in Lowndes County, Alabama (which had 15,000 people and 2 doctors 35 miles apart), by a Yale professor of pediatrics. He reported:

> *Eighty percent of these children . . . had anemia sufficient to require treatment in any doctor's office anywhere in the country.* [*But*] *90 percent of the children said they had never seen a doctor. One of those who answered "yes" to the question said: "Yes, he pulled my tooth."*
>
> *. . . Twenty-five percent of the children . . . needed further referral for glasses. One child out of 709 I examined had glasses.*

Human Resource Development in the South

A study of four South Carolina counties by Dr. John Lease of the University of South Carolina, published in the February 1970 issue of the *Journal of the South Carolina Medical Association,* suggests that the problem of intestinal parasites remains widespread throughout the South. It found that of the children tested in elementary schools, day-care centers, and Head Start programs, 13.5 percent of the whites and 22.5 percent of the blacks had Ascaris intestinal roundworms. The rate of infection in rural areas was higher than these averages. These studies make it clear that much of the fatigue and apathy among rural Southerners is due to health and dietary inadequacies.

Southern political leaders have kept welfare payments low because of resources insufficient to finance adequate programs, but the influence of racial prejudice is too obvious to be questioned. Many apparently hoped that low welfare payments would induce welfare recipients to move to other states. Policy built on that notion was not only morally indefensible, but very shortsighted, since out-migration merely resulted in draining away many of the region's most productive Negroes, leaving the South with both a heavy welfare burden and a residual population which is not attractive to industry. Between 1955 and 1960, for example, the South lost 20 percent of its nonwhite men 25–29 years of age who had some college training, but only 6 percent of those with only elementary school training.

SPECIFIC PROGRAMS

The economic, education, manpower, nondiscrimination, and health and welfare programs discussed above are necessary but not sufficient conditions for improving the lot of poor people. Experience with social change demonstrates the need for specialized programs and organizations which take people where they are and work from there. The best of these programs will simultaneously initiate procedures to modify those institutions which cause poverty and unequal opportunities. For example, programs dealing with the upgrading of Negro doctors or other professionals, upgrading cultural policies and more resources for technical and financial assistance to poor farmers. Similarly, specific programs to get more help for small business enterprises are needed. Some of these businesses might require permanent subsidies in the form of technical assistance and low-interest loans, but many of them can, with proper help, develop into viable economic enterprises. At the worker level, special programs might concentrate on such narrow objectives as better placement of graduates from Negro schools, the upgrading of Negro doctors or other professionals, upgrading journeymen and skilled workers, and the like. In short, specialized programs and strategies should be initiated to accelerate whatever changes are considered desirable.

Experience in the rural South makes it clear that permanent organizations whose members have political influence—such as the Manpower Development Corporation in North Carolina—will be required to institute the kind of comprehensive human resource development programs necessary to bring about significant change in the lives of poor people. At the same time, it is equally clear that these organized pressure points must have as much economic independence as possible. This is why many specialists believe it necessary to create, wherever possible, economically viable organizations among disadvantaged people in urban and rural areas. Where such organizations are not possible, others which are only partially self-sustaining can be started, and society would gain if the subsidies required to keep them alive produced greater cost-benefit ratios than could be produced by alternative expenditures elsewhere.

Clearly, the time has come when we can no longer ignore the economic crisis our region is confronting. The South's potential greatness lies in its people—a vast resource of untapped wealth which now lies dormant. We must begin *now* to take measures to upgrade our region's underdeveloped human resources, white and black, if the South is to succeed in its climb to national equality.

EXPANDING OWNERSHIP IN THE DEVELOPING SOUTH

Stewart Gammill III

[At a session of the Southern Governors' Conference scarcely two years ago, I had just finished my brief remarks introducing the paper of Dr. Ray Marshall. One of the governors was quick to take issue with me.

The subject was rural economic development in the South. The governors in my audience—it was the fall of 1970—included Lester Maddox of Georgia, John Bell Williams of Mississippi, Claude Kirk of Florida, and John McKeithen of Louisiana. I had prefaced my remarks with the statement that I was qualified neither by education nor experience as an expert in the field. I had further stated that my first reaction to the invitation to speak to the conference was to decline, a remark that brought friendly laughter from the governors.

I went on to state, "We Southerners are a sensitive people, sensitive especially to criticism; and yet I think most of us would agree that by almost all standards, we *are* a poor region, *materially*—and the rural South is certainly no exception." I quoted my friend Tom Naylor's description of how the destiny of the South has been controlled for the past hundred years, during which its natural resources have been exploited as "the allocation of land, timber, mineral, and human resources in the South . . . was determined primarily by forces outside the region."

My remarks continued, "There were, certainly, many other factors during those years. At least within the last twenty, much of our time, and effort, and other resources have been devoted to attempts to maintain a segregated way of life. In fact regardless of your position, or mine, on the subject, I think it would be fair to say that *this* has been our number one priority for some time. Many other problems, meanwhile, have gone unsolved because of lack of resources or determination. But, gentlemen, more and more the dynamics of our society are demanding new solutions, or at least new efforts, and unless responsible Southerners step forth with constructive, honest efforts in the many areas which need attention, we will surely see the destiny of the South continue to a large extent to be determined by others.

"You know much better than I the many problems facing our region and the demands they place on us.

"We are a poor region, and we have limited material resources with which to work. But we have, on the other hand, *a vast human resource,* which, if adequately developed, can become a contributing part of our society.

"In conclusion, in planning a strategy for rural economic development, and for most of the other potential solutions to the South's many problems, I believe that the development of our human resources, so long neglected, should without question be our number one priority."

After introducing Dr. Marshall, I, somewhat relieved, took my seat.

It was then that one of the Governors spoke up. He wanted, he said, to ask some questions.

He wanted to know where someone like me could be from; and when I replied that I was born, raised, and received most of my education in Mississippi and that I lived just three miles from his own state, in an area not too unlike his own, the Governor dropped that issue and proceeded to tell me of the vast mineral deposits and other resources in his state.

He turned to the Governor of Texas and asked, somewhat

facetiously, if they didn't have a little oil and gas out their way, too. He asked me if I knew of these vast resources and if I had taken them into account in my statement that the South was a poor region.

I was completely dumbstruck by his remarks. Apparently I had failed miserably to get across the simple points I had sought to make. I responded very briefly to the Governor's last question and sat down to hear Dr. Marshall's paper.

During his presentation, Dr. Marshall took a very realistic look at problems facing the rural South, stressed limited resources in the region as a major obstacle, documented the fact that the South is the nation's poorest region by almost every measure, and concluded with rather convincing recommendations for comprehensive, coordinated policies stressing the promotion of public and private labor-intensive activities aimed at raising the per capita income of the region.

At the conclusion of Dr. Marshall's presentation, I waited for the Governor who had questioned me to differ with him. But there were no questions.

Perhaps I misread the Governor's response to my remarks. Perhaps they just illustrated that "we Southerners are a sensitive people, sensitive especially to criticism." And possibly that sensitivity goes far to explain why most of the assembled governors appeared to give little attention to Dr. Marshall's paper, and why the reporters present at the conference gave it almost no coverage. The *Anniston* (Alabama) *Star,* one of the few Southern newspapers that did cover it, commented in a critical editorial that the governors were more interested in passing ineffectual resolutions than in substantive discussions, and that the press found better copy in Governor Maddox's informal press conferences, which were "long on beguiling folksiness but short on problem-solving ideas." But be that as it may, let us hope that both of us—the Governor who took issue with me and I—at least recognize that there *is* a problem, whether we wanted to admit it publicly or not.

The fact remains that low per capita income continues to plague the South; that the South's natural resources are continually exploited; and that the allocation of land, timber, mineral, and human resources in the South continues, to a large extent, to be determined by forces outside the region.

Meanwhile, nothing has so dominated the lives of Southerners or had a greater impact on the institutions of the region than the relationship of blacks and whites. Politically, this has been the issue upon which dynasties were built. Socially, it has dominated the regional dialogue on education and pubic accommodations. Economically, it has had a profound impact on jobs, housing, and ownership patterns. The psychological results on both sides have been devastating. And yet many Southerners, still preoccupied with race and empty rhetoric, fail to see our real problem for what it is: by and large, the lack of capital resources with which we could and would determine our own destiny as individuals and as a region. It is not enough to have jobs for a significant percentage of our labor force. For although jobs may provide the necessities of life, they do nothing to alleviate the economic powerlessness inherent in any system that lacks a basic program for the acquisition of capital through indigenous ownership, or at least for the development of a stake in the success of local economic institutions.

Indeed, economically, the South is like a colony of a foreign power, controlled to a large extent by foreign corporations and outside interests. And unfortunately, many of these "foreign"-owned companies have, through the years, had little if any concern for the natural resources, the level of education, or the quality of life in the South. On the contrary, it has been in their interest to maintain a low level of achievement and limited political awareness among both blacks and whites. To have it otherwise would directly threaten long-term profits and growth potential—for as aspirations and sophistication rise, so do demands for higher wages and ecological responsibility. This, of course, is not to say that all "foreign" corporations are bad or that they are totally insensitive, for more and more outside owners are becoming aware that their own enlightened self-interest dictates that they respond to the needs of the people of the area in which they operate.

Indeed some were responding at least fifty years ago. My wife's grandfather, L. O. Crosby, combined some Northern capital, a cutting contract on timber owned by Northern interests, a contract with International Harvester of Chicago, and all the other elements necessary to build one of the most successfully locally owned companies in the South.

And numerous outside corporations are continuing to respond to the needs of the South in furnishing both capital and technical know-how to developing local enterprises. Most recently, Crown Zellerbach, a San Francisco-based corporation with extensive timberlands in south Mississippi and Louisiana and two paper mills nearby, elected to contract with a local lumber company to build a new mill to utilize timber now going directly to Crown's own mill. Even though the local company is one of my own close competitors, the construction of this mill will not only help to build the local economy through local business, but will also mean better utilization of one of the most important natural resources in the South—pine forests.

In Mississippi, in fact, 36 percent of all manufacturing plants are timber-based and account for 28 percent of all manufacturing employment, while in south Mississippi, where the state's pine resources are concentrated, most of us are involved with timber at one level or another. In addition, the pine forest, until maturity, produces significant quantities of oxygen, and the conversion of mature trees to lumber consumes considerably less energy than the manufacture of competing unrenewable resources such as metal and petroleum-based products. Furthermore, wood by-products, such as bark, wood chips, and sawdust, are used for yards and gardens, other forest products, or as fuel for steam or electric power for the mills.

This is not to say all is well in our area. On the contrary, some interests appear to be totally insensitive to not only the future but the present needs of the area, stripping the land of timber, hauling it miles away to be used for the least valuable pine product, taking jobs and taxes away from the local area and often leading smaller timber owners to follow forest practices from which they receive minimum return on investment. As a result, those owners often convert their land to other uses, or let it remain idle and unproductive.

Local concerns, made up of individuals whose assets and life's work are wrapped up in the community, are much less likely to operate that way. Their interests are very closely aligned with the interests of local people, their neighbors, with whom they have much at stake.

I intend no reflection on the many fine people who work for "foreign" corporations and devote so much of their time and honest effort toward building their community; but when it comes right down to the hard issues affecting the community and the corporation it is unrealistic to expect most corporation representatives to give first priority to community interests.

If, therefore, we are to see the South begin to reach its full potential we must continue to welcome all interests locating facilities in the South which demonstrate responsibility to the people of the area in which they operate, *discourage those who do not,* and at the same time do everything possible to promote the development of responsible local concerns.

Success for these new enterprises will not come easily, even with help. It never has. Business is a deadly game in which strong outside forces or weakness within can spell disaster for the best intentioned efforts. And the failure rate is high. A leading business service reports that 50 percent of all small businesses fail within the first eighteen months, and 80 percent are out of business within five years. But the potential returns are good, for there are important economic and social benefits in having a strong indigenous entrepreneurial class in the region. For example, the decision-makers in most communities, from the membership of the trade associations to the boards of directors of the local banks, are drawn largely from local business and professional people. So also are seekers and holders of public office.

If this decision-making "establishment" is locally sensitive and involved, the likelihood of community progress is considerably enhanced. If, on the other hand, the local Chamber of Commerce and the bank boards are dominated by the managers of local "foreign"-owned plants and businesses, there is less chance of local interest being paramount in their deliberations.

The concept of development through the small enterprise is not new. In fact, it represents the traditional approach to business development in our country, through which millions of people have had an opportunity to determine their own destiny by individual and collective efforts. To a large extent, small local enterprises, farms, and businesses of all kinds have been the sturdy blocks with which our nation was built, and in which even the giant corporations had their beginning.

What is new, if anything, is the idea of promoting the development of local enterprise as a matter of public policy through both government programs at all levels and direct participation by the people as promoters, developers, owners, operators, employees, suppliers, and customers.

There are of course government and private agencies and organizations already dedicated to helping the developing business. Before discussing some of these, however, I would like to acknowledge my indebtedness to Alan Steelman, a native of Arkansas now living in Dallas, who has served as Executive Director of the President's Advisory Council on Minority Business Enterprises. Alan has been most helpful in providing me with information concerning some of the organizations with which he has had contact, and especially in sharing with me his thoughts on the role expanded local ownership can and must play if the developing South is to reach its full potential.

To help develop this potential, programs of assistance are available in many areas of concern to new ventures.

In the vital area of capital acquisition for the new and growing enterprise there are various sources other than commercial banks. Government agencies, such as the Small Business Administration, the Economic Development Administration, the Department of Agriculture, and the Veterans Administration, as well as small business investment companies, are good examples. A highly successful technique for raising capital among middle-income and poor people has been the 10-36 Plan developed by Dr. Leon Sullivan in Philadelphia. The community residents are informed of the objective of the proposed corporation and are asked to invest $10 per month for thirty-six months in a capital pool to be used as financial leverage by the corporation. Two hundred participants operating in this fashion could amass $72,000 in thirty-six months, an amount which provides approximately $500,000 worth of leverage on the commercial real estate market.

The Small Business Administration also offers counseling services in the areas of feasibility analysis and management and technical assistance. Trade associations are frequently good sources of management counseling and assistance. In establishing a market for a product, the entrepreneur should also consider the federal government's 8 (a) Procurement Program, in which the government contracts on a preferred basis with small businesses.

A second important strategy for the expansion of local ownership is offered by the Community Development Corporation. Unlike individual ownership enterprises, the CDC is participated in by a large number of community residents who not only profit from it economically as shareholders, but also profit from the social services it performs, such as health care, preschool education, and day care.

The CDC's distinguishing characteristic is the way the profits or proceeds are used. A portion of the proceeds, after the financial obligations of the corporation are met, are plowed back into the community in the form of social services which benefit the entire community.

CDCs serve several purposes. The corporation can be a source of jobs for people normally denied access to the job market; it can attract more outside funds for community services by having its own matching funds; and it can provide an object lesson in the management of money, the value of coordinated action, and the necessity of capital accumulation. Not least important, a successful CDC is an effective source of community pride and solidarity.

The cooperative, like the CDC, is broadly based and offers great potential for mass participation. The cooperative is a form of local ownership already relatively well-established in the South, and cooperatives have been a source of great benefit to the region. The electric co-op, the agricultural buying and selling co-op, and the credit union, which will be discussed at some length later, are examples of cooperatives with widespread use and familiarity.

Cooperatives open their membership to all people in the community with a common economic interest. They incorporate the one-man, one-vote principle, and surplus profits are distributed to members in proportion to their use of cooperative goods or services. If credit is needed, it is arranged through a credit union which, in many cases, is affiliated with the cooperative.

There are two common types of cooperatives: the consumer cooperative, in which the producers of the product or service band together to sell to the public, and the credit union. Cooperatives have proven themselves an adaptable and practical means to economic self-determination. The credit union answers one of the greatest needs of many people—access to credit at a reasonable rate of interest and for a reasonable term. The members of a credit union are encouraged to save a given amount of money regularly. The members are entitled to borrow, and the money lent is the members' money. The more saved, the more there is to lend.

The members of the credit union are both savers and borrowers, and therefore the union can make loans available to some people who otherwise would have to rely on a high-interest source of credit. Emphasis is placed upon building a credit standing and teaching habits of thrift and saving among the union's members, in contrast to the conventional practice of insisting upon a demonstrated credit record before a loan can be made. In addition, the members are entitled to a dividend on their savings.

The goals of a community credit union include encouraging financial independence among its members, building a strong community organization, and providing experience in operating a community financial institution. Initial and continuing technical assistance is available to community groups from state and national credit union trade associations.

Like the CDC and the cooperative, the credit union is a good vehicle for broad and social and economic participation. A bank examiner visiting the Richmond Federal Credit Union in the Appalachian poverty area of Kentucky was astonished at the religious and social mix he found among the management and membership of the credit union. In reporting back to his home office by phone, he allegedly said, "I'm here in a black minister's Baptist church talking with a Catholic priest, with a Methodist minister sitting across the table, and, so help me, they've got a Jewish boy keeping the books!"

The Richmond Credit Union operates on a countywide basis and has grown from ten members and $4 in 1966 to $34,478 in assets in 1970. As with all credit unions, a single individual is limited to outstanding loans amounting to no more than 10 percent of the union's total assets. The Baptist minister is the bad debt collector. He doesn't call on anyone, however, until a name has been posted on the bad debt board in the office for a while. The bad debt board is a pretty effective collection method in its own right. In the words of the treasurer, "The word gets around and people who are behind in their payments usually come in and pay up right away."

The employee stock participation plan is another strategy for expanding indigenous ownership and is a good example of a way in which the workers in an enterprise can share in the profits of their labor. This plan can provide a good middle-ground or bargaining position for communities which are approached by outside-based companies seeking to locate plants in the South. The plant is asked to put aside a certain amount of company stock for its employees either as options or as bonuses for reaching certain production quotas. This is of mutual benefit. When a certain amount of the stock is worker-owned, there is also an incentive on the part of the worker to produce a quality product at a reasonable cost.

Another form of expanded participation in the company is employed by mutual savings and loan associations, in which the association's profits are paid back to the depositors as dividends. Such associations have the additional benefit of representing an important source of financing for housing.

For these various organizations, agencies, and strategies to be effective in moving the South toward its full potential, we Southerners as a people must face our problems together and seek practical solutions for them.

And if we agree that expanded ownership offers a solution to some of our problems and decide to make it a matter of public policy, there are several specific steps which federal, state, and municipal governments, in cooperation with the private sector and the people concerned in Southern communities, can take to expand ownership, economic participation, and economic independence. State industrial development commissions should be urged to reexamine their policies toward the location of outside-based companies in the South to assure that local development is getting priority treatment, and that those outside interests who are locating in the South are serving the public good while pursuing their own private gain. State governments providing financing or tax incentives for the location of firms owned by non-Southerners should insist on certain conditions, including employee stock participation plans, recruitment of local personnel as part of the management team, and adequate environmental protection agreements.

In the areas of management training and assistance, basic business and economic education can be made an integral part of public school curricula, and business can be promoted as an attractive career alternative. School facilities should be made available after school hours for compensatory economic education for adults. The President's Advisory Council on Minority Business Enterprise has recommended that federal assistance be granted to school systems to assist in curriculum development in this area.

Furthermore, management training for prospective entrepreneurs should be made a high priority program item for the private sector in the South. Local Chambers of Commerce and trade associations, in cooperation with colleges and universities, are probably the best channel for this training and are best equipped to provide it. In several Southern cities, including Atlanta, Dallas, and Houston, there are programs already underway which could be used as pilot projects. The Dallas Alliance for Minority Enterprise is a good example of a public–private coalition of businessmen and government agencies whose objective is the promotion of business ownership through management education and assistance.

In addition, management assistance to existing business should be provided by other successful businessmen and trade associations. The local Chambers of Commerce are usually staffed professionally and the coordination of such management assistance could be provided by this staff.

The federal government, through the Small Business Administration and the Economic Development Administration, could be urged to put more of its management and technical assistance monies into the South. Those who are providing management training could seek federal and state funding for the program operating costs. The National Business League chapter in Atlanta and the Dallas Alliance for Minority Enterprise are both federally funded and have had a major impact in their respective cities.

As for financing, private corporations could be encouraged to form Small Business Investment Corporations (SBIC) to serve as sources of equity and debt for entrepreneurial development. The federal government, through the Small Business Administration, will match private funds two to one, the only requirement being minimum assets of $150,000 by the sponsoring corporation. The government share brings the initial capitalization to $450,000. There are several successful SBICs already operating in the South.

Also, commercial banks could be urged to follow the lead of the more progressive Southern banks in adopting new lending priorities toward owned enterprises, giving preferential treatment where possible. Furthermore, federal, state, and municipal governments should be urged to make deposits in those banks with demonstrated records of strong commitment to local ownership development.

Federal agencies, particularly the SBA, EDA, the Agriculture Department, and the OEO, could be urged to organize extensive periodic "show-and-tell" visits to small towns and rural areas to acquaint the people with the federal financing programs available and to provide technical assistance in making application for such funding.

There are, in addition, various less formal steps which can be taken. Government agencies and the private sector in the South could be encouraged to buy from local suppliers, including cooperatives and community development corporations, since money used to purchase equipment or supplies from concerns outside the South is lost to the region and its people. Furthermore, government agencies, private companies, foundations and universities can be encouraged to deposit funds in local credit unions as a means of improving the viability of these important community institutions.

Much of this, of course, is already being done; and people in the more progressive areas of the South are becoming aware not only of the various programs and assistance available but of the significant contribution made by the development of indigenous enterprises.

Yet there is still much more to be done, both in disseminating factual information and in obtaining a firm commitment to maximum resource development as a top priority. And, in each instance, there remains to be found the one element perhaps most important of all to the success of any enterprise: the entrepreneur, the man with that rare combination of exceptional drive, ambition, perseverance, and faith which distinguish the successful from their fellows; a man who can organize, manage, and assume the risks and responsibilities of the enterprise.

A full commitment to the maximum resource development, therefore, necessarily implies a commitment to adequate food, housing, educational, creative, and recreational resources, for a developing society demands better and better qualified people.

We Southerners have come a long way in recent years toward a willingness to look together at our mutual problems and to work together toward their solution.

Perhaps we have come far enough to make a major commitment to maximum resource development.

HUNGER? LET THEM EAT MAGNOLIAS

Jack Bass

[IN Beaufort County, South Carolina, there stands a large grove of wild-growing magnolia trees, some as high as one hundred feet, and in the spring the giant white blossoms bloom with pristine beauty. The Spanish moss and the expansive sea marshes add to the haunting lure of the South Carolina low-country coast.

The casual visitor pays little attention to the dirt paths that lead off the main highways. But Dr. Donald Gatch—a Nebraska farm boy who interned in nearby Savannah to see the South and then decided to practice medicine in tiny Bluffton (population 529)—developed a habit of taking field trips down the winding dirt trails. He found they lead to huts of poverty, to people who don't go to doctors, to hovels where breakfast for a shack full of kids is grits and lunch is grits with a bit of fatback added—if there is lunch.

The houses are crude affairs, lined inside with cardboard boxes or perhaps with the *Savannah Morning News.* Running water doesn't exist; sometimes there is no electricity; the shallow wells

A complete list of references and data sources for this paper may be obtained from the L.Q.C. Lamar Society, P.O. Box 4774, Duke Station, Durham, North Carolina, 27706.

themselves are a source of disease. In many cases, even an outdoor privy is lacking.

The quiet life of Donald Gatch, country doctor, ended November 9, 1967. In a soft, almost listless voice, Dr. Gatch that day described the serious malnutrition and high incidence of intestinal parasites among Negro children that he found in everyday observation.

At a hearing in Columbia sponsored by a national Citizens Board of Inquiry into Hunger, Dr. Gatch told of eight Negro children, three in one family, who died from worms and other parasites before he stopped counting. "If eight white children in Beaufort County had died of parasites, something would have been done eons ago," Dr. Gatch said. Then in a rising voice that cracked with emotion, he declared, "There's no damn sense in people going hungry in this country."

The *Beaufort Gazette* blasted Gatch for "running his mouth" too much and the fourteen other doctors in the county issued a statement which concluded, "An objective analysis of the various allegations made reveals no factual substantiation."

Despite the reaction of the Beaufort doctors and the county seat weekly, Gatch remained "good ol' doc" in Bluffton. Not long after the furor, three white public health nurses at a local clinic said they had been told not to discuss the feud between Gatch and the other doctors, but one of the nurses confided to a reporter, "We all use him as our doctor and our families do, too. That's what we think of him."

Gatch's friendliness with Negroes didn't seem to bother the whites in Bluffton, who were too close to the conditions to doubt the accuracy of his testimony. Few towns the size of Bluffton could boast of a fulltime doctor, and an acquaintance of Gatch's there said, "One would be ill-advised to talk unfavorably about Dr. Gatch around Bluffton."

Although Gatch was hounded out of Beaufort, where he had moved and opened a second office, accounts of his testimony in newspapers in the Carolinas and in *The New York Times* provoked an interest in hunger and malnutrition that eventually evolved into recognition that the conditions he described were accurate. They reflected conditions that existed, in varying degrees, all over the state, a manifestation of a regional problem that covers the entire South.

A half century earlier, the recognition of widespread pellagra and hookworm in the South resulted in public health measures aimed at eradication. Over the years, however, the question of hunger had been neglected.

Dr. Raymond Wheeler of Charlotte, North Carolina, a practicing physician who served four years as a member of the Citizens Board of Inquiry into Hunger in the United States—the body before which Dr. Gatch originally testified—is among those who have done most to discover the extent of hunger throughout the South.

"Wherever we went, in the South, the Southwest, Florida, or Appalachia, the impact was the same," said Dr. Wheeler, "varying only in degree or in appalling detail." As for evidence, he declared, "There is an abundance of statistics available to document the fact that there are people in our nation and especially in our region who are hungry, malnourished, and who do not have available to them either food or medical care which is required to restore them to a condition of health or productivity."

Statistics on infant mortality show that the number of infants who died in the first years of life was 21.7 per 1000 for the United States, which ranks thirteenth among the countries of the world. Every Southern state exceeds that mortality rate, and in states where infant mortality is given by race, a black baby is roughly twice as likely to die within his first year of life as a white child.

Statistics from the National Nutrition Survey obtained from testing low-income families in Louisiana, Texas, and South Carolina are broadly representative of the region. In Louisiana, 42 percent of those examined had unacceptable levels of hemoglobin, an index of anemia, and a rate of occurrence of anemia eight times higher than in Honduras. The rate was 38 percent in South Carolina. A third of the children examined showed evidence of retarded growth. In South Carolina, the unacceptable rate for riboflavin was more than 25 percent.

Dr. Wheeler has concluded, "The people of the South are among the most malnourished in the nation."

South Carolina is an interesting state to look at, both because of the widespread scope of the problem there and the fact that once public awareness of actual conditions developed, responsible political leadership began to take action. The scorn that greeted Gatch's original charges changed to sober recognition that hunger and malnutrition were serious statewide problems in South Carolina. It was Senator Ernest F. (Fritz) Hollings who, more than anyone, forced the public to face and accept the truth, though many still refuse to accept conditions as they are.

Early in 1969, Hollings toured four sections of the state for a first-hand look at conditions of hunger and malnutrition, travelling with the Reverend I. De Quincey Newman, then the veteran field secretary for the N.A.A.C.P. in South Carolina. That February, Hollings told the United States Senate, "There is substantial hunger in South Carolina. I have seen it with my own eyes."

The next year, he wrote a book, *The Case Against Hunger,* in which he lashed out at myths about the hungry, myths he admitted he believed until he saw for himself the starkly inhuman conditions inside the shacks of urban and rural slums in his own state. With documented detail, Hollings described the effect of malnutrition upon the mental development of infants and small children and the growing evidence that links mental retardation in many cases with malnutrition. As an example of "hunger myopia," Hollings wrote: "Within a 40-mile radius of Timmonsville, South Carolina, there are 40 farmers who each received last year over $40,000 from the United States government—for not working. This doesn't affect the character of the farmer. He's still as red-blooded, capitalistic, free enterprising, and patriotic as ever before. But give the poor, little hungry child a 40-cent breakfast and you've destroyed his character. You've ruined his incentive. You've taught him bad habits. You have developed a drone society. 'This food stamp program is a plot of the Communists.' There are too many people all over America who believe this."

As governor, Hollings lived four years in the governor's mansion on the edge of Columbia slums. He had seen the hungry, but he wrote, "I still believed the poor could climb to prosperity all by themselves if they would just follow the old Horatio Alger formulas." In a vivid recollection of his first trip to a slum area in his native Charleston, Hollings wrote: "I saw what all America needs to see. The hungry are not able-bodied men, sitting around drunk and lazy on welfare. They are children. They are abandoned women, or the crippled, or the aged. They are that part of America for whom civil rights or first class citizenship is not a part of their wildest dreams."

After Hollings asked for a county-by-county analysis of how many South Carolina residents were going hungry, Dr. E. Kenneth Aycock, Harvard-trained State Health Officer, gave a "conservative estimate" of 300,000—or 11 percent of the state's population.

Even the doctors in Beaufort County eventually came to terms with actual conditions, once they got over their anger at Gatch's implied accusation that they weren't doing their job. Under federal funding, the Beaufort County doctors cooperated in planning a comprehensive health care program for the poor.

When Governor John C. West was inaugurated in January 1971, he pledged, "We can, and we shall, in the next four years eliminate hunger and malnutrition, and their attendant suffering, from our state." Three weeks later, West looked South Carolina poverty in the face and appeared stunned. After stepping from a windowless, unpainted shack on John's Island near Charleston, in which the only light came from a single kerosene lamp, West declared, "That'll tear you up. Fifteen children live in there." The forty-eight-year-old Governor added, "I wouldn't have believed it if I hadn't seen it, and I thought I had seen a lot."

West was accompanied by Hollings, a former classmate at The

Citadel, Dr. Aycock, and state welfare Director R. Archie Ellis. Mrs. Ida Magwood, who was cooking a meal for the children, told the Governor, "Some of them sleep on the floor, wherever they can find room." The primary source of food was $125 worth of food stamps each month. What such families did before food stamps is uncertain. Many, of course, simply moved north, a journey Claude Brown, describing the flight of his own parents from Sumter County, South Carolina, in *Manchild in the Promised Land,* said was going "from the fire into the frying pan."

The next household West and Hollings visited offered a more chilling alternative. There the older children had come home from school one day and found their mother dead, clutching an infant still trying to feed from the breast. "We're told she died of starvation," Ellis told reporters.

When Dr. Gatch testified in Columbia, there were 24,017 persons participating in food-stamp programs in South Carolina. Only thirteen of the forty-six counties had programs. There were no other food subsidy programs in the state and South Carolina participation was the lowest of any Southeastern state. By the time of West's inauguration three years later, the food-stamp program had expanded statewide with 270,000 participants whose food budgets had expanded by more than $60 million annually. Moreover, state officials from West and Ellis down were finally acknowledging that the food-stamp program by itself was inadequate.

Meanwhile, field research by two University of South Carolina scientists—Dr. E. John Lease, a nutritionist, and Dr. Felix H. Lauter, a parasitologist—basically confirmed Dr. Gatch's reports, and Dr. Lease and Dr. Lauter went to work on the parasite problem, beginning in Beaufort County. Years earlier, Dr. Lease had helped push legislation to require enrichment of all grain products in the state, part of the battle that controlled pellagra, a disease that affects the central nervous system and is associated with a diet deficient in niacin, an acid of the vitamin B complex.

Hunger? Let Them Eat Magnolias

Pediatricians at the Medical University of South Carolina in Charleston later became interested in the parasites, especially after analyzing the number of cases of children being brought into the hospital because of intestinal blockage caused by worms. One professor of pediatrics estimated that as many as 25 percent of the children in South Carolina suffered at some point from worms. They not only can cause death by obstructing vital organs, but—as Dr. Gatch put it—they "eat the food before the child gets it digested," thus adding to the problem of hunger and malnutrition.

In control groups, Dr. Lease found some schools in which more than half the children had worms and responded to treatment. But applied research on treatment for the parasites and their eradication, as well as a search for a form of immunization, have been quite limited. One public health official commented, "Worms are too horrible to become a popular issue." But the South Carolina legislature was shocked into setting up a study committee on hunger and malnutrition after Representative Travis Medlock of Columbia held aloft a bottle containing a ten-inch Ascaris worm as thick as a pencil, an example of the parasites Dr. Gatch talked about.

Beaufort County legislators took an active interest in these problems, and their county became a center for pilot programs in feeding the hungry. One was a free food-stamp program for the very poor who could not afford even a token payment to buy stamps, which are sold on the basis of a formula based on income and family size. Another program involved recruiting of workers from the poor by Clemson University and training them as home nutritionists.

One of the most shocking aspects of the hunger problem is the developing scientific evidence of permanent brain damage in infants and young children who suffer from malnutrition. The human brain reaches almost full growth before the age of four years. Qualified researchers have found that the brain is unlikely to develop fully if a child has an insufficient intake during those years. They have found that small brain size in malnourished children is linked with increased frequency of impaired visual perception and other evidence of organic brain damage.

Another of the Beaufort County programs provides "food by prescription" for pregnant and lactating mothers and children under six. Low-income mothers become eligible by reporting to the county health office. There, the children are weighed, measured, given blood tests and a dose of medicine for worms. Then they are given a chit good for a variety of special packaged foods of high nutrient value that are furnished free by the United States Department of Agriculture.

An estimated 170,000 persons were eligible for food chits statewide, but plans for statewide implementation were dropped because of the administrative problems and costs of storage and distribution of the food, costs the state would have to pay. Despite the potential for salvaging thousands of youngsters who otherwise face the prospect of mental impairment, the "food by prescription" program received little study or evaluation from either state or federal officials.

In addition to the physical damage and impairment of the ability to learn, there are also profound behavioral implications for a child who does not get enough to eat in infancy. Dr. Robert Coles, a child psychiatrist at Harvard, described what happens: "A child learns to trust the mother who feeds him. If a child does not get fed when he is hungry, if he does not get alleviation of his pain when he suffers, he may develop a basic mistrust of adults which in later life is difficult to correct."

Distribution of food stamps also presents problems. Governor West inaugurated a system under which welfare recipients could have the cost of stamps automatically deducted from their monthly checks and the checks then mailed to them, thus saving travel costs to food-stamp offices. Another problem involving transportation is that the rural poor often have no means to travel to neighboring towns, not only to buy food stamps but to shop at large supermarkets. Small country stores invariably mean limited selection and higher prices and usually lower quality.

The problems of hunger not only create a major tragedy in terms of blighted lives and economic waste in lost income and productivity by people who are sick or incapable of performing adequately; they contribute directly to the national crisis in the cities. Dr. Carlos Krumdiek of the University of Alabama Medical Center has assembled impressive data to support the hypothesis that malnutrition in rural areas plays a key causative role in the worldwide phenomenon of urban migration and slum formation. He finds malnutrition in the South a major contributor to the problems of the urban ghetto as well as of the rural slum.

During 1967 in Jackson, Mississippi, the late Senator Robert F. Kennedy asked a witness, "Do I understand that really for many of these families it is a question of starvation or trying to leave and go to some other part of the country?" Her answer was, "They are starving, and those who can get the bus fare to go North are trying to go North."

Yet it is foolish to suggest that poor states such as South Carolina or Mississippi have the resources to deal with the problem. The thrust of the Hollings book is that hunger is a major national problem affecting millions of people, that it will cost far more to let it go unsolved than to solve it, and that the key to a solution is leadership. Hollings asserts that the Nixon administration has failed to provide leadership because it became appalled after looking at the facts that reveal the full dimension of the problem. The facts are suppressed because of fear of the cost, charges Hollings, and presidential rhetoric on ending hunger is unsupported by presidential commitment.

In January 1971 Dr. Arnold Schaefer, who headed the National Nutrition Survey, quit in disgust after charging that the Nixon administration was suppressing his data. Results from only two of the ten states surveyed were reported, and Schaefer was said to have been offered a job with the Center for Disease Control in Atlanta on condition that he neither write, speak, not testify further about the survey.

"I'll be damned if I'm going to go under those conditions," he told a reporter. Schaefer quit after his recommendations of "action programs" to deal with findings of the study were ignored. Instead, additional money was provided to keep studying the problem. The survey results were later released, but as statistical tables with little interpretation. They attracted little attention.

At the federal level, there is a need for executive leadership to recognize the scope of the problem, to make the public aware of it, and to commit the resources of the nation to develop solutions. The experience in South Carolina proved that public exposure of conditions and political leadership are needed to tackle the problem.

James E. Clyburn, a black aide to Governor West who set up his joint tour with Hollings, believes the impact of the first-hand visit strengthened West's role of leadership with state agencies. Clyburn believes the problem at the state level is basically one of leadership to develop and implement programs that are available through federal resources. For example, he feels a statewide breakfast program in the public schools, with free and reduced price meals for poor children, is needed. He also believes that school lunchrooms can be utilized as feeding centers for the aged poor.

Early in 1971, reporter Jay Gross of *The Charlotte Observer* went back to visit some of the families that Hollings had seen two years earlier on a publicized hunger tour in Chesterfield County.

His findings: "The people are still hungry."

Mrs. Minnie Buie of Chesterfield, head of a fifteen-member household living three blocks from the county courthouse, said, "We don't have any more food since last year—there's less now, I reckon . . ."

Hollings said he wasn't surprised. "I would like very much for one article, or one tour, or one series to solve this problem . . . but it's an uphill fight, you've got to keep beating [the public] on the head, making them wake up to the fact that there is a problem," he said.

"I've still got it [malnutrition] in my own county to show," he said. "We've made progress, but there's still a hell of a lot of hungry people—I'd like everywhere I go to change overnight, but it doesn't work that way."

For the hungry, the answer can only come with food. You can't eat magnolias.

The southern past

THE SOUTHERN HISTORICAL PERSPECTIVE

James S. Ferguson

[In the opening paragraph of a brochure setting forth the objectives of the then recently organized L.Q.C. Lamar Society, one finds these words: "The . . . Society is a nonprofit, tax-exempt, educational organization committed to the premise that Southerners can find practical solutions to the South's major problems. The organization is comprised of members whose common bond is a desire to see the South achieve its full potential." Thus is asserted an assumption of regional distinctiveness. Thus is implied that Southerners can attack the problems of their homeland with special insight and understanding.

Is the South distinctive? If so, what makes it so? Is this singularity waning or is it simply awaiting the birth of a new "New South" to find its highest level of fulfillment?

C. Vann Woodward, writing in *The Burden of Southern History,* warns that few scholars have succeeded in explaining "why the heritage, or the collective character, or the general outlook of a particular geographical grouping of people is distinctive." Nevertheless, he asserts a belief in the cultural distinctiveness of the South and sets out to explain it. Numerous other writers have

A complete list of references, tables, and data sources for this paper may be obtained from the L.Q.C. Lamar Society, P.O. Box 4774, Duke Station, Durham, North Carolina, 27706.

pursued the same theme. Edgar T. Thompson at one point speaks of "an irreducible core" that is Southern, and in another instance states that "the South has seemed to live inside its people like an instinct."

Other geographic regions of the United States have their distinctive features, too, but none has felt its differences to the degree that the South has. Only the South has at one point in its history sought to make itself a separate nation, engaging in a bloody war to uphold its separateness, "only for defeat that brought a strengthening of the Southern mind, and a glorification of the concept of 'Southern-ness.'"

Such distinctiveness does not necessitate unanimity of thought. There are many threads of history that run through the Southern fabric, some complementary, some conflicting, but the incidence of common concepts is great enough to produce a regional ethos.

What are some of these threads in Southern history? What are the enduring belief and value systems that would-be leaders of a new New South must take into account? Are they subject to metamorphoses that will fit them to the life of a new day?

The roots of Southern sectionalism are deep in history. Even in the colonial era the region diverged somewhat from its sister colonies, depending primarily upon staple-crop agriculture and a system of slave labor for its economic development. It is in this genesis that Ulrich B. Phillips finds the key explanation. "Let us begin by discussing the weather," said he. Long growing seasons and a fertile, virgin soil made it possible for early English settlers to grow tobacco, sugar cane, rice, indigo, and eventually cotton. All of these were money crops sold in a world market, and their production required an assured labor supply. Only briefly in the South did this come from indentured servants. By 1700 the South was depending on African Negro slavery for its labor supply, and it imported blacks in substantial numbers, thus creating a society in which two decidedly different races lived in close proximity.

It was in the consequent biracial adjustment ("Whites and Negroes intertwined, but separated") that Phillips found his "central theme of Southern history." "What is its [the South's] essence?"

> *Not state rights . . . not free trade . . . not slavery . . . not democracy . . . not cotton. Yet it is a land with a unity despite its diversity, with a people having common joys and common sorrows, and* above all, as to the white folk, a people with a common resolve indomitably maintained that it shall remain a white man's country. *Whether expressed with the frenzy of a demagogue or maintained with a patrician's quietude, [this] is the cardinal test of a Southerner and the theme of Southern history.*

The slave system, the thought control of the last three decades before the Civil War, secession, and the war itself, defiance of the first reconstruction, the substitution of sharecropping and segregation for the slave system, white primaries, Senate filibusters, reluctance to embrace social change—all at bottom, in Phillips's view, have been outgrowths of the South's fundamental resolve to maintain white supremacy.

That preoccupation with race has been a continuing characteristic of the South is, of course, unquestionable. That it will ever be so is another matter. The Phillipsian doctrine would suggest, however, that if the South should abandon segregation, not only as practice but as principle, it would cease to exist as a distinctive region. And there are scholars of today who would agree. Harry Ashmore, former editor of the Little Rock *Arkansas Gazette,* makes this assertion in *Epitaph for Dixie,* and predicts that when the South reaches such a point of development, it will blend into the mainstream of American life, losing its separate identity.

But a host of historians has taken issue with the Phillips thesis. A counter view was set forth by William E. Dodd, Frank L. Owsley, Avery O. Craven, and others. They had a predilection for an agrarian society, and they explained the pre–Civil War South in such terms. Phillips, said they, while not completely ignoring the yeoman farmer, nevertheless wrote as though the Southern pattern had been determined almost exclusively by the Southern planter, thus suggesting a society ruled by a few and tending toward an aristocracy. Throughout the ante-bellum period, Dodd and his associates maintained, nonslaveholding whites outnumbered the slaveholders by a wide margin, and among the slave masters of 1860 less than one third owned five slaves or more.

The pre–Civil War South, in this view, should be thought of as the domain of white yeoman farmers living close to the soil and emphasizing self-sufficient agriculture, individualism, and independence. Conforming to the Jeffersonian ideal, these small farmers sought the advancement and extension of democracy. They were the primary power base for liberal national leaders like Thomas Jefferson and Andrew Jackson, and locally they gave their support to Southerners like Joseph E. Brown of Georgia and Andrew Johnson of Tennessee when they sought to liberalize constitutions or moved to establish public schools. The strength of the South, said these historians, was to be understood more in terms of its folkways than through its energetic and restrictive defense of slavery.

For these authors, the crisis preceding the Civil War provided an occasion when the liberalism of the South was subverted by the forces of aristocracy, hierarchy, and slaveholding. They think of the war itself and the period following it as a time during which the opportunistic Northeast overcame the agrarian South and imposed its commercial-industrial society on the South and on the nation as a whole.

David M. Potter accuses Dodd and his associates of engaging in wishful thinking. They claimed, said he, that the normative South was that of Jefferson and not Calhoun. They believed that that which is agrarian is Southern, that which is not is extraneous, "a cowbird's egg in the Southern nest." They failed to recognize, Potter cogently asserts, that the South's one-crop economy was almost the antithesis of agrarianism, and could more accurately be described as agricultural capitalism, much closer to the Calhoun than to the Jeffersonian ideal. Furthermore, says Potter, the Dodd-Owsley group treats Southern biracial society almost as an afterthought, which seems untenable in view of the energies Southerners have expended on the race issue and the frequency with which they have abandoned liberal efforts in the face of racial fear.

Distorted or not, the agrarian theme is one that recurs with regularity in Southern history. Following the Compromise of 1877 in which local government was placed in the hands of the Redeemers and the white South was allowed to pursue its own "racial solution," Southern leaders seemed intent on gaining for their own region many of the economic benefits of the Northeastern commercial-industrial society. Through the Populist revolt many Southerners challenged at least the methods and the form of the new economic order, if not its fundamental objectives. C. Vann Woodward, who has researched this movement more thoroughly than any other historian, calls it "the most serious indigenous political rebellion an established order ever faced in the South."

In 1930 there was a resurgence of defense of the old agrarianism, at least agrarianism as it was idealized in the minds of a group of scholars centered in the Nashville area. In that year appeared the symposium, written by twelve Southerners, entitled *I'll Take My Stand: The South and the Agrarian Tradition.* Under the leadership of John Crowe Ransom, Donald Davidson, and Allen Tate, these scholars in brilliantly written essays set forth a critique of the new industrial order that had fastened itself on the South. They warned against a new South that would "be only an undistinguished replica of the usual industrial community." Thinking in terms of the quality of life, they urged a return to a folksy, ordered, conservative, soil-oriented way of life which they identified with the old South.

They denounced the Southern Redeemers of 1877 who had struck a bargain with the industrial order. They castigated the "apostles of progress" then associated with Howard Odum's school of regionalists at Chapel Hill. The new Agrarians were bona fide agents of the Southern literary renaissance, and they were then on the threshold of distinguished literary careers. They were taken seriously by their fellow writers, but they suffered a different fate in the body politic. Even in the light of the economic collapse of the new order during the Depression, their concepts seemed unrealistic to common men and leaders alike.

Some of their ideas were to recur in historiography, most notably in the writings of Francis Butler Simkins. His concept of Southern history was a blending of Phillipsian and agrarian interpretations.

Simkins described a South that was "a unique blend of race and family consciousness, personal violence, protestant orthodoxy, political conservatism, and economic colonialism . . . of literary genius in the midst of intellectual indifference and nonliteracy, [of ready reliance on thought suppression whenever the status quo was challenged], of implacable sectional loyalty entwined with national chauvinism; and of drawling speech, feminine women, and hot biscuits." To Simkins, the most formative influence in Southern distinctiveness was biracialism, but second only to that was the region's devotion to fundamentalist religion. He accepted the South's predilection for social hierarchy, but depended even more heavily on the folkways to assure continuity in Southern institutions.

He thought of the South as being "everlasting." In his mind Southern society had a remarkable capacity for absorbing outside and even alien influences and of translating them into forms essentially Southern. He even spoke of the extent to which non-Southern regions, particularly the great cities of the North, were taking on some of the characteristics of the South. Southernness was being exported. His was the perverse and enduring South.

In view of the events of the last thirty years, it is not surprising to find most scholars in disagreement with Simkins about what constitutes Southern distinctiveness. Of course, if all historians agreed on this subject, it would be disastrous, says David M. Potter. "It would be as bad as if all the theologians had agreed upon the nature of the Trinity." But to most of us, he asserts, the identity of the South is less important than its destiny.

Is there a view of Southern distinctiveness that will give the region a realistic self-concept, that will enable it to relate to the broad range of national and international life and yet allow it to make its own contribution?

The view of C. Vann Woodward holds such promise. The distinctiveness of the Southern people, he says, arises from their unique historic experience. Alone among Americans, Southerners have experienced defeat in war and have lived with its consequences. America is the land of plenty and success. The South in contrast has endured long periods of poverty and has encountered frustration and failure in efforts to cope with social and economic problems. America, at least until recently, has enjoyed an illusion of innocence and virtue, based upon its supposedly superior moral position. The South, on the other hand, has had to endure "the corroding effects of the sense of guilt and evil which accompanied the caste system." This total experience has bred in the Southern people a consciousness of history and of tragedy.

"From a broader point of view," says Woodward, "it is not the South but America that is unique among the peoples of the world." Poverty, defeat, and frustration are to be found in the histories of most people of the earth. If the South will learn from its experience, it can provide mature and realistic leadership to the nation in attacking both domestic and international problems.

Until the very recent past the South has been an abnormally static segment of a larger American community that was remarkably dynamic. In the last four decades, however, the dimensions of change in the region have been enormous, with hardly any sector of society being spared the agonies and the excitement of change.

The tendency is for the South to move into "the mainstream of American life" and to lose some of its distinguishing characteristics. It is hard to pick and choose what will survive from history and what will not. Nevertheless, says Woodward, "it would take a blind sentimentalist to mourn the passing" of certain of the monuments of regional distinctiveness: "the one-horse farmer, one-crop agriculture, one-party politics, the sharecropper, the poll tax, the white primary, the Jim Crow car, the lynching bee. But until the day before yesterday there they stood, indisputable proof that the South was different."

Other traits showed a greater staying power, however. George B. Tindall, who has made an authoritative study of the era from 1913 to 1945, saw a stubborn persistence of the Southern ethos. He recognized "an erosion," but maintained that a central core of Southernness remained. The region was torn, said he, between responsiveness to the new order and reaction to its own responsiveness. "Caught between the past and the future, the South struggled painfully to know its own mind."

Much of the pressure for change came from the outside—the influences of the New Deal, World Wars I and II, outside investment in industrial development, and the urgings for the elimination of racial injustice. But there was also a growing internal impetus for change. Southerners moved to gain for themselves some of the abundance of America to counteract poverty and its close companions, ignorance and ill health.

The industrial impulse in many ways took over the Southern mind. There was widespread promotion of industrial growth and development—in chamber-of-commerce terms. The apostles of Henry W. Grady were in full cry.

And though the South still lagged behind other sections in such development, industry did move in. It was still controlled primarily from the outside, for the region lacked sufficient capital. But even in the accumulation of investment reserves, the section moved closer to the national pattern. By 1970 most parts of the South had been touched and radically altered by the industrial surge.

The rural character of the South is fading rapidly. As of this date, fewer than 10 percent of its population is engaged in agriculture, and it is expected that by 1975 the figure will drop to 5 percent. An urban sprawl has developed as erstwhile farm workers have moved to the city. In the South as elsewhere, the inner city is frequently the new home of the Negro migrant, if he has not gone North. The urban style of life has become dominant.

The region has made substantial economic gains. In per capita income the Southern states still occupy the bottom rungs of the ladder, but they have narrowed the gap between their own position and that of the United States as a whole. In comparison to the national average, income per person in the South rose from 61 percent in 1940 to 79 percent in 1969, but poverty remained the lot of many Southerners, particularly those in agricultural regions.

As might be expected, the movement that caused the greatest resurgence of traditional Southern feelings was the national effort to eliminate racial discrimination. Political revolt on the part of the white South appeared as early as 1944 and was intensified as issues connected with school desegregation, public accommodations, and Negro voter registration developed. Conservative reaction took its most extreme forms in the Deep South. Thought suppression and violence in harsh forms reasserted themselves as parts of Southern life. But along with all the rancor and bitterness there was nevertheless a great change in the regional pattern of race relations as the legal supports of segregation were swept away. The marvel, in the opinion of William C. Havard, a Louisianan now teaching at Virginia Polytechnic Institute, is that so many changes, inconceivable a generation ago, have occurred.

The industrial crusade had its effects in reducing resistance. New investors were not readily attracted to a location characterized by racial turmoil and violence.

Much of the pressure for racial change came from the outside, especially from the federal government—but not all of it, for an impulse toward racial justice was native to the South. From the time of the formation of the Commission on Interracial Relations in 1919 (and even before that) to the present, native whites in increasing numbers have cooperated with Negroes to alleviate the effects of racial bias, and despite local pressures and numerous reorganizations, these groups have continued their efforts to promote harmony. Regional and racial studies in Southern colleges and universities eventually affected attitudes among whites. Dewey W. Grantham points out that a majority of the scholars who aided Gunnar Myrdal in his publication of *The American Dilemma* were Southerners.

The 1950s and 1960s witnessed the emergence of Southern Negro leadership in the drive for racial justice. The legal actions of the National Association for the Advancement of Colored People were taken through local blacks who were, of course, challenging the age-old structures of Southern society. Negroes responded by the tens of thousands to the leadership of Martin Luther King and his Southern Christian Leadership Conference in their use of nonviolent pressures for change, and much of the federal civil rights legislation of the 1960s could be attributed directly to their efforts.

If Woodward's *Burden of Southern History* has validity, Southerners, black and white, because of their centuries of association and their repeated frustrations in dealing with vexing problems, may develop realistic solutions for the region and for the nation. As the racial problems of non-Southern cities come more clearly into focus, the dimension of national need for insight and patience increases.

The Negro himself as voter, officeholder, laborer, union member, or middle-class professional is having more and more to say about what the Southern racial settlement will be. The political alliances he makes are halting and sometimes ephemeral, but the South of today is experimenting with new forms.

It would, of course, be premature to declare that a majority of white Southerners are no longer wedded to biracialism, but Ulrich B. Phillips would have difficulty recognizing in today's South the "indomitable resolve" of his central theme.

The Southern Historical Perspective

Still another factor moving the South toward the pattern of life in the nation as a whole has been the impact of education. Poverty and ruralism have held back educational development of the region at least since the Civil War. Despite much progress in the public schools and in colleges and universities in the fifty years following 1900, the South in its industrial revolution of the 1950s and 1960s found itself short of persons with adequate technical and professional knowledge. More and more, leaders recognized that a scientific-urban culture cannot exist without both general and specialized knowledge. Southerners retained a lingering suspicion of free investigation; nevertheless, the region's legislatures stepped up their investment in colleges and universities and in the public schools as well. Scholarly work emanating from the universities tended to reduce the effects of provincialism.

The South in the last three decades has become more like the society of the nation. As it becomes more industrialized, its people richer and better educated, is it destined to lose its distinctive qualities? Is the New South to be, in the words of the Agrarians, "only an undistinguished replica of the usual industrial community," its air and water polluted, its central cities marked by the problems of the ghetto?

There are scholars who still recognize sectional distinctiveness in the South. David M. Potter, as noted before, sees limitations in the agrarian theme of Southern history. Nevertheless, he detects certain qualities among Southerners which are redolent of a lately rural society. He writes:

> *On the face of it, it seems a matter of observation and not of theory to say that the culture of the folk survived in the South long after it succumbed to the onslaught of urban-industrial culture elsewhere. It was one aspect of this culture that the relation between the land and the people remained more direct and more primal in the South than in other parts of the country. . . . Even in the most exploitative sit-*

> *uations, this culture retained a personalism in relations of man to man, which the industrial culture lacks.*

Potter goes on to suggest the possibility that modern man in his mass civilization is yearning for the life of a folk culture that may indeed be a part of Southern life.

Louis Rubin, in evaluating the work of the Nashville Agrarians, declared that their image of the South was "a rich, complex metaphor" through which they "presented a critique of the modern world."

As Dewey Grantham says, "The South will take much of its past into the future." That the region's future destiny lies in an expansion of the urban-industrial society can hardly be debated. It is difficult to predict what qualities the Southern component will contribute to the national mixture. For example, the South's fear of change could encourage America in what Frank Vandiver would call "another faulty response"—the stifling of needed self-criticism with pressures for conformity. The vestiges of the South's agrarian past may not have the supercultural power to turn back trends toward depersonalization in a mass culture.

But what more worthy burden could an emerging South accept for itself than the encouragement and promotion of a society that values personalism and the dignity of the individual?

REFLECTIONS ON SOUTHERN SOCIETY

Frank A. Rose

[AMERICA is touted as the richest and most powerful nation in the world, and that much is certainly true; but it is equally true that America is in many ways the most irresponsible and neglectful of nations. Given our vast natural and material resources, we do far too little to achieve the democratic goals of mass education, widespread economic security, general health service, and orderly freedom under good laws. Pockets of problems persist throughout our country.

In two locations, the problems of poverty, disease, changing laws, and social stratification—or problems of education, economics, ethics and ethos—are geographically visible. These two areas are the urban centers across the nation, and the South—those states of the old Confederacy bound together by geography and history.

The South is the last frontier for regional studies in America. While urban studies must consume a large part of future university development everywhere, studies of the South will be colored by the cultural context in which they are undertaken. Too, one will soon discover that there is a direct relation between the ghettos of the North and the problems of the South, as studies of black and white migration demonstrate.

You Can't Eat Magnolias

Southerners have written hundreds of books to help their fellow Southerners understand themselves, where they came from, and where they ought to be going. Practically all of these writers deal with three themes, all of a distinctly regional nature, which appear to be most central to an analysis of the average Southerner: historical consciousness, racial consciousness, and economic hardship. And most of these books leave the reader with no clear answers to the questions they pose.

An exception is Wilbur J. Cash's *The Mind of the South,* which ought to be required reading for any Southerner with a high-school education or better. Unfortunately, Cash wrote the right book at the wrong time. When *The Mind of the South* was published in 1941, Pearl Harbor came close behind. Whatever effect the book might have on that generation of Southerners is impossible to gauge. Standing midway between the Lost Generation of the twenties and thirties and the Beat Generation of the fifties and sixties, the book may have been some sort of revelation to those Southerners involved in the search for values; and not just to the novelists—the Faulkners and Wolfes—but to the larger public as well.

Age has not impaired the validity of Cash's work for the present generation of Southerners, nor for the present generation of non-Southerners who are also concerned with understanding the South. *The Mind of the South* is an excellent study of the Southerner, who he is and whence he came, the problems of sociology and history. The question of where the Southerner ought to go, the problem of ethics, is left to the reader.

Where should the South be heading? It is a relatively simple question, although some Southerners are reluctant to accept the answers. The South ought to become part of the nation again, something it has not really been since the generation of Jefferson. The South wants to obliterate poverty, that swamp of evils which stands in stark contrast to the image of America as the richest land in the world. In a word, the new South wants to be free—

free from its past, free from fears, free from wants, free from prejudices.

The goals are easily stated, so much that they seem idealistic and glib. Cash's second unanswered question is the harder of the two: How can the South reach these ends?

The problem of *how* goals are reached is the problem of will and policy-making. It may well be that Cash himself has provided a start towards a solution by popularizing the efforts of the social sciences. History, sociology, economics, and political science are the methods of analysis without which policy-making is shallow and futile. The answer to what needs to be done is always dependent upon a realistic analysis of the *status quo.*

Cash's analysis of the South should be particularly helpful for policy-makers through its two major points. First, Cash shows that the South has been, since 1830, a generally closed society, in contrast to the democratic norm of an open society. Second, and more important, Cash reduces this Southern system to its component parts, so that the region's weaknesses are laid bare and the possibilities for change become apparent.

Except for the Tidewater plantations of Virginia, the South remained largely an American frontier until the 1830s. Land was still plentiful, fortunes were still being made and lost, immigration was still widespread on the part of white people (and involuntarily on the part of blacks), and life was in general rugged, individualistic, competitive, and personal. With the combination of fertile land, slavery, the cotton gin, the cotton market, and frontier industriousness, the social system began to settle into a distinctive pattern.

Today, the South is caught in a web of economic "necessities" not entirely of its own making. In order to progress financially to some semblance of equality with the rest of the nation, the South has often had to ignore some of the ethical questions of economics: What about labor, its just wages and bargaining powers? What about the blacks, their right to equal job opportunities? What about taxation, the light loads on industries and the heavy loads on consumers? What about overall profits, the using of Southern resources to make profits for absentee landlords and other places?

"Necessity" is not always the mother of invention; sometimes "necessity" is the defender of the *status quo.* If the South has exploited lower classes, it has not always been out of malice, but out of "necessity." The Communist analogy of the poor being used by the rich does not generally apply in the South; it has been more like the poor using the poorer.

Franklin Roosevelt's analysis of the South in the 1930s is still valid to a great degree:

> *It is my conviction that the South presents right now the Nation's number one economic problem—the Nation's problem, not merely the South's. For we have an economic unbalance in the Nation as a whole, due to this very condition of the South. It is an unbalance that can and must be righted, for the sake of the South and of the Nation.*

But necessity is not the only argument Cash finds in favor of the Southern class system. Reinforcing economic necessity, and almost as important to the Southern mind, is the argument of Southern tradition. After all, this is the way that things have been for 125 years.

Poverty, defeat, and defensiveness go together. The political idea of the "Solid South" as a continuation of the Old South is primarily a defense mechanism used by the South against its feelings of despair. While the South has always had its social and economic classes, it has never had any significant class consciousness. The lower classes have been kept in their designated places by the arguments of necessity and patriotism, by paternalism from the "haves" toward the "have-nots," by the split between the blacks and the whites of the lower classes, and, in short, by the simple ability of the system to perpetuate itself.

Reflections on Southern Society

Two historical forces of particular significance in sustaining the class system are theology and the military. Southern theology has tended to be a balancing of Calvinism and Arminianism, by which Southerners accept their social status as that given them by God (predestination), while at the same time and without contradiction an individual's labors in his social station are seen as being rewarded perhaps by a higher status in this world but assuredly with recognition in the next (free will). Such theology has dominated Southern pulpits since the demise of Deism in the South about the time of Jefferson's death in 1826. The result has been an acquiescence in the *status quo* and the hope for "a better life in the next world."

The ideal of military organization has exerted the same pressure toward complacent acceptance of one's station. John Hope Franklin's study on *The Militant South* traces the regimentation of Southern society back to the gradual institutionalization of the early Southern frontier violence. The military motif permeated the whole Southern way and still does to a great degree. Education, the family, the one-party political system, organizations, social groups, and all of the ordinary groupings of life have been united in a military-style system in which the necessity of accepting one's rank is unquestionable. The lower classes are foot soldiers serving under captains of politics and business; to question a maneuver is tantamount to treason, punishable in assorted ways.

The net result of this closed organization has been a heightened sentimentalism, a proud refusal to face the reality of poverty, a complacency with social evils as the "givens" of God; an interpretation of "progress" as meaning more money but no change at all in the social structure and class system; a militant reaction against self-criticism from within the South, and a chauvinistic reaction against anything that hints of changing social structures, especially "outsiders" and the federal government. In a word, the South clings to an exaggerated myth of a closed and happy society.

Yet it should not be assumed too quickly that the Southern

system is so tightly closed that seeds of change have found no soil to grow in. Tools of sociology and history are most helpful in showing that the dominant image of the South is not the only image. V. O. Key, Jr., for example, in his impressive study, *Southern Politics,* traced state by state the various centers of political and economic opinions, arriving at the eventual conclusion that the conservatism of Southern politicians is out of proportion to the strength of liberalism and populism among masses of Southern people. Furthermore, he concludes that some politicians often are but mouthpieces for the vested interests of business and political groups, keeping alive the phantom of racism as a weapon to subdue massive discontent and preserving the one-party political system in order to control patronage. Urban areas and depressed mountain regions are especially victimized by the oligarchic power wielded by necessity and history.

The social scientists have, piece by piece, reconstructed a picture of the South which stands in stark contrast to the contention that the South is now and has always been "solid." Francis Pendleton Gaines, in *The Southern Plantation: A Study in the Development and Accuracy of a Tradition,* showed that the Old South ideal is more a product of novels and Hollywood than of fact. Frank L. Owsley, in *Plain Folk of the Old South,* rediscovered the lost middle class of the yeomen, the nonslaveholding Southern farmers. Clement Eaton, in *Freedom of Thought in the Old South,* traced the thread of liberalism in the South up to the Civil War; and Virginius Dabney, in *Liberalism in the South,* complemented Eaton's work and extended it into the 1930s. William R. Taylor, in *Cavalier and Yankee,* deromanticized the long-cherished myth of Southern white descent from English aristocracy, and showed that, interestingly enough, much of the myth was created by the North. C. Vann Woodward's studies on Southern populism and Jim Crow history, and his essays in *The Burden of Southern History,* illuminated numerous paradoxes in the Southern image of self-containment. T. Harry Williams saw in Huey Long a Southern effort at economic realism, an attempt to arouse the Southern people to the dangers of a closed social and economic system, using the weapons of the demagogue but lacking the program to carry it through.

Nor is the sanctity of the Southern system being exploded only by historians. If the Southern image of the past does not correspond with the historians' facts, neither does the image of the present correspond with the sociologists'. The conservative performance of Southern legislators and executives does not reveal the widespread discontent with platitudes and promise and the unorganized yearning for a New South.

The Southern system is not closed to expressions of discontent, but it may appear to be. In the long road from 1830, discontent has noticeably threatened the static structure only twice: in the Populist uprising of the 1890s and in the crisis of the Great Depression. Discontent had never risen to revolutionary proportions until the black revolution of the present day, because discontent has never had the organization and the power to make itself heard, especially against the arguments of expediency and loyalty.

The rumblings of disenchantment today are not confined to any particular class of white people. The lower-class workers often lack the bargaining groups they have elsewhere; the intellectuals often lack the methods and contacts for significant action; the students often are not yet able to articulate their uneasiness. This lack of solidified opposition to the *status quo* can at best only chip away at the system. Inner-South restlessness cannot produce a dramatic transformation in Southern mores. Its most realistic hope is for a gradual evolution of Southern structures into the more open structures of the rest of America. To that end, the two effective means most acceptable to the South are education and sustained communication with the rest of the nation, by which the stark contrasts between the region and the rest of the nation will gradually become apparent and abhorrent. Without massive capital of its own, the South alone cannot alter the economic system or solve the problems of unemployment and migration of talent and labor.

You Can't Eat Magnolias

Though the South may lack the means of self-correction, there still remain two other forces which act upon the Southern system. One is the process of industrialization. The other is more deliberate: the process of responsible planning and action.

The opening of the Southern system to industry is most closely associated with Henry Grady, the Atlanta publisher and prophet of the New South during the last decades of the 1800s. Grady's industrial theory was based on the premise that the South's social structures could remain essentially permanent while the economic structures were being uplifted, using the increased benefits of industry. The effect, as Cash pointed out, was to transplant the plantation system from the cotton field to the cotton mill. The owner of the mill was the new aristocrat, the white working class was the new labor force, and the blacks stayed behind on the farms as tenants or as house servants. In this way the folk values of the old Solid South were preserved while the economic strains were lessened. In 1889 Grady wrote:

> *I attended a funeral once in Pickens County in my state. This funeral was particularly sad. It was a poor fellow like most Southerners. . . . They buried him in the midst of a marble quarry: they cut through solid marble to make his grave; and yet a little tombstone they put above him was from Vermont. They buried him in the heart of a pine forest, and the pine coffin was imported from Cincinnati. They buried him within touch of an iron mine, and yet the nails in his coffin and the iron in the shovel that dug his grave were imported from Pittsburgh. They buried him by the side of the best sheepgrazing country on the earth, and yet the wool in the coffin bands and the coffin bands themselves were brought from the North. The South didn't furnish a thing on earth for that funeral but the corpse and the hole in the ground.*

Reflections on Southern Society

In retrospect, Gradyism seems partial in goals, provincial in scope, chauvinistic in economic motivation, and prejudiced in social understanding. In the long run, the plight of the working classes did not decline impressively, and the interests of the South continued to be associated with the ruling classes—in this case, industrialists—many of whom were from outside the South. The problems of subsistence-level living continued to plague the majority of Southerners, and a reserve army of unemployed still stood ready to fill the gaps created should the factory workers falter and decide they were entitled to a larger share of affluence, and thereby lose their jobs.

There is, however, a way of looking at this period of Southern history other than as one of sheer exploitation. One may also see here a decisive step upward for the South.

H. Richard Niebuhr's study of American churches, *The Social Sources of Denominationalism,* develops a theme which may prove helpful as an analogy. This study shows the movement of various American church groups up an evolutionary scale from sect to denomination. The pattern of movement is generally the same for all churches, but the time factor varies according to the assorted influences of numerous conditioning factors.

By comparison, the Southern regional economy can be seen as a sort of sect moving upward to nationalism, and it can also be demonstrated that the Southern social system follows a similar pattern. If such evolutionary trends were charted, they might look something like this:

Plantation	*Transition*	*2nd Frontier*	*Transition*	*3rd Frontier*
1830–1865	1865–1880	1880–1930	1930–1970	The National Pattern
Cotton Slaves Yeomen Militancy	Reconstruction No Slaves Outsiders	Gradyism Local Industry Tenant Farms	Depression New Deal Mississippi Plan Desegregation	

David M. Potter describes this process as the movement toward abundance, and he specifically points to the lag between the South and the nation as the gap between a harmonious folk society and a bountiful, but dynamically diverse, mass culture. If the folk society has built-in inequalities, it also has security of station, a powerful factor inhibiting the movement toward a mass society with greater equality of opportunity but insecurity of social station.

This demonstration of the tension between the *status quo* and change is significant for understanding the Southern dilemma. Because of the gulfs of time which separate the Southern economic process from the national norms, the South cannot be expected to conform readily to non-Southern standards.

The extent to which the South has become industrialized and urbanized is illusory. According to the 1960 census, the South had only twenty-nine cities with a population over 100,000 (in the thirteen Confederate states and Kentucky). This means that a sizable share of the Southern labor force has had to move northward to find employment. It also means that most Southern cities and towns have to rely upon local industries and those they can entice from outside at great local sacrifice. The largest Southern cities are those with a combination of resources, both natural and manmade: oil, water power, shipping facilities, trained labor, recreation facilities, good schools and colleges, good housing, and so forth. Especially crucial to the rise of industry and urbanization is progressive local government.

It is this last factor which deserves the South's closest attention, because it is the mechanism through which community resources are coordinated, developed, and improved. Responsible industrialism cannot be separated from responsible community and state government and from the interests of the whole community. Policy-making must take into account all facets of a community's life, and this can best be achieved by representation of all community interests in the processes of decision-making. Especially when the community must make sacrifices, such as higher taxes for community improvements and the dropping of the color line in hiring and educating, all aspects of public life should be heard.

One of the factors most severely inhibiting the South's rise to prosperity is the virtual political monopoly of the Democratic party. Southern loyalty to the one-party system began during Reconstruction, when a solid South seemed essential to expose and oppose Republicanism; but by the Great Depression the policies of the Southern Democrats had become amazingly similar to those of Northern Republicans. The coalition of these two groups is still in force today, and the Southern Democratic party is dominated by leadership which would be more at home with the recent principles of the Republican party.

The logic used against the two-party system in the South stems from the same factors which have influenced Southern economic policy: necessity and tradition. The argument of tradition has great appeal to most Southerners. Voting the Democratic ticket is the "Southern way," a test of one's loyalty to one's father and grandfathers and to the "Southern" system. The argument of necessity can be both economic and racial. It is assumed that a one-party system will keep blacks in their place and will deter the actions of outsiders, such as the federal government.

Today, the Congressional power of the one-party system is on the verge of a breakdown, largely as a result of the 1962 Supreme Court decision on reapportionment. All the implications of the Tennessee case of *Baker vs. Carr* are not yet visible, but one definite effect is certain. The shifting of Congressional districts in an effort to approach the goal of "one man, one vote" has removed some of the rural power and transferred it to the urban centers. The result has been a reshuffling of Congressmen and a loss of Southern Congressional seniority. The transfer of Southern voters to the Republican party, which has already begun in Presidential elections, is gradually expanding to state and local elections as well.

This development may prove to be a hidden blessing for the South and the nation. It may well be that the South will gain more by the competition of two parties for the vote than it has ever gained under the seniority plan of one-party politics. In the past, the South has been seen as a lost cause for the Republicans and a certain victory for the Democrats. The lack of competition between the major parties in the South has reduced the pressure on national party leaders to distribute patronage in the region, and funds have been diverted to those states where voting competition was heaviest. It is true that federal aid to the South is higher than the Southern share of the tax burden seems to warrant, but that argument fails to consider that the Southern standard of living and per capita income are below the national average. If the South gets more than it puts in, that "more" amount is still not enough to solve its economic problems. There are still vast areas of need for federal assistance, such as education, manpower training, flood controls, conservation, housing developments, development of the South's coast line for shipping, and the establishment of an internally sound transportation network.

Other benefits follow from the two-party system. The general elections, formerly empty ceremonies, are transformed into battlefields of political philosophies, and the voter's sense of participation in government is heightened when he has a choice. Minority opinion becomes more significant in formulating platforms, and interest groups are more evenly balanced. Officials become more conscious of their responsibility to all interests rather than just to those which were fortunate enough to carry the primaries, because promises in a two-party system have to be backed up by performance.

The South stands with one foot on the threshold of social change and the other rooted in the past. This clashing of the past with the future has precipitated a Southern debate, with all of the existential excitement and tensions of those long-ago duels under the giant oaks. One tempter whispers, "Stand fast"; another counsels, "Rush on." For the conservative, it is a duel between an orderly society and an uncontrollably mobile society. For the liberal, it is a duel between government by an aristocracy of power and government by democracy, or between a subsistence culture and an abundant culture. Some simplify it and call it a duel between agrarianism and industrialism, or between regionalism and nationalism. Both sides test their weapons, take practice shots, get the drift of the wind, confer with their seconds; but they know, and most of the spectators know, that the duel must never come to actual bloodshed, because 1861 is still too fresh in their memories. Both sides are right and both are wrong. Only the lunatic fringe, concealed behind false slogans and organizations, shouts for blood.

To the rest of America, Southern conservatism about the benefits of affluence may be incomprehensible. This is because the rest of the nation has not shared in the Southern stability of status and thereby lacks the perspective of the Southern mind. As C. Vann Woodward points out, it is America which is unique in world history, not the South. America has never lost a war; the South has. America has grown accustomed to prosperity; it is new to the South. American idealism has never suffered serious setbacks; the South has had little reason for optimism and has found its survival in accepting its suffering.

Poverty and defeat have forced the South to find new values—or, if not new values, values different from those of the industrial nation. Granted that these values were the products of an agricultural regionalism, as the Agrarians were quick to point out in 1930, the South is convinced, even as it pushes into modern society, that some of these values are valid today. Among these "goods" were personableness, neighborliness, a leisureliness in work and movement, a willingness to share the last cup of meal with one who needed it, personal dignity and courage to keep trying when the boll weevil and the drought came, closely knit family ties, and a willingness to practice religion as the minister said it ought to be practiced. The list grows long, and there is much truth in it. Maybe the virtues have been romanticized and generalized too much, and maybe they have been used to conceal a multitude of sins, but the stratum of truth remains. The "good society" for the South would be one in which the spiritual values dominated, and if material blessings could be added without altering the basic way of life, then well and good.

For these reasons most Southerners fear the coming of the new as much as, or more than, they desire it. They are torn between economic necessity and tradition. Can prosperous men master their machines? The prospects of dealing with a complex and uncertain future are frightening: countless decisions will have to be made, endless adjustments will have to come.

And on the other side of the Mason-Dixon line, the North produces its own value theories. For the North, prosperity is the means to democracy, to the opening of society to all men. Prosperity brings freedoms: freedom from want, freedom from hopelessness, the freedom to carve out one's own niche in society rather than to be assigned one by birth or color. Perhaps the North also romanticizes and generalizes, paints a picture in exaggerated lines; but there is a core of truth in the North as well as the South.

The conflict is one of clashing ideologies, of demands for freedom with demands for order. Can the nation, after much trial and error, develop a balance of freedom with order, some middle road that avoids the tyranny of too much order and the anarchy of too much freedom? The complexities are enormous, but democracy in this day and age is impossible without the willingness to deal with complexities. To hesitate because of the fear of complexity is to admit that democracy is impossible.

Let the North bring to the nation its technological know-how and its experience; let the South bring its needs and its questions; and perhaps both will find prosperity. A mobile society needs to learn again the values of family and community life, especially as working hours shorten and leisure time increases. An abundant society, rich in material blessings, needs to learn again the abundance of blessings which cannot be bought; the dignity of *all* men everywhere, the rights of *all* men everywhere, the respect due all men by all men everywhere.

The lessons to be learned are not just for the North nor for the

South, but for both. Thomas Wolfe, who was both a North Carolinian and a New Yorker, but more American than either, asked the question that needs asking again today, when the South holds too tightly to its orderliness and when the North exults too loudly in its prosperity:

> *Which of us has known his brother? Which of us has looked into his father's heart? Which of us has not remained forever prison-pent? Which of us is not forever a stranger and alone?*

In the long run, the success of the nation in the development of national values will hinge on how able the nation is in answering Wolfe's question. Prosperity without community responsibility is just as dangerous as social order without guarantees of freedom and equal opportunity. When abundance can be seen as more than an end in itself, as a means to social harmony, it can take on new dignity.

The assimilation of the South into the nation can follow no generalized timetable. Assimilation-on-paper has just come for one portion of the South, the black people. It is also evident that some larger Southern cities are already indistinguishable from those of California or New York, while rural areas are just beginning to feel the restlessness of progress. The majority of Southern communities stand at various stages along the way.

By allowing the evolutionary process to work itself out, it may be that each Southern community will have time to ask itself how prosperity's blessings can be extended to the whole community and how the community can be made safe for democracy. The strengthening of respect for the individual's needs, talents, and rights is the first step in responsible community policy-making. At this particular juncture in Southern history, the local community can best serve itself by insuring a broad interest base in the power structures, as illustrated in the examples of industry procurement and two-party politics. Responsibility will accompany prosperity, not inevitably, but to the extent that community leadership is willing to question its motives and its means. To accomplish this, the community power structures must be expanded to include men willing to ask the questions and informed enough to settle on answers.

It has been said that there is nothing more powerful than an idea whose time has come. There is a reverse side of the coin: there is nothing more dangerous than an idea which the human mind tries to ignore. We can no longer back into the future.

The southern future

THE END OF THE MYTHS: THE SOUTH CAN LEAD THE NATION

Terry Sanford

[SOME years ago I took a train to New York, waking up in the early dawn to peer out on the New Jersey countryside. There I saw the familiar wastelands—stagnant winding streams colored by chemical wastes, the backside of a city with dirty streets and dingy tenements crowded against each other. The purpose of my train trip was to visit some corporate officers, to urge them to bring industry to North Carolina. My impulse was to turn around. If this, I thought, is industrialization, then why do we want it? Do we really have to kill our land? I did not have an answer—because, in addition to all our other troubles, we desperately needed jobs.

I know we in the South are given to myths. I have certainly perpetuated my share. I have in time blamed every difficulty of the South—including low income, weak schools, even hookworm—on the discriminatory freight rates, the oppressive credit restrictions, the failure of the North to help with educating the freed slaves, and the so-called "Reconstruction."

We were poor and put upon, or so we felt, and myths came easy. Consider the Georgia driver of a sight-seeing bus at Gettysburg who continued to recite Southern victories in skirmish after skirmish until one offended Yankee lady demanded, "Didn't the Union forces win anything here?"

"No, ma'am," he said, "and they ain't going to as long as I'm driving this bus."

We still feel put upon. Just last year a National Farm Organization field man told a group of Alabama chicken farmers to join up and strike, for they were to be "the last slaves freed in the South." A tall farmer with high-water overalls unfolded and stood up and yelled to the crowd: "Y'all better hurry up! They've already freed the mules!"

The fertile earth of this lush and ruddy land of our South has always been remarkably productive, and our agrarian atmosphere seems also to stimulate creative imaginations, including a disposition for nourishing mythology. Especially during this past century, we have too often committed ourselves to myths—whether those of our own making or those imposed on us from afar—so loyally that we have become enslaved by them. The legend of the Old South nourished and languished over by the distending nostalgia of so many writers, the "Cavalier Thesis," as W. J. Cash titled this myth, is a most obvious example.

In the early sixties we began to rend the curtain of racial discrimination, a cloth woven out of long strands of various mythologies, and glimpsed behind it—for the first time in a century—the real South. Once we began to remove that curtain and to reconcile ourselves to reality, our revelations seemed to force a similar reassessment on the North.

I see many possibilities because of these developments, and I hope I am not indulging in new myths. The result of the South's new awakening, as the whole world knows by now, has been that we, as an entire country, have had to admit that racism is not an exclusively Southern dishonor, but a tragic national blight.

But our progress is encouraging. The April 18, 1971, edition of *The New York Times* cited figures showing that the South has now moved *ahead* of the rest of the country in school desegregation. "Two years ago at this time, according to the federal government, 18 percent of all black pupils in the South were attending integrated schools; today, 38 percent are. In the North and West, during the same period, the figures remained almost static at around 27 percent."

To cite the corresponding change in attitude toward school desegregation among white Southerners, a 1963 Gallup Poll showed that six out of ten white Southern parents said they would object to having their children enrolled in an integrated school. A similar poll taken last year indicated that only one parent in six objects. According to George Gallup, "This finding represents one of the most dramatic shifts in the history of public opinion polling."

This new awakening, while it does not mark the end of prejudice and discrimination, does make it possible for us to intensify our interest in other concerns. How do we turn now to challenge those other forces that threaten to suppress us as the race issue has for so long? One of our most pressing concerns at this time is the rapid and haphazard growth of Southern cities. How can we profit from the urban mistakes of the rest of the country and find ways to keep our cities clean and livable? How can we avoid slums and ghettos and stacking people up in "glass-and-steel filing cabinets," as Lewis Mumford called the urban high-rise concentrations?

I cannot inventory everything the South should do to avoid the urban problems of the major cities in the rest of the country. I cannot even catalogue everything that is wrong with those cities. We know that they are in deep trouble, both in finding enough money to keep up the present services, and in seeking ways to make the cities more livable. We know their troubles include crowding, slums, smog, sprawl, pollution, transportation, crime, drug traffic, insufficient medical services, a lack of open space, playgrounds, and parks, and, worst of all, the lack of mobility for disadvantaged citizens to leave the city for jobs elsewhere.

We also know that some of the remedial answers lie in low-cost housing, open space acquisition, stern zoning laws, comprehensive transportation arrangements, and urban renewal projects. But the frightening thought is that we never will have enough money to bail out all the cities and keep them bailed out. Too many cities have grown to be irreversibly unmanageable accumulations of too many people.

We need to find for the South, while there is yet time, some workable plan that will have the effect of directing the location of population centers. The plan must have restrictive features to eliminate the self-destructive practices of cities, but it must also include attractive alternatives in the areas of transportation, housing, new towns, and plant location, all with special concern for human considerations.

Horace Barker, in *South Today,* noted that the new governors across the South have been pledging to work against racial discrimination. "What did they mean?" Barker asks. "They perhaps could find no better place to apply themselves than in ridding the region of discriminatory housing practices, and the field is wide open."

This would be a tremendous step in avoiding the development of ghettos and the flight to the suburbs. The same is true of the consolidation of school districts. As Joel Fleishman points out in his essay in this volume, "An example of valuable opportunity already lost is housing patterns. Perhaps the most disturbing respect in which Southern metropolitan areas differ from those in other parts of the country is the extent to which racial segregation in housing has been increasing in the South within the central city and between central city and suburbs. . . ."

But these measures, although both essential and urgent, are merely corrective. To avoid the blight, to protect the earth, to save the magic of the ecology, to enhance the civility of life, what do we do? If I were one of the Southern governors today, I would not be so concerned with federal grants for roads and dams in the Coastal Plains or Appalachia or other regions. We have been down that road. I would be concerned with Model City programs and urban renewal—but only as necessities, and not as preventive strategies.

The End of the Myths: The South Can Lead the Nation

We can now see beyond the half-myth that held for scores of years that our best path of progress, toward full recovery, was greater industrialization. We paid rather simplistic allegiance to that principle for too long. Now (and, I believe, just in time) we have become aware that industrialization in itself can be highly detrimental to our region and our people, unless we ourselves regulate it to our best interest. We are, therefore, much more concerned today with the job-training programs which companies may offer, the wages these incoming industries will pay, the revenues they will provide (in fair-share arrangements, not in tax-reducing enticements), their effect on our air and water, and their practices in equal employment opportunities. Even a good record on all these points should not signal clearance to a new industry, because its ultimate location, we now understand, can create problems beyond solution.

Our hope, our only hope, is to direct our own population growth and location.

I would have us in the South start a new approach toward saving the nation. We, that is, all the citizens acting through their governments—state, local, and national—must have something to do with arranging where people are going to live. Please note carefully that I do not mean that we are going to have to tell people where to live. But right now forces not directed by anyone tell us where to live. I would have us bring those forces under our own control.

Cities act as natural magnets, drawing more industry, more commerce, more people, more jobless, more welfare recipients, more problems. Far from offsetting this magnetic force, we encourage it. What mayor (now a few hopeful exceptions) does not want to see his city grow and grow? What Board of Realtors does not feel the divine mandate to add and add to the city? What Chamber of Commerce does not want to jump from thirty-second largest city to twenty-fourth largest city? What city promotional brochure does not boast of size?

If I were to declare public policy at any level, state or local,

I would decide that first, before we decide how to get better garbage collection, or how to cut down on air pollution, or how to get another freeway stretched across the city, we would declare one aim: *Stop the growth syndrome.* We need growth, and will get it in any event; but growth cannot be our primary ambition. We must learn to control the direction and rate of growth.

Let the mayor of every city declare that they have enough quantity and that they now seek quality. Let the state and national governments use the tax power to control plant location. Either the plant fits population needs where it is to be located, or there is no depreciation write-off. This is simply one example of the means that might be used to shape the future size of metropolitan areas. And it probably will work—but it is not likely to work unless we can find a way to make it part of an overall plan. How do we develop such a plan, and how do we start?

A popular remedy has been to suggest consolidation of local governments and the creation of metropolitan governments; and while I do not think this long line of thinking and writing is all bad, I have a suspicion that we are not eliminating the problems, merely spreading them over a larger area. Of course, consolidation does establish a broader capacity for planning, it does improve the tax base in support of the core-city operations, and the suburbanite must pay some of the costs of the place where he works but doesn't live. Consolidation of fragmented governmental areas makes a lot of sense. However, no matter what good might be accomplished by consolidation, it is not the way to arrange population patterns for the future. It would help certain areas somewhat, but it would not help much in shaping a decent face for the South as a whole in the year 2000.

To do something significant about where people live and work and how they travel back and forth requires a larger piece of real estate than a county or two. Furthermore, it takes more legal and governmental powers than a state is likely to give its municipalities, and indeed more than perhaps it can. In any event, it is essential for wholesome and orderly growth to have the broader overview of the state, with its powers of eminent domain and taxation, and its regulatory authority.

It is assumed that the national government will continue to be concerned with population patterns, although nothing substantial has been done and nothing substantial is reasonably anticipated. I have my personal doubts that we can expect much efficacy from Washington programs until the federal government is reorganized away from its present fragmentation into bureaus, departments, and agencies with conflicting and cross-flowing authority and responsibilities. But that is another subject for another time. The question now is, What can the Southern states do about their own urban future to avoid repeating the mistakes of the North?

I want to present a plan that we as Southern states might undertake together, as a regional endeavor; then I want to suggest one project as an example of what a state might undertake on its own.

Let us develop our own cooperative effort among the Southern states, using the familiar interstate compact as our means, much as we developed the Southern Regional Education Board to look to our cooperative needs in higher education. Why not have a Southern Regional Growth Board? The governors could organize it, and together the governors and the legislatures could make it work.

A Southern Regional Growth Board, acting for, of, by and through the states, would draw interest and help from the national government. It could take care of our own regional growth opportunities, and, moreover, it could set an urban pattern for the rest of the nation.

A Southern Regional Growth Board could plan and suggest the legal devices and public policies to provide for orderly growth, and to decide where a new industry should go too slow or accelerate growth as the need may be. The patterns of highways and public rapid transit systems could be planned and designed to attract population growth to appropriate places. The incentives for new towns, the maintenance of clean water supplies, and the preservation of natural resources could be planned, suggested to the individual states, and coordinated. In addition, such an organized effort would give us a handle on housing, school districting, medical care, jobs and job training, rural life enrichment, population control, the acquisition and preservation of open space, and the preservation and development of cities as cultural centers. Most of all, it presents exciting alternatives for providing mobility for those now locked into the ghettos of the cities or confined to the uneconomic rural areas. This new mobility, carried forward in the concept of retraining and relocation, subsidized and promoted by the individual states, with federal financial aid if available, would provide one of the best hopes for members of minority groups who now are destined by forces beyond our present control to live where there is no hope for realizing individual opportunity.

To achieve all this, we need an overall design plan, one that sees cities the size they should be, that sees industry located where it promotes healthy growth, that sees highways placed where they encourage livable housing and commercial patterns, that looks to the future and draws the plans for the society we would like to be when this century ends. Who is wise enough to sketch out such a broad and long-range plan? We Southerners are, and the Southern Regional Growth Board established by compact is a workable method. What we presently lack is the determination, a mechanism for such planning, and the belief that we can control our destiny rather than having it directed for us by uncoordinated forces we set in motion by not knowing where we are going.

A regional approach is desirable. No state can take the necessary steps alone. We are too interrelated, and, in a sense, states are too competitive. On the other hand, a national plan would be too cumbersome, and it would take too long to set it in motion. We can start a regional growth-planning operation immediately.

The main function of a Southern Regional Growth Board would be planning—in particular, planning for the location and quality of population groupings. The execution would be left largely to state and local initiative, and the Board would have only the authority granted it by the states entering into the compact for its creation. The Board, just as the Southern Regional Education Board, really needs no powers in itself, since the power, force, and authority of the individual states must be relied upon in any event. In addition to planning, the Board would assemble the expert advice needed for execution and furnish the coordinating devices the individual states would need as they followed a general overall regional plan of population placement.

Planning is no longer a feared word, or a feared undertaking. It is now an undeniably essential part of any sensible approach to complex societies. The only questions remaining are whether or not we make the effort to plan—or to whom we forfeit if we neglect to plan—and whether we, collectively, can muster the desire to make plans for our future.

As Dean John C. McKinney has pointed out, "Planning is neither ivory-tower speculation, intellectual star-gazing, nor utopian thinking. Essentially it is a practical and instrumental activity. Its criteria and style are pragmatic." Moreover, he points out, "There is no shortage of basic knowledge and no necessary shortage of data for the conduct of planning for change." And this kind of endeavor—for all its long-range benefits—can be started simply, and *now.*

Now let me give one example of one project, for one state, that would probably fit well into a regional plan. In eastern North Carolina, where I was born and now live, we have been beset with all the ills of the rural South—not enough jobs, not enough transportation, not enough medical care, schools that are not good enough, out-migration of our talented young people, to name a few. One way out of some of these problems, and one way to spread out future population growth that otherwise will choke our cities, can be found in looking at two corridors leading to the central part of the state. One is from the northeast, the Elizabeth City area just south of the Norfolk area, and the other leads from our Wilmington and Morehead City ports. We do not have highways of interstate standards in these corridors, and our rail transportation is antiquated. We need to build superhighways through these corridors, connecting with the interstate system in the center of the state, and thence with the heartland of America. We could build them with tax funds, or with bonds sold to private investors, and they would pay for themselves just because they would connect our ports and the Virginia ports with the Midwest centers of population, such as Cincinnati and Chicago, as well as with Charlotte and Atlanta.

But let us add another ingredient. Let us build new towns along those highways. We know how to build new towns, and most experts concerned with future population patterns agree that a substantial part of our new growth must be absorbed by new towns. In acquiring the right-of-way for the highways, land for new cities could be acquired at intervals of every twenty-five or so miles. We would not, of course, expect to populate them all right away, but they would be there, ready, connected with each other and the rest of the state by good roads and eventually by other means of transportation. While designing our roads, we could reserve space for rapid mass transportation for the future, perhaps a monorail riding over the highways. Present rail facilities would inevitably be improved.

We could develop the new cities much in the manner we develop urban redevelopment sections of old cities. The infrastructure could be put in, the necessary industry could be recruited, while the actual building of plants and houses and buildings would be left to private enterprise according to community plan. The original owners of the land, already having been paid a fair price, could perhaps be given a residual interest in the enhanced value of the land after the improvements were paid for.

These are just examples of some of the things the South might do to avoid the evils of population concentration that now plague other parts of the country. In essence, we must control the forces that now cause people to crowd together in unmanageable masses. While the urban states must be concerned with urgent corrective programs, we can, if we start now, dedicate ourselves to preventive practices.

I am not suggesting, and never have, that the South should set itself apart from the remainder of the nation. We have been working too hard to get back into the Union for the past hundred years. As a matter of vivid fact, I think we have a responsibility to give the nation the benefit of some of our own learning and peculiar capacities.

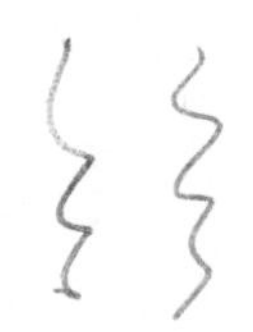

There is in the South a civility, a reasonableness, a certain graciousness, a patience born of travail, and a sensitivity to minorities because we have been one. I do not believe that this is all part of the myth, or myth at all. I acknowledge the abuses, the perversion of legal justice, the oppression of the blacks and the warped attitudes that have been peddled. The point is that we have been through the racist experience, and our leaders have struggled for years to reverse these attitudes. The success of desegregation of the schools in contrast to the rest of the nation, the victory of Governor John West over the traditional campaign of hatred and racism, are typical of the evidence that we are reaching the top of the mountain. Out of our travail, we do have something to say to people elsewhere, especially now. We do have an example to set in assuring a wholesome future, especially now.

The American political system is tired, or so it seems. And well it might be, for it is carrying an overburden of governmental maze and programmatic antiquities. Or maybe more than the system, it is the people who are tired, the people who are supposed to direct the system—which is to say, all the people. In any event, the American people have recently found it difficult to get up the spunk to ask the questions, to answer the questions, to drive forward with the creative, effervescent spirit of America. We are sluggish, we are drooping, we are tired.

The freshest, most hopeful, most energetic section of the country right now is the South. Witness the recent elections where the people took charge. Witness the vitality of the economy. Witness the willingness of people of all classes to seek as well as accept dramatic social change. This is not old myth resurrected. It is the fresh wind that should begin to blow across the nation.

D. W. Brogan, professor of political science at Cambridge University, talks of the South and its need for

> *the preservation of the many things that the region has and ought to preserve.... Some of them are in short supply in the triumphant North, not to speak of censorious Europe. I have in mind its genuine tradition of civility that has survived such defiances as the Bull Connors and the Jim Clarks and the Wallaces, some skepticism of the more foolish promises of the prophets of a technological paradise, some feeling for the tragic side of history which the North has not experienced and consequently does not realize it needs.*

All these aspects seem relevant today.

Reese Cleghorn asserted two years ago in *Atlanta* Magazine that the South has something unique to offer the nation, although

> *in recent years the South's noisiest defenders have not been working to defend this humanistic, religious, and history-conscious uniqueness, but to defend the South's old wrongs. These defenders of the worst in us now are being slowly overcome or outlived. And as the frenzy dies, it may be possible for the South to stop fighting changes that are good, and start fighting changes that are not, to rediscover and nurture its special virtues rather than compulsively defend its anti-human, antidemocratic aberrations.*

Then, citing Martin Luther King as a true Southerner, Cleghorn said, "With the end of the old tyrannies, King thought the South might become a redemptive force ('black and white together') against the impersonal, mechanical, amoral forces of our time."

The End of the Myths: The South Can Lead the Nation

He asks: "Can the South ultimately help the country work its way out of that trap?" And he answers: "A growing number of diverse people think that maybe, maybe, it just may. Their belief in the region is a far cry from the guilt-ridden defensiveness that produced the white-supremacy tyranny, violent deeds, violent tongues, and political backwardness that have characterized the worst of the South's recent history."

We in America are overwhelmed by problems which are complicated and difficult, but only partly as complicated and difficult as we manage to make them. We cannot make our domestic system responsive. We do not want people living with rats and filth. We do not want teen-agers resorting to drugs in bewilderment and confusion, yet somehow we cannot get rid of the slums and cannot inspire greater aspirations and hope among our young.

We need a freshening of spirit. We need to find a better way to make a free society function in a technological age. We need to win the awesome race with time to save the cities and to preserve the countryside. Now is the time, and the South can lead the way.

The South's time has come, after a century of being the whipping boy and the backward child. The time has come, finally come. The South can lead the nation, must lead the nation—and all the better, because the nation has never been in greater need of leadership.

EDITOR'S NOTE: The central idea of this chapter became a reality on December 16, 1971. On that date, at a meeting in Atlanta, the Southern Growth Policies Board was organized as a compact among Alabama, Arkansas, Florida, Georgia, North Carolina, South Carolina, Virginia, West Virginia, and Tennessee. Its mission is described in detail in Mr. Sanford's chapter. Because of his leadership the idea came to life, as he led an alliance of Duke University, the L.Q.C. Lamar Society, and others in developing the project to the point of its acceptance by nine governors.

WHY GO BACK SOUTH?

Luther Munford

[THE South is my briar patch. At least seven generations of my ancestors, on both sides of the family, were Southerners. Before that, they were Europeans, not Yankees. My great-grandfathers owned slaves, cleared ground, and fought for Jeff Davis. My grandmother still cherishes the silver her grandmother buried in the red hills of north Georgia to hide from Sherman's army. I was raised with Br'er Rabbit stories, grits for breakfast, double names, and a black woman servant paid $4 a day whom the whole family called "Josephine."

If it is possible to think Southern, then I probably think that way—not even four years at what my New York friends deride as the "Northernmost Southern College" could change my point of view. Yet the title of this essay, "Why Go Back South?," has a question mark at the end, for I have sincere doubts about life in the South, doubts that began when, as a thirteen-year-old errand boy in the Mississippi House of Representatives, I watched the political leaders of my state bray like jackasses over the admission of a black man to the University of Mississippi, and doubts that surfaced again one day two years ago when I came across two United States maps displayed in a Princeton hallway.

From a distance I thought the maps marked the counties that supported the Confederate rebellion, or those that voted for Breckinridge in 1861, because appropriately shaded in black, gray, and brown was much of the Old South. A closer look uncovered my mistake. True enough, the maps identified the South, but not as the Confederacy. They pictured the South as the area in the United States having the most "Counties in Which One-Half the Families Have Incomes Less Than $3,000" and the highest proportion of "Persons Twenty-Five Years and Over Who Have Completed Fewer Than Five Years of School." As I later learned, they could just as easily have shown the counties with the highest infant mortality rates, or the fewest registered voters, or with the highest incidence of violent crime. Outside of a few high-priced suburbs, the South is not a place where my neighbors are likely to be well-educated, well-fed, or healthy.

The South is also not a place where I am likely to be very well-fed or healthy, especially if I try being both a liberal and a journalist. One fellow writer, an Atlanta correspondent for *The New York Times,* surveyed the region for a job in hopes of leaving that paper and its heavy travel demands. He found salaries so low and tolerant managements so few that he stayed with the *Times* and was transferred North. The same money problems exist in other professions—Southern newspapers are filled with speeches by prominent leaders bemoaning the exodus of state-college graduates, from teachers to engineers, who leave their homeland for high-paying jobs in the North or West.

In short, the centers of power, fame, and fortune in America are not in the South. If I wanted to be editor of the best magazine, or chairman of the biggest corporation, or even the most respected historian of the South, chances are that my career ambitions would quickly lead me either north of the Mason-Dixon line or far west of the Mississippi. Even for less lofty apsirations, the trend of the past twenty-five years is clear—unless you have a business to inherit, or a girl to fall in love with, you don't return to Columbia, or Greenville, or Jackson.

Moreover, despite the many older friends who each time I visit home urge me to "come back to Mississippi . . . we need you," I know that wherever I go in the South I am not likely to find very many neighbors, or relatives, who share what I have grown to consider most important—freedom of expression and association, respect for human dignity, respect for minority rights and for civil liberties.

To go South would mean to sacrifice many things which I value, but I am considering it, and I'm also thinking about bringing some of my Northern friends with me. Our generation has often been portrayed as the disillusioned idealists. The rosy world we saw in our 10th-grade civics books, our Sunday school classes, and the Fourth of July speeches of our politicians was a cruel joke, and it didn't take much more than a trip across the railroad tracks in our home town for us to find the punch line. Raised in affluence, never seriously hungry, or powerless, or in jail, we discovered that those afflictions are the day-to-day lot of many Americans, black and white. Whether we put our stock in political action or cultural transformation, in the "Princeton Plan" or *The Greening of America,* we are a generation of reformers, and the South is the one part of America where a Great Reformation is brewing.

For years the South has been vilified for allegedly holding a monopoly on the collective vices which agonize the American conscience—racial discrimination, poverty, repression of dissent. Only recently has the nation been willing to admit, as the *Saturday Evening Post* did in 1965, that, "We are all, let us face it, Mississippians." Bull Connor and Sheriff Rainey aren't too far away from Mayor Daley.

For reformers, however, there is a crucial difference—Mayor Daley is still in office. The Northern city and suburb are ossified creatures, slowly strangling themselves with ropes of concrete highways, poisonous smog, and unresponsive political systems. Many seem to have a structured incapacity to deal with their inhuman and brutal way of life. After Birmingham had its police riot, the voters turned City Hall upside down. But Chicago had its police riot, and the Daley machine is as powerful today as it was in 1968.

Why Go Back South?

The South today is changing, becoming more democratic and more humane. There are some, particularly among my black contemporaries, who say the South's evils are the same today as they were ten years ago—Southerners today have just learned a few Northern tricks, like saying, "No, sir," when denying a black man a job instead of, "No, nigger." I think they are wrong. The South is today going through what my fellow Mississippian Willie Morris calls a "true revolution." Although the word "reformation," with its peaceful and theological connotations, probably better describes what is happening, the thrust of his description is correct.

It is a reformation not just in terms of lunch counters, but of lunch boxes. Seven years ago there were four black lawyers in the state of Mississippi. Today, there are twenty, and another twenty-three blacks—all natives of the state—are enrolled in the Ole Miss law school. It is also a reformation of the spirit. Seventeen years ago N.A.A.C.P. leaders bravely submitted desegregation petitions in several Mississippi towns and had three of their number murdered in as many months. But last year not a threat was made when three black Mississippians, one of whom had returned from an exile in the North, went on statewide television to ask that the governor of Mississippi be impeached. Despite all the rhetoric of the "Southern strategy," there seems to be a national determination that this reformation continue. Federal programs are at work today reshaping the South, some openly, in the newspaper headlines, and others quietly, in the voter registration books and tax records.

In education, in housing, in voting, in putting food on the dinner table, life is getting better for Southerners who are poor or black or both. The South I might return to will have a rising group of educated middle-class black citizens given access to the most important tools of power in society, and a group of whites who have learned to treat their black contemporaries as human beings, not anonymous serfs. Many in the two groups may not like each other, but they will learn to live with each other. Those twenty-three black law students in Mississippi are not only going to have some clients when they graduate, they are going to have some constituents as well.

The direction of the Southern Reformation is set. But how it will affect the everyday lives of Southerners is still uncertain. It will take large numbers of public-spirited persons with compassion, courage, and wisdom to keep those who have been so ingenious for so long at preserving a rigid social order from frustrating the Southern Reformation and using it for their own ends. As Kenneth Dean, former director of the Mississippi Council on Human Relations, said of the proposed Family Assistance Act, "Without community organization this will be a landlord's and merchant's program, not a people's program."

Moreover, in some areas, particularly the majority-black counties, it will take equal amounts of compassion, courage and wisdom to insure that the sons of those who held power in the past have a chance to play a role other than that of the benevolent retreating colonialist preparing the blacks for independence.

There is much to be learned from past efforts. Community organization is not going to be accomplished in a "Freedom Summer" or a VISTA sabbatical from Scarsdale; organizing a community will take a lifetime. Southerners also need to see the mistakes Northern city builders have made, with a realization that Atlanta editor Henry Grady's 1890 "New South" vision of every small town's becoming an industrialized city leads to ecological and spiritual disaster.

There is another reason the South should attract our generation. Repulsed by the unlivableness of most Northern and Western cities, young Americans can still look at the South as a frontier that might be developed along lines more compatible with a humane society. *The New York Times* has discovered what it calls a "new generation of expatriates" which includes "many of New York's most capable citizens" who are leaving that city for Europe to look for:

> *forms of self-realization they find either difficult or impossible to achieve here. . . . Some deplore the passing of civility, gracious manners and common courtesy. Some find the frenetic pace of life frightening and unsettling. Some hunger for the freedom and openness of a frontier society.*

Many, the paper says, are going to Israel, to "participate in building a new country." Those same impulses could lead not to Europe, but to the American South, where many black and white Americans can find a frontier homeland where personal values are still treasured and the air is still worth breathing.

Southern culture values personal relationships—the big city, Northern, mechanical culture, doesn't. In the South, one person can make the reformation work in his town; one body makes very little difference in Chicago. Like William Alexander Percy, legendary planter-poet of the Mississippi delta, I have come to believe that "you can't do anything on a grand scale. But you can work for your own people, in your town. It isn't national leaders we need so much as men of good will in each of the little towns of America . . . [that] can make the kind of country we want or don't want." Large federal programs attacking social problems are useless without local people willing to put the program into action.

Percy placed his emphasis where I think it belongs—on "men of good will." The South is in a very troubled period. It would be foolish to expect such a wide-ranging reformation to be accomplished without tremendous unrest. As Alexis de Tocqueville wrote, "Only consummate statecraft can enable a king to save his throne when, after a long spell of oppressive rule, he sets to improving the lot of his subjects." It will not be easy for me, much less a white Southerner raised in an earlier, less turbulent era, to learn my new role as a black man's or a poor man's equal. It will not be easy for the black or poor man to learn his new role either. But it must be done—and done with good will.

That is the challenge, and the promise. An opportunity exists today to shape the South for the better that did not exist twenty years ago, and may not exist twenty years hence. "There's one thing for sure," a seventy-two-year-old friend told me when I asked him for advice, "if you come back, you'll never be bored." He was right. Of all the cruel adjectives hurled at the South, one has seldom been used—dull. The South is a region of dark drama, a land where people are passionately struggling with the most common needs and conflicts of human flesh. The struggle that faces my generation of Southerners, whether or not I accompany them, will continue to be that kind of battle, of "the human heart in conflict with itself," as Faulkner put it.

One hopes that the Southern creative genius, long recognized in literature, will be able to make that struggle productive of the best things man hopes for. Perhaps the reformation can somehow capture the spirit of the young white boy from my neighborhood in Jackson, Mississippi, on his first day at a newly integrated school. As he got off the bus, he briskly stepped up to the biggest black boy on the playground, stuck out his hand, and introduced himself. "Hello," he said, "my name is John Stephens. When the trouble starts, I'm on your side."

A SOUTHERN STRATEGY

Thomas H. Naylor

[IT was on a cold and rainy night in Jackson, Mississippi, that I finally began to appreciate the elusive nature of the changes now taking place in the South. In the course of a few hours I saw the vision of the "new South" as it can be, and confronted the ghost of the old politics as it still is in some parts of Mississippi. I spent the early evening in the home of a professor at Tougaloo College, a predominately black college just north of Jackson, which had for years been a vexation to white Mississippians. The host was a delightful German Jew named Ernst Borinski who has taught sociology at Tougaloo since shortly after World War II. Ernst's party was a kind of milestone for me, for it was the first integrated party I had ever attended in Jackson, where I had spent the first twenty-one years of my life before going on to graduate school and teaching in another part of the South.

Any uneasy feelings I had about being at Tougaloo were quickly dispelled by Ernst's fascinating guests, many of whom could remember when no white man could enter the Tougaloo campus without risking censure in the pages of the *Jackson Daily News* and being accused of the one unforgivable sin in Mississippi—being a "nigger lover." As the Jack Daniels began to flow, there were signs that maybe things really had changed in Mississippi.

I would be remiss if I did not acknowledge Judy Naylor's substantial contribution to this essay, as well as to the entire book.

A prominent white businessman was engaged in serious conversation with the black President of Tougaloo. A white professor from Jackson was discussing politics with a black Tougaloo professor. And everyone was enjoying himself—a phenomenon which would have seemed impossible as recently as five years before—and no nightriders were waiting on the lawn. The ghost of the old politics was not welcomed in the home of Ernst Borinski.

My vision of a new Mississippi and a new South was soon shattered. We left the party early, for my wife had promised an old college friend we would stop by for a drink, and drove back into Jackson feeling quietly satisfied, at home.

It happened that the husband of my wife's friend was an official of one of the major political parties in Mississippi, a bright, energetic conservative, about thirty years old. After we exchanged the usual Mississippi niceties, the conversation turned to politics.

In response to my question about whether his party would continue to follow the philosophy of Bilbo, Ross Barnett, John Bell Williams, and Big Jim Eastland, my charming young friend quietly proclaimed that these gentlemen were all liberals (except on the race issue) and that what Mississippi needed was some "real conservatives." His argument seemed to hang on the fact that Big Jim Eastland had accepted several hundred thousand dollars from the United States Agriculture Department for not planting cotton on his Sunflower County plantation during the past few years. I could think of several words to describe Eastland's behavior, but "liberal" wasn't one of them. Mostly, I remembered demagogic harangues by Eastland and Barnett against every progressive program the federal government offered, particularly if the program provided any assistance to poor people, black or white. Yet my friend construed their behavior as "liberal."

(I was reminded of a conversation some years earlier with the first Republican elected to the Mississippi legislature since Reconstruction. I had raised with him the identical question about the fundamental differences between the major political parties in Mississippi. To my complete amazement he had replied that he really didn't know what the differences were but that his party literature contained the answer; he would be glad to send me some. The literature never came and some years later he was soundly defeated in a race for Congress. Perhaps the people in his district raised the same question and got the same answer.)

Continuing my conversation with the Mississippi party official, I asked what issues he considered important for Mississippi during the 1970s. Specifically, I asked what his party would say about such problems as rural poverty, substandard education and housing, unemployment, low wages and per capita income, an increasing rate of population growth, and environmental pollution: all barriers to any humane society's achieving its potential. He responded that his party was going to say absolutely nothing about these problems, because election to public office in Mississippi depends more on personality than on issues. To get involved with specific issues was risky business. The party would seek candidates with attractive personalities and say little or nothing of substance about anything else—except for vigorous opposition to the federal government and all programs originating in Washington. The scenario was exactly the same as the Congressional campaign I had witnessed in North Carolina in 1966 when a friend of mine was elected as a Democrat by managing not to take a stand on Vietnam, tobacco, labor, O.E.O., or any other issue relevant in North Carolina. What my Mississippi friend had described was not a new strategy, but a strategy with a proven record of success in the South for the past twenty years. Incidentally, my Mississippi friend was a Republican, but he might very well have been an official of either the Democratic or the Republican party in virtually any Southern state.

At this point I was not very optimistic about finding any significant differences between Republicans and Regular (Wallace) Democrats in Mississippi. (Of course, there was considerable difference between the Republicans and the Loyal Democrats led by Charles Evers and Hodding Carter III.) Perhaps George Wallace was right when he said, "There's not a dime's worth of difference between the Democratic and Republican parties"—at least not in the South. It brought to mind the story of the Mississippi politician who, without changing his party registration, served as a delegate to both the Democratic and Republican state conventions in the same year. And there was the case of the registrar of voters who changed his registration to Republican in 1960 in anticipation of becoming postmaster after a Nixon victory. When this strategy failed, he proceeded to register in the next Democratic primary and was elected clerk of court.

I finally turned to the race issue. Surely it was impossible for the Mississippi Republican Party to challenge old-line Democrats such as Ross Barnett and John Bell Williams on that issue and perhaps, I reasoned, they might even seek to attract some Negro votes through a more moderate stand. (Winthrop Rockefeller had applied this strategy with considerable success in Arkansas in his gubernatorial campaigns in 1966 and 1968.) Whereupon the party official told me Republicans in Mississippi were neither segregationists nor racists, they were neutral on the race isue. "The race issue is a *tool* which should be used only when it is necessary to win elections. Otherwise, it should be ignored, and the less said about it the better." Did this point of view reflect the "Southern Strategy" we had all read about during the past few months—the strategy designed in Washington by those who claim to speak for the South? Was this the essence of the master political plan for the South being skillfully carved out by the Watergate clique in Washington and the expensive public relations firms? The answer was "Yes": that is precisely what the "Southern Strategy" is all about and the proof of its success will be the defeat of George Wallace in Alabama in 1970 and the election of Republican governors in South Carolina, Georgia, Florida, and Texas. None of which, of course, came to pass.

The names were different, but the game was the same one that Democrats like Herman Talmadge, Orval Faubus, Ross Barnett, and Lester Maddox had played in the 1960s. The "Southern Strategy" was nothing more than a variation on an old theme that has pervaded Southern politics for nearly two decades: antagonism toward all federal programs and unremitting opposition to integration. What had been called the "Southern Manifesto" in the 1950s and the "Southern Coalition" in the 1960s was to be known as the "Southern Strategy" in the 1970s. Only this time the "never-never" tune was coming from outside the South and was only being echoed by Southerners.

It can be argued that Southerners have had very little to say about their own destiny at any time during the past one hundred years. Consider the following historical periods. Immediately after the Civil War, during Reconstruction (1865–1877), the South was still under the direct control of the federal government. Federal troops were still on the scene. Although in theory the reins of political power were transferred back to the South around 1877, in practice the region remained at the mercy of Northern business interests for nearly fifty years. The period between 1877 and the late 1920s was characterized by the exploitation of the South's natural resources by Northern capitalists seeking a short-term payoff without regard to the long-term implications of their actions. The allocation of land, timber, minerals, and human resources in the South during this period was determined primarily by forces outside the region. In the 1930s the South was dependent on the New Deal; major decisions affecting it continued to be made by outsiders rather than by Southerners. And of course the story of the 1950s and 1960s is well known.

The ideological polarization so characteristic of our nation in the 1970s had become an established pattern in the South by the early 1960s. The political intransigence of Southern "liberals" and "conservatives" fostered an *ideological isolationism* that resulted in communication barriers on the political, business, and social levels.

The response of white conservatives to the Supreme Court decision of 1954, the Civil Rights Acts of 1964 and 1965, and the entire civil rights movement has been one of reaction and negativism. The term "Southern conservative" came to represent a bastion for the *status quo,* and the party line for both Southern Democrats and Southern Republicans was pure racism. In the name of "states' rights," "racial integrity," and "individual freedom," Southern segregationists fought the civil rights movement every inch of the way.

The white South was swept again into an era of defensive introspection. While the times cried for objectivity and critical self-analysis, Southern political rhetoric and Northern superciliousness only produced frustration, rationalization, and blatant hostility. It was not a new theme in Southern history; the tragedy was the frequency with which it occurred. The only issues were preservation of segregation and hostility to the federal government—issues kept alive by such politicians as Ross Barnett, Orval Faubus, John Bell Williams, George Wallace, and Strom Thurmond.

But while the majority of white Southerners embraced the cause of Southern conservatism, black Southerners and a small number of whites were becoming increasingly liberal. With the success of the sit-in movement, Dr. Martin Luther King, and the Civil Rights Bills of 1964, 1965, and 1966, there came a spirit of renewed optimism on the part of Southern liberals. With John Kennedy and Lyndon Johnson in the White House, they possessed a degree of political clout disproportionate to their limited voting power. As a result, they became so preoccupied with their own political ideology that they failed to realize they were sowing the seeds of their own destruction. For a time between 1964 and 1966, it was possible for Southern liberals to ignore the fact that most of the Southern Congressional delegation was decidedly conservative, because the liberal majority in Congress generally prevailed on gut issues.

Thus, as the programs of the Great Society were being written into law (over the objections of Southern Congressmen), Southern liberals, with a heightened sense of self-importance, became more didactic. Their ideological purity had few mediating qualities, it allowed no compromise, and its abrasive aura of self-righteousness did little to build bridges of communication. And like their conservative counterparts, liberals failed to subject their own programs to scrutiny and self-criticism.

As the tide of the Great Society began to fall and the nation as a whole came to have doubts about the Great Society and its sponsor, Lyndon Johnson, Southern liberals responded with the same platitudes they had used in the early 1960s. Only this time the balance had shifted; many white Southerners who might have been sympathetic in 1962 now chose to take no position or moved into the mainstream of conservative opinion.

The unwillingness of Southern liberals to acknowledge the deficiencies in some of their programs and to seek practical remedies to alleviate these shortcomings left them quite vulnerable. The result was the conspicuous defeat of liberal political candidates on the national, state, and local level throughout the South in the 1968 elections. It is difficult to say whether these results should be credited to the political astuteness of George Wallace and Strom Thurmond, to a protest against government and the system itself, articulated through Wallace, or to the naïveté of Southern liberals.

But despite its adversities and its adversaries, the South has, on a number of occasions, reflected an optimism, a belief in its ability to assume its rightful place in the Republic, no longer burdened with the image of economic backwardness and political reaction and intransigence.

Traveling through the area in 1927, a journalist made this observation: "Down in Dixie they tell you and always with cheerful pride that the South is the new frontier. . . . There is a feel in the air: Big tomorrows seem to be coming around the corner." Unfortunately for the South, that particular "big tomorrow" turned out to be the great depression of the 1930s.

As the distinguished Southern historian C. Vann Woodward has observed, however, the many Southern converts to the gospel of progress and success could never carry a reluctant region with them. There were too many reminders of the Southern experience, an experience that could not be shared with any other part of America: military defeat, occupation, Reconstruction, and moral self-doubt. These experiences can teach us, and the rest of the nation. They are close to the real human experience, closer than most other Americans have gotten. They can form attitudes towards life, if we *recognize* them and *use* them.

Will there be a new South? Mississippi editor Hodding Carter offers us constructive optimism. "The statistics cannot be evaded," says Carter. "It is useless for Southerners to pretend that the region we love is not identical with the region whose faults and needs have been so thoroughly tabulated. But the past does not endure even when men insist that it is unending. The Southern legacies are not eternal and need not be accepted when reason suggests their rejection; *but before rejection or retention, they must be inspected and evaluated and their sources understood.*" I believe that the statistics of the South can be changed—but not until practical solutions are found for the problems of the South which we have previously defined. In particular, we must generate a new breed of political leaders in the South who are long on imagination, innovation, and professional competence and short on political dogma.

For too many years the ground rules for competition between and within the Democratic and Republican parties in the South have been purely racial. The results of the 1970 elections provide substantial evidence that an increasing number of Southerners would like to see these ground rules changed. The Bumpers-Rockefeller campaign in Arkansas demonstrated rather conclusively that it is indeed possible to have a gubernatorial campaign in the South in which race is not an issue. Defying the "Southern Strategy," nonracist moderates were elected in Arkansas, Florida, Georgia, South Carolina, and Texas, joining moderate Republican Linwood Holton of Virginia and moderate Democrat Bob Scott of North Carolina, who were already in office. And to the amazement of everyone, for the first time in as long as people can remember, race was not an issue in the 1971 Democratic primary in the Mississippi gubernatorial contest. With the election of moderates William Waller and William Winter to the positions of Governor and Lieutenant Governor respectively, there is a distinct possibility that the state of Mississippi may once again return to the union.

There are signs that the collapse of the "Southern Strategy" in the 1970 elections may have set loose forces that can liberate both the Democratic and Republican parties in the South from the bondage of racism and reaction. Consider the case of Jim Gardner, the former GOP Congressman from North Carolina who "retired" from politics after failing in 1968 to become governor of the state. Shortly after the November elections in 1970, he returned to the political arena with a speech in Asheboro. Gardner, whose previous political career had been highly racist, surprised North Carolinians by saying that he felt the Republican Party in the state was not representative of minority groups and young people. "Tonight as we gather in Randolph County there is not a black face in this crowd. How can we go out to the people and say we can cure the ills of this state if we cut off 24 percent of our population?" If the Republicans in North Carolina and other Southern states do openly court the Negro vote, the ground rules for competition between the parties could literally change overnight.

Such a strategy would obviously be enhanced if Southern blacks would discontinue their present policy of always voting Democratic. All too often the black vote has gone to the Democrats almost for the asking, without the extraction of any firm commitments from party politicians. But there were exceptions to this rule even in 1970. For example, State Representative Curtis Graves, a leading black politician in Texas and a Democrat, supported Republican George Bush in his Senate race, and Memphis businessman Harold Whalum broke with tradition and supported Winfield Dunn in his successful race for the Governorship of Tennessee. An open Republican party and a more critical black electorate could bode well for the future of politics in the South.

Southern Democrats would have little choice but to emulate the Republicans if they wanted to survive. Politicians might actually be forced to discuss issues other than race and "big government." And for once the Southern people would be the "winners" rather than the party hacks.

Increasingly, a large number of Southerners have a strong desire to seek realistic solutions to the South's problems. Among these Southerners are the moderate governors recently elected in half a dozen Southern states, and the members of the L.Q.C. Lamar Society, whose goals are constructive change through practical solutions to the South's major problems. These individuals (and many others like them) recognize the South's great potential in terms of both human and natural resources. That the South still has a chance to avoid some of the urban and environmental problems of the North is well understood by this new breed. Governor Jimmy Carter of Georgia summarized the philosophy of the Lamar Society at its 1971 Symposium in Atlanta when he said, "I think Southerners now realize that the solution of our problems is our own, and that we can no longer berate the federal government, the Supreme Court, or any other 'outside group' for our own problems, our own needs, our own shortcomings. We are witnessing the birth of a new awareness of the personal responsibility that we share for solving our own problems."

People like these are committed to the premise that Southerners can find practical solutions to such problems as poverty, low per capita income, inadequate schools and housing, inferior health and sanitary conditions, and an excessive rate of population growth. If there is to be a "Southern Strategy," it should be and will be designed by Southerners for the benefit of *all* the people of the South and not merely feed the old retarding mythology which has sustained visions of the past by starving the imagination of government and people alike. Many desire to see the South achieve its full potential, to replace romantic rhetoric, so long the solace of our region, with pragmatic dialogue, and to tell both the Democratic party and the Republican party in the

South that time is running out and that if they want to survive they must replace their racist politics with practical, hardnosed programs capable of yielding positive, progressive solutions to the South's many socioeconomic problems.

Concerned Southerners of either political persuasion and every ideological bent must therefore enter the decade of the seventies by asking themselves some very difficult questions.

The first question is long overdue. "Can political ideology provide the answers to the really pressing problems in the South during the 1970s?" In reality, is it not the *institutions* of our society which serve to interpret and direct our lives? Does not their level of performance in large measure determine the "quality of life"?

One thing seems certain. Our institutions in the South will face new demands in the 1970s. Richard Goodwin, speaking of the nation as a whole, warns us that "many of our institutions, including our political parties themselves, are led by men who developed their ideas in response to earlier demands and are therefore unable to understand or cope with a newer set of problems. . . . When institutions and leaders are faced with demands they barely understand, their reaction is often to become rigid and defensive, and even angry. . . . A people suffering from institutions that can't respond, problems that are mutually left untouched and the myriad of uncertainties in their own private and public existence must inevitably rise in protest." No matter what label we use—"student radicals," "white backlash," "black militancy," "silent majority," "hard hats"—all are responses to and symbols of the institutional crisis in our nation. The South is no exception.

What can be done to ameliorate the problem of *institutional obsolescence* in the South without further contributing to the problem of *ideological isolationism?* We shall examine some of the important institutions as we outline a Southern "strategy for change" based on two simple premises. *First,* Southerners should spend more time discussing the common problems of the region and less time arguing political ideology. *Second,* Southerners need to learn to ask the right questions about their region and its problems.

High on the list of problems about which Southerners need to become more perceptive is education. In the heat of the school integration debate, we have all but lost sight of the more fundamental problem of quality education. Only recently many Southerners have become aware of the significant differences between the educational system of the South and educational systems in other parts of the country. Although these differences are partly attributable to the economic inefficiency of attempting to operate a dual school system, they also reflect a number of other factors, not the least of which is that the South is the poorest region in our nation. Long before the integration crisis in the South, teacher salaries and expenditures per pupil were lower there than elsewhere. Compulsory education laws were not enforced, and dropout rates were noticeably high. All too often our public education leaders have been bound by tradition and have been reluctant to experiment with new concepts and ideas at times when they were needed most. Although it may be accurate to say that most Southerners were not really aware of the inadequacies of their educational system, it might also be argued that the region as a whole was not fully committed to the concept of a first-rate educational system for all of its children. Now that racial integration is the rule rather than the exception, the South may find it possible to focus more attention on questions relating to "quality education." The list is long and complex, including such issues as curriculum reform, educational parks, preschool programs, a twelve-month school year, school board representation, and student rights and responsibilities, to mention only a few. Surely the development of an educational system that will serve the region well requires a total commitment on the part of every community. No school board, superintendent, or PTA can be expected to achieve these results without the kind of public support that thus far has not been in evidence in the South.

A Southern Strategy

Perhaps each Southern state should assemble a broadly-based citizens' committee on public education to (1) define some new goals for public education during the 1970s, (2) evaluate critically the existing educational system, (3) design a prototype educational system to achieve the educational goals, and (4) attempt to sell the new educational program to the state legislature, county commissions, city councils, and the "educational establishment."

A disturbing by-product of the integration crises in the public schools of the South is the renewed growth of private "segregation academies" for children of white, middle- and upper-income diehards. Although these underfinanced, ill-equipped, understaffed institutions serve a relatively small (but increasing) percentage of the population, their generally inferior quality lends support to the argument that Southerners have not always been judicious in evaluating the quality of their educational program. These segregation academies represent a serious threat to the survival of good public education in some areas of the South. Numbered among the students in these private academies are children from some of the more influential families. Without the support of these families, school bond elections are defeated, the quality of representation on school boards deteriorates, and the entire public education program suffers. Southern educators and journalists need to examine closely these segregation academies and the impact they are having on the attitude toward and the quality of public education in the South.

Higher education in the South suffers from many of the same problems plaguing the public schools: a lack of economic resources and a poorly defined concept of quality education on the college and university level. The latter can be explained in part by the preponderance of "inbreeding" within the educational institutions themselves and the strongly political overtones attached to the appropriations a state legislature makes to its colleges and universities. The universities are the favorite football tossed about in the ideological and political forays of a state legislature. Even so, while no Southern university has achieved a position of national eminence, some of our universities are highly respected for a number of excellent departments.

As we enter the seventies, perhaps the distinguishing characteristic of Southern universities in the mind of the general public is not their level of academic achievement but the absence of a large and vocal radical student element. But no Southerner, be he a college administrator or a taxpaying citizen, should feel smug. We have no reason to believe that Southern students will be any less angry than their counterparts elsewhere when they discover how badly managed are our institutions of higher education in the South.

Serving to compound the problem of misallocation of resources in the South, a new trend emerged in the state university systems —multiple universities or the "regional university." State colleges began seeking ways to increase their prestige, their enrollments, and their budgets, and the most popular method was the establishment of new or larger graduate programs and increased political pressure for university status. That such a trend developed throughout the South is not surprising, given the competition that has always existed in educational circles and between geographical regions. Some of the poorest states in the South attempt to support the largest number of universities, which vary significantly in quality.

Among many state universities in the South one finds a near obsession with intercollegiate athletics, particularly football. A view widely held by Southern state university administrators is that success on the football field yields immediate access to the legislative purse strings. Commenting on the fact that the bulk of a $3.5 million gift to the University of South Carolina was to be used for expansion of the football stadium, a university trustee said, "To put that kind of money into a concrete memorial [to a former University athletic director] instead of building additional classrooms or creating a scholarship fund for needy students is stupidity at its highest."

A Southern Strategy

Higher education in the South (and in the nation) suffers from a lack of imagination and innovation, poor economic policies, antiquated management techniques, and a frantic competition for funds and prestige—realities that taxpayers, alumni, and students are beginning to recognize. University reform will become an even greater issue, both on and off the campus, in the seventies. It would appear that the South has only two options with regard to higher education. It can maintain the *status quo* and surely invite the explosive events of Berkeley, Columbia, Harvard, and Madison, or it can begin to seek reform in organization, administration, curriculum, and student representation in university affairs. The latter course of action will not only serve to mollify students, alumni, and taxpayers; it will also greatly strengthen the basic foundations of the university and serve to attract noted scholars from other parts of the country. Finally, Southern colleges and universities need to become more outward-looking in their relationships with the communities and states which they serve. It is crucial that they strengthen their ties with the rest of the nation and indeed the rest of the world. It is a formidable task; but regional development demands a quality educational system.

The 1960s represented a period of dynamic growth for the South's economy. Median family income increased 48 percent, a more rapid rate than in any other region. The median income for Negro men rose 178 percent. Personal income in the South increased more rapidly than in the rest of the country, and there was a significant decrease in the number and percentage of persons in the region living in poverty. But despite substantial improvement during the 1960s, the South still lags behind the nation in per capita personal income, with a 1970 average of $3062, compared to $3910 for the nation as a whole. The range ran all the way from a low of $2358 in Mississippi to a high of $3372 in Florida. Regardless of the measure used, the South is still the poorest region in the United States. Why does it continue to lag behind the rest of the nation in economic well-being? What are some of the causes of the South's retarded economic growth? What policy alternatives are available which might lead to accelerated economic growth and to a more equitable distribution of income in the South?

The South has never fully shared in the affluence of the nation. C. Vann Woodward notes that this aspect of the Southern experience has contributed significantly to the Southerner's strong sense of identity with his region and its people. Historical evidence indicates that the Southern economy, with its dependence on a one-crop agricultural economy and absence of industrial development, was in decline before the Civil War, which only hastened a process already begun. The closing decades of the nineteenth century were a crazy juxtaposition of economic exploitation by Northern capital, Southern "New South" spokesmen vigorously asserting the region's economic growth potential, and an economic depression that gave rise to a strong Populist movement in several Southern states.

Agriculture continued to dominate, with industrial gains made primarily by low-skilled, low-paying industries. Virtually all capital came from outside the South, and control rested in the corporate offices of New York City.

State legislatures contributed to this demoralization by demonstrating appalling ignorance of economic policy and the economic structure of their own region. Because of the adoption of regressive tax structures, tax revenues were dependent on high sales taxes on such essential items as food and clothing. On the other hand, elaborate schemes were developed to serve as financial incentives for industries relocating in the South, often without a careful evaluation of the social costs and social benefits of such inducements.

Southern labor, while plentiful, was unskilled, adversely affecting the quality of industrial growth. Instead of bolstering public education, developing more vocational programs, or fighting illiteracy, Southern Congressional leaders concentrated their efforts on the "pork barrel," with such success that the South became a favored location for large military complexes. In more recent decades the aerospace industries and related government agencies have had a tremendous effect on the economies of several Southern states, especially Alabama, Florida, and Texas. But "defense industries" are subject to such uncertainty that an economy dependent on them is extremely unstable.

An important task for state planners, industrial boards, and economists is to determine what sort of industrial "mix" is best for their respective states. The recent growth of high-skill and research-oriented industries is an encouraging sign that the South can and must diversify. This will require imagination and entrepreneurship by private and public sectors in the Southern states. But, more important, it will require skilled labor, strong and progressive educational systems, and harmonious racial relationships.

Economic development should be based on sound planning rather than intuition and political pressures. The interests of each state would be better served if state governments concentrated more on competent planning departments and less on "industry-hunting boondoggles." (The latter approach, a favored alternative of many Southern states, may very well be the least efficient means of attracting new industry.)

Jon Nordheimer of *The New York Times* offers us some well-chosen words of caution:

> *If the vices of the old economic system are simply replaced with the vices of the new—pollution, unrooted families, and de facto segregation—the South will have missed an opportunity. But if it seizes every chance to improve its condition, it could very well emerge from the 1970s in a position to challenge the leadership of the North for the first time in more than a century—not to secede from the Union but to help salvage it.*

You Can't Eat Magnolias

Despite the typically Southern images of a North Carolina tobacco field, a Delta plantation, or a Tennessee hill farm, the fact is that the "New South" will be an urban South. During the past decade, for the first time since Reconstruction, more people moved into the South than out of it. Furthermore, the population of the South is becoming urbanized at twice the rate of the North. While cities like Houston, Dallas, and Atlanta are obvious manifestations of the new urban South, a more interesting phenomenon has been the emergence of smaller cities such as Charlotte, Memphis, Columbia, Jackson, Little Rock and Nashville, on a scale unheard of in the Northeast and North Central United States. The South, through a fortuitous chain of events, has established the overwhelming preponderance of its population in smaller cities. But in addition to their size, Southern cities enjoy other advantages. First, they are less dependent on heavy manufacturing as a major source of employment. Second, they are less densely settled than cities in the tradition of New York and Chicago. Third, Southern cities have been spared the maze of governmental bureaucracy that paralyzes so many cities, as they have opted for fewer governmental units with a wider range of authority. Fourth, they are fortunate in having been built later, and thus have less decay.

But, as Joel Fleishman has noted, "To the extent that our cities are different from other cities in the country, and to the extent that those differences are potentially advantageous to us, the main reason for the difference is time. . . . What time has given us, time itself will take away." The continued urbanization of the South at an accelerated rate poses new problems and new opportunities. To prevent urban growth from becoming urban sprawl, to continue the practice of minimal governmental units, and to maintain a diversified economic and residential base within the central city, there must be a rational and systematic growth policy. Now that in-migration into the South exceeds out-migration and our rate of urbanization continues to grow, we may be faced with a population problem in our urban areas comparable to that of the cities of the

North. Perhaps the South can lead the nation in the development of rational population policies which provide family-planning information and services and legalized abortion.

In the early 1930s a group of Southerners wrote a book extolling the virtues of Southern agrarianism. Entitled *I'll Take My Stand,* it was based on the premise that the life style of the Southern agrarian was to be desired over the emerging patterns of urban life and served as an eloquent apology for the relatively slow rate of economic development in the South. But since that time the influence of agrarianism has been rather clearly on the decline. We have already acknowledged the fact that the "New South" will be an urban civilization. But will it be a humane civilization?

Some social scientists have argued that the best way to help the rural poor in Appalachia and the Mississippi Delta is to encourage them to leave these areas and to move to locations where opportunities are greater. However, the rapid growth of Southern cities and the problems that accompany such growth (including problems of environmental pollution) require one to take a second look at this policy. Perhaps we should seek ways of attracting more people to rural areas so that Southern cities will not become unmanageable monoliths of congregation and confusion. (Terry Sanford's proposed Southern Regional Growth Board gets at the heart of this problem.) In his article entitled "The New Agrarians," Taylor Branch says, "No system exists that can guarantee both the secure tranquillity of the farm ethic and the material advancement and change of the hustlers. The challenge—to have economic growth without environmental or ethical damage—is a personal one." Perhaps we can "even discover a new entrepreneurship, creating enterprises that give people enriching work without making the world ugly or dangerous."

But while planners, journalists, economists, blue-collar workers, bankers, and even Southern expatriates dream of what the South might become, the politicians continue their harangues against the federal government, "outside agitators," or any individual who attempts to illustrate institutional deficiencies. As Richard Goodwin has observed, "Asking many of today's institutions to respond to new needs is a little like putting a man on a windowsill and asking him to fly. Not only was he not built for flight but if you keep insisting he's likely to turn around and punch you in the nose." Southern educational institutions, like the economy of the rural South, were not designed to carry the burdens they are being forced to assume. The same can be said of state legislatures that must act upon questions of great importance with little or no information from professional consultants or a qualified staff, using archaic administrative and parliamentary procedures, working under severe time constraints, and representing electoral districts of disproportionate sizes.

Institutions should serve the people—not vice versa. The history of our nation has been of evolutionary institutional change. But institutional change in the South has more often been the result of precipitous events than of pragmatic goals. It is time for Southerners to initiate their changes in a thoughtful and judicious manner. It is time for men of good faith to reason together.

One of the ironies of Southern history is that a people with such a fierce desire to shape their own destiny have, in reality, abrogated their responsibilities in a tragic quest of racial illusions. The South's "mythology" has blurred the vision and consumed the energies and imagination of her native sons. Southerners have always sensed that the real decisions affecting their lives were being made in places far from home. (Therefore, it seemed logical to assume that anyone advocating change in the South was by geography, or frame of mind, an outsider.) In the words of Lucius Quintus Cincinnatus Lamar, one of the South's most gifted statesmen, "Our people have suffered so much, have been betrayed so often by those in whom they had strongest reason to confide, that it is but natural that they should be suspicious of any word or act of overture to the North by a Southern man.... It is time for a public man to try to serve the South, and not to subserve her irritated feelings." It is time for problem-solving to replace political ideology as the focal point of Southern politics. If the South is to determine its own destiny, then the people of the South must see and understand the choices. It is conceivable that this time it is the South's turn to save the Union.

I believe that both the "Americanization of the South" and the "Southernization of the Nation" are goals worthy of pursuit by all Americans, whether they happen to live in the South or not. And the model set so eloquently by L.Q.C. Lamar in 1878 may still be applicable today: "The liberty of this country and its great interests will never be secure if its public men become mere menials to do the biddings of their constituents instead of being representative in the true sense of the word, looking to the lasting prosperity and future interests of the whole country." Both the South and the nation need more public men.

APPENDIX: EXCERPTS FROM THE INAUGURAL ADDRESSES OF FIVE SOUTHERN GOVERNORS

GOVERNOR LINWOOD HOLTON
Richmond, Virginia
January 17, 1970

. . . AT the dawn of the 1970s it is clear that problem-solving, and not philosophical principles, has become the focal point of politics, both in Virginia and in the nation.

No longer can we be divided into opposing camps of political philosophy. No longer is there complete disagreement between "conservatives" and "liberals" about the problems confronting us or the need for their resolution. Old clichés have now blurred and old dogmas have died.

The common belief is that state government must act, that the future of states' rights rests upon the success of state efforts. No more must the slogan of "states' rights" sound a recalcitrant and defensive note for the people of the South. For the era of defiance is behind us.

In its place is the challenge posed by the late twentieth century. Moreover, it is evident that the federal government alone has not coped and cannot cope with this challenge. So much of the national government's attention must be given to our commitments abroad; and even its massive domestic programs have failed to halt the decay of our cities, the exploitation of our rural resources, the rising crime on our streets, and the befoulment of our environment.

John W. Gardner, chairman of the Urban Coalition, recently spoke on the nation's apparent incapacity to launch meaningful solutions to its problems. "We know our lakes are dying," he said, "our rivers growing filthier daily, our atmosphere increasingly polluted. We are aware of the racial tensions that would tear the nation apart. We understand that oppressive poverty in the midst of affluence is intolerable. We see that our cities are sliding toward disaster. . . . But we are seized by a kind of paralysis of the will. It is like a waking nightmare."

The great task of state government is to dispel this nightmare, to overcome this paralysis of the will. We are fortunate in Virginia. Environmental decay has not yet beset us as it has the great cities of the Northeast and southern California. There is still time here to see that Virginians have both material progress *and* a dignified, enjoyable, and lastingly productive place to live.

This administration intends to move forward immediately on all fronts against the deterioration of our environment. We are determined to make the quality of our air and water, the safety of our streets, the core of our cities, the development and preservation of recreational areas top priority public concerns.

We intend further to continue the development of our educational system at every level. We must see that our youth are prepared for the complexities and changes their generation will face; and we must engage them actively in the identification of major concerns and in finding solutions to those problems. We must make our highway system adequate for the demands of a mobile population, and we must find some way to save our urban areas from traffic strangulation. We must develop fully the potential of our great natural harbors and waterways. We must offer every incentive possible to persuade industries to locate in our rural areas so that their young people will not migrate to cities already overpopulated. We must seek a new partnership with the federal government to insure that Virginia will receive the full benefit of federal funds and programs available to it. . . .

The durability of our nation and civilization will be in the end determined by how we have responded not only to external problems but, more importantly, to our problems from within. One of the foremost of these is obviously that of racial discrimination.

Here in Virginia we must see that no citizen of the Commonwealth is excluded from full participation in both the blessings and responsibilities of our society because of his race. We will have a government based on a partnership of all Virginians, a government in which there will be neither partisanship nor prejudice of any kind.

As Virginia has been a model for so much else in America in the past, let us now endeavor to make today's Virginia a model in race relations. Let us, as Lincoln said, insist upon an open society "with malice toward none; charity for all."

To succeed, this quest for an open society must involve all of us, not just the leaders of government. We earnestly ask the active participation of our business and professional leaders, the heads of our schools and universities, our labor chiefs and legislators, our local governments, leaders of minorities, and all individual citizens. Let our goal in Virginia be an aristocracy of ability, regardless of race, color, or creed.

It is now almost two hundred years since Thomas Jefferson and George Washington, Patrick Henry and James Madison inspired the birth of our nation. All through the early years of our Republic, it was Virginia which guided the nation's destiny. For long after the Civil War, Virginia's people had to overcome the hardships of poverty and defeat. But they succeeded.

Today a new vigor, similar to that of two hundred years ago, has caught our people. It is an honor to become governor at such a time. We accept a challenge which Daniel Webster once expressed in these words:

"Let us develop the resources of our land, call forth its powers, build up its institutions, promote all its great interests, and see whether we also, in our day and generation, may not perform something worthy to be remembered."

This challenge summons us forth again today, and, with God's help, we shall succeed.

GOVERNOR REUBIN ASKEW
Tallahassee, Florida
January 5, 1971

... Florida, for all of its virtues, has one of the poorest tax structures in the country. We have stacked burdensome consumer taxes and property taxes on middle- and low-income families while granting special tax favors to the politically influential.

The time has come for this to end.

We said several months ago that, if we were honest with ourselves, we would have to admit that this is going to be one of those years in which the question would not be whether there will be new state taxes—but, rather, who will have to pay. The hard facts of the financial crisis that faces us today are now dawning on even the most optimistic among us.

Some have said that instead of closing the loopholes and requiring profit-making corporations to pay their fair share, we should once again raise the sales tax to solve our revenue problems. Let me say that for the legislature to *even consider* increasing the sales tax in Florida to 5 percent, while our tax inequities still exist, would be a complete travesty of justice. Continually turning to higher consumer and property taxes to pay for needed public services without facing up to tax inequities is the answer of yesterday....

You Can't Eat Magnolias

It has been said that government cannot solve all of society's problems. In that, I could not agree more. But political leadership can provide a commitment to progress and it can, by its own success, restore confidence in what can be done by individuals.

None of the responsibilities before us today will be carried out by words or platitudes. It is not enough merely to acknowledge the problems of our senior citizens—or to give pious lip service to the justifiably urgent needs of our black citizens—or to be aware of the miserable living conditions of many of the migrant workers who help bring our crops to market. The commitment to make government work will not be meaningful without the courage to face squarely and honestly the difficult issues before us. And, as we outline the goals of this administration, it should be clearly understood that we are not blind to the controversy and difference of opinion which may result. We are not blind to the fact that all will not agree with the course we are setting. But we see the responsibility of this administration to provide the leadership and the direction for this state and its people.

And, regardless of the difficulty or the controversy, *we will not abdicate that responsibility*.

The journey of a thousand miles begins with the first step. We take this step with optimism, confident that man—who has touched the stars—can reach back to this earth and solve the problems confronting us. We take this step with the realization that this is the greatest country on this earth, with a foundation built on the dignity and the highest aspirations of man. . . .

GOVERNOR DALE BUMPERS
Little Rock, Arkansas
January 12, 1971

. . . I consider the solution to all of these problems both progressive and forward-looking necessities. But the realization of these will not depend on me alone. It must be a group effort. To fund some of these programs will require still another look at our projected revenues and the probability of additional revenues. I hope the General Assembly will invite me back in about two weeks to present precise concrete proposals on the revenues I believe will be necessary and the sources I believe best from which to derive them.

The people of Arkansas are looking for new approaches, new attitudes, and new initiatives. To help in this search our administration will be one of open minds and open doors. The future we envision must be shaped and shared by all Arkansans: old and young, black and white, rich and poor. I appeal to the best in our people to meet this challenge.

I believe that the collective thought of our people is that we are capable of mastering our own fate in a manner befitting the highest humanistic principles. This administration will be one of concern, compassion, and reality. Our mandate is to correct or eliminate those things which are wrong and build on those things which are right.

I invite you all to join me in a rededication, in a covenant for the good of our state. . . .

GOVERNOR JIMMY CARTER
Atlanta, Georgia
January 12, 1971

. . . Our people are our most precious possession and we cannot afford to waste the talents and abilities given by God to one single Georgian. Every adult illiterate, every school dropout, every untrained retarded child is an indictment of us all. Our state pays a terrible and continuing human and financial price for these failures. It is time to end this waste. If Switzerland and Israel and other people can eliminate illiteracy, then so can we.

At the end of a long campaign, I believe I know our people as well as anyone. Based on this knowledge of Georgians north and south, rural and urban, liberal and conservative, I say to you quite frankly that the time for racial discrimination is over. Our people have already made this major and difficult decision, but we cannot underestimate the challenge of hundreds of minor decisions yet to be made. Our inherent human charity and our religious beliefs will be taxed to the limit. No poor, rural, weak, or black person should ever have to bear the additional burden of being deprived of the opportunity of an education, a job, or simple justice. We Georgians are fully capable of making our own judgments and managing our own affairs. We who are strong or in positions of leadership must realize that the responsibility for making correct decisions in the future is ours.

Georgia is a state of great natural beauty and promise, but the quality of our natural surroundings is threatened because of avarice, selfishness, procrastination, and neglect. Change and development are necessary for (our) growth . . . for the progress of our agricultural, recreational, and industrial life. Our challenge is to insure that such activities avoid destruction and dereliction of our environment. . . .

GOVERNOR JOHN C. WEST
Columbia, South Carolina
January 19, 1971

. . . It is appropriate on this occasion that we set for ourselves certain goals, goals whose urgency and priority at this moment in our history cannot be questioned. The time has arrived when South Carolina for all time must break loose and break free of the vicious cycle of ignorance, illiteracy, and poverty which has retarded us throughout our history.

If to some these goals seem too lofty, impossible of achievement or unrealistic, I submit that nothing is impossible if we unite together with energy, determination, and dedication toward a common cause.

Appendix

We can, and we shall, in the next four years eliminate hunger and malnutrition and their attendant suffering from our state.

We can, and we shall, in the next four years initiate new and innovative programs which will in our time provide adequate housing for all our citizens.

We can, and we shall, this year initiate far-reaching programs to provide more doctors, nurses and health personnel as well as better systems for delivery of health care to each citizen. Our goal shall be that each citizen may live with proper protection from disease and proper treatment of illness for his full life expectancy.

We can, and we shall, in the next four years eliminate from our government any vestige of discrimination because of race, creed, sex, religion, or any other barrier to fairness for all citizens.

We pledge to minority groups no special status other than full-fledged responsibility in a government that is totally colorblind.

We can, and we shall, accelerate programs of industrial and agricultural development until every citizen who is underemployed has the opportunity for full and rewarding employment and every young person has a job opportunity that is productive, meaningful, and challenging.

We can, and we shall, strengthen our law enforcement system by providing better training, better pay, and better equipment for our officers; by strengthening our laws and court procedures dealing with criminals; and by working for the removal of the root causes of crime.

We can, and we shall, seek and channel the energy, dedication and social consciousness of our young people into solving the problems of our times.

We do not need—and we cannot afford—an alienation of the generations, and I pledge that this will be an administration which actively seeks the involvement of the young and old alike.

We can, and we shall, in the next four years take whatever action is necessary to assure the preservation of our living environment and to provide the type of resource management which will make it possible for all interests in our society to live in harmony with each other. There need not be—and there shall not be—economic or ecological sacrifice in the progress of South Carolina in the next four years.

Finally, and perhaps most important of all, we can, and we shall, provide a better educational opportunity for all citizens of whatever age or status, from a comprehensive preschool program for the very young to a continuing educational program for adults ranging from basic literacy to sophisticated, advanced research-oriented graduate programs.

The setting of these goals is in itself an important first step toward their ultimate accomplishment, and—in all candor—this first step is perhaps the easiest. Certainly it is the simplest. But if these words can launch our state into positive action, if they can unleash the energies of our people and their government toward solutions, then they will have proved to be a valuable first step.

More important than action and good intentions at this point must be the establishment of guiding principles to direct and channel our efforts in this undertaking. Basically, I see three principles to be of immediate and primary importance.

First, the goals as stated must be accorded priority status. In today's complex society with constantly increasing demands and expectations of people, there is a tendency to overlook fundamental problems and to scattergun society's thrust on less essential, but more glamorous functions. In a state with limited financial resources, we must concentrate with laser-beam accuracy on the basic human problems, using the constant criterion of progress for people toward these stated goals.

Second, the achievement of these goals can become a reality only if the people of this state unite and work together, putting aside differences of race, politics, generation, or other. Two thousand years ago, the greatest philosopher and teacher who ever lived said, "And if a Kingdom be divided against itself, that Kingdom cannot stand, and if a house be divided against itself, that house cannot stand." The politics of race and divisiveness have been soundly repudiated in South Carolina. We are all one—God's people—and our differences, whether they be age, sex, religion, or race, should be considered as blessings and strengths. . . .

Third, in directing our efforts toward achievements which have eluded man throughout his time on earth, we must have the active involvement of all citizens. Government is but the instrument of the will of the people—having no power in and of itself, deriving not just its power, but its will and its effectiveness from its citizens. It is not our purpose to change that relationship; it is our goal to strengthen it. What we outline today in terms of human progress are not simply governmental projects. If we are to eliminate hunger, provide better housing, improve the delivery of health care for all, we must have the deep involvement and commitment of the private sector working in close cooperation with the public sector and providing necessary support from our whole free enterprise system.

If we are to bring the generations together, if we are to eliminate discrimination, it requires more than a law or mandate from government. Basic to all our hopes and aspirations is the willingness of our people to accept change and to gain a new respect for the opinions and the rights of all people. . . .

THE L.Q.C. LAMAR SOCIETY

[THE instincts which produced this book are rooted in a specific time and place. The people who wrote it were brought together as a result of new stirrings in the region, a growing belief that to be a Southerner in the 1970s is to know that more things are possible for us than they were for our fathers and grandfathers. Southerners of our generation and those to come will not have their energy caged by a "way of life" that was morally barren. No longer will we have to bear the mark of a historic sin, nor will we have to starve our imagination by feeding the old, retarding myths. In the words of the spiritual, "We are free, thank God, free at last."

But what were we to do with that freedom? That was the question which on November 21, 1969, brought us to Quail Roost, a country estate outside Durham, now owned by the University of North Carolina.

We were there to define a role for a proposed new Southern organization, the L.Q.C. Lamar Society, named for a Mississippi statesman who had been a fire-brand secessionist but who, in the 1870s, became a spokesman for reconciliation between the races and regions.

As the debate developed, two distinct definitions of the proposed organization emerged. One side, impatient with temporizing educational organizations, wanted the Lamar Society to become an activist ideological and political association. They saw great potential in an organization which would raise money and perform other supportive tasks for candidates whose views the Lamar Society approved.

That view did not prevail, for the majority was skeptical about the effectiveness of such an organization. Their skepticism was fed by visiting the graves of ideo-political groups of the right and left which had sprung up in the South, lived a short, frenzied life, and then perished with few mourners and fewer good works. It was predicted that a regional political organization would die of implosion, sucked to death by its members' fights over ideological purity and the insistence of the directors from each state that their own candidate for governor should have first priority.

By the morning of November 23, the issue was resolved. The Lamar Society would welcome men and women who believed the South could achieve practical solutions to its problems, regardless of whether these men and women were liberal or conservative, white or black, Democrat or Republican, establishment or student. The Society would be a network of Southern competence, linking educators, political leaders, the professions, communicators, businessmen and students of the states of the old Confederacy plus Kentucky. It would spread confidence among Southerners seeking constructive change through knowledge that they were not alone, that there were thousands from Dallas to Miami, Atlanta to Louisville who shared their ideals. It would be a conduit which could trap and disseminate good ideas before they were lost in the journals of professional and learned societies. It would be a meeting place drawing together many different talents and instincts to examine our society, applying intelligence to define the traditions worth perpetuating and the changes that would replace old ways with something of value. Finally, it would be a catalyst which actually *made things happen.*

Late that morning a temporary board was selected under the chairmanship of W. J. Michael Cody, a prominent young Memphis attorney. It was a representative group which included a congressman, three blacks, editors, educators and businessmen. Watts Hill, Jr., chairman of Home Security Life Insurance, whose father had given Quail Roost to the University of North Carolina, was there. Willie Morris, one the South's best known literary expatriates, was there, too. But perhaps most symbolic was the presence of two young men from Mississippi: Hodding Carter III, editor of the *Delta Democrat-Times* and courageous spokesman for young white liberals in the South, and Stewart Gammill III, chairman of Interpine, Inc., a young man of considerable means, finely and genuinely conservative in manner, dress and politics.

All the prospective board members were as diverse as Hodding and Stewart, yet a common denominator revealed itself when Mike Cody asked each one at the table to say what he thought the Lamar Society could do for the South. As they talked I wondered if the idea for *I'll Take My Stand* hadn't grown out of some similar setting at Vanderbilt. I remembered that the Agrarians were mostly young men. Their views were not identical, but there was a kind of corporate communion among them, an agreement more instinctive than verbal, a shared reverence for the permanence of nature and devotion to a certain kind of South.

The views they held in common were expressed with great literary distinction by men of integrity and sensitivity. There is some advice still worth heeding in *I'll Take My Stand,* advice which has survived the forty-one years since it was published. On the whole, however, the Agrarians spoke of a people and a place that never existed and could never have, and in some respects never should have.

Perhaps it is time, I thought, for a new definition of the South, by a new generation of Southerners, just as deeply devoted to their region as the Agrarians but more democratic and realistic. When I suggested the idea for this book to Tom Naylor, the real founder and energy cell of the Lamar Society, he took it up immediately. It is mostly because of his persistence and organizational ability that this new voice is raised, not defensively, in answer to the

Agrarians, but as a positive new statement about the South in our time.

Like the Agrarians, the authors of this volume achieved a common approach, even though they never met formally to discuss the book and they come to their different topics from a variety of backgrounds. There is agreement achieved by a deeper understanding, the consensus which produced the Lamar Society and that is rapidly reshaping the politics of the region.

What follows are the dry details of the lives of the contributors. The personality of each cannot be reduced to any abstract collection of facts but speaks through what each has written here. There is one name missing from the biographical list. Betsy Morton is not the author of any single chapter but her editorial assistance was literally invaluable to the editors.

—H. B. A.

Anniston, Alabama
June 17, 1971

BIOGRAPHICAL NOTES

[WALLACE M. ALSTON, JR., Senior Minister of the First Presbyterian Church of Durham, North Carolina, was born in 1934 in Lexington, Kentucky. He received his B.A. from Emory University and his B.D. and Th.D from Union Theological Seminary in Virginia. He has also studied at the Harvard Divinity School and the University of Zurich in Switzerland. Mr. Alston is a member of the Council on Church and Society and the Joint Advisory Committee on Worship and Music of the Presbyterian Church of the United States, and is chairman of the Urban Council of the Granville Presbytery.

H. BRANDT AYERS was born in Anniston, Alabama in 1935, and was graduated in journalism from the University of Alabama. He has served as a capitol and legislative reporter for the *Raleigh* (North Carolina) *Times* and as Washington correspondent in a news bureau serving Southern and Southwestern newspapers. Now editor and publisher of *The Anniston Star* and vice-president of the Anniston Broadcasting Company, Mr. Ayers was the 1968 recipient of the National Headliner Award for an exposé of corruption in the Anniston city government. During 1967–1968 he was a Nieman Fellow at Harvard. He was the founding president of the Alabama Journalism Foundation and a member of the board of Talladega College and the advisory board of the University of Alabama in Birmingham. Mr. Ayers is a member of the board of the National Conference of Christians and Jews, President of the L.Q.C. Lamar Society, and a former member of the Board of Directors of the Society.

Biographical Notes

JACK BASS was born in South Carolina in 1934 and was graduated in 1956 from the University of South Carolina School of Journalism. He was a Nieman fellow at Harvard in 1965–66 and is now Columbia Bureau Chief for the *Charlotte* (North Carolina) *Observer* and part-time lecturer at the University of South Carolina. In 1968, Mr. Bass was named South Carolina newspaperman of the year by Sigma Delta Chi. He is co-author with Jack Nelson of the recently published *Orangeburg Massacre,* a book based on the events surrounding the 1968 killing of protesting students at South Carolina State College. Mr. Bass is a member of the Lamar Society.

NORTON L. BEACH, Dean of the School of Education at the University of North Carolina at Chapel Hill, was graduated from Boston University in 1938. He did graduate work at Boston University and Columbia University, where he received his Ed.D. degree in 1949. Dr. Beach has collaborated on a number of community survey reports and several books on education. He is a former member of the Chapel Hill School Board and is a member of the Lamar Society.

RONALD S. BOROD is an attorney in his native city of Memphis, Tennessee. A *magna cum laude* graduate of Princeton University in 1963, he received his J.D. degree from Harvard Law School and his LL.M. degree in taxation from the New York University School of Law. His articles have appeared in the *New Republic,* the *New York University Law Review,* and the *Southern Journal.* He is a member of the boards of the Memphis and Shelby County Legal Services Association and the Health and Welfare Planning Council of Memphis and Shelby County, and is a member of the L.Q.C. Lamar Society.

VIRGIL CHRISTIAN is associate professor of economics at the University of Kentucky, from which he received his B.A. in 1947 and his Ph.D. in 1955. He has served as a statistical consultant to a number of Kentucky legislative research commissions and as codirector of Negro Employment in the South, a project sponsored by the Office of Manpower Administration. His publications include articles on Negro employment and the Southern economy. His paper with Dr. Marshall, "Human Resource Development in the South," was presented at the April 1970 Lamar Society symposium in Memphis and at the Southern Governors' Conference in Biloxi, Mississippi, in September 1970. Dr. Christian is a member of several honorary and professional organizations and of the L.Q.C. Lamar Society.

REESE CLEGHORN was born in 1930 in Lyerly, Georgia, and received a B.A. in journalism from Emory University and an M.A. in public law and government from Columbia. An experienced journalist, Mr. Cleghorn is currently editor of the editorial page of the *Charlotte* (North Carolina) *Observer.* He was previously director of the leadership project of the Southern Regional Council and editor of its monthly publication, *South Today.* He is coauthor with Pat Watters of *Climbing Jacob's Ladder,* a book on the civil rights movement and the South, and has contributed to several other books. In addition, his articles have been published in *Esquire,* the *Saturday Review, The New Republic,* and *The New York Times Magazine.* He is a member of the L.Q.C. Lamar Society.

JAMES CLOTFELTER, assistant professor of political science at Emory University, is a native of Birmingham, Alabama. He studied at the University of Wisconsin and at the University of North Carolina at Chapel Hill, where he received his undergraduate degree in 1965 and his Ph.D. in 1969. A member of the L.Q.C. Lamar Society, Dr. Clotfelter has published articles in the *Journal of Politics* and the *New South,* and has contributed to a number of books. He was formerly a reporter for the *Atlanta Journal* and for *Time* Magazine.

W.J. MICHAEL CODY, a Memphis native, was graduated from Southwestern University at Memphis in 1958 and holds a law degree from the University of Virginia Law School. Now an attorney in Memphis, Mr. Cody is a member of the National Board of Directors of the American Civil Liberties Union and is founder and past president of its West Tennessee branch. In addition, he is vice-chairman of the Greater Memphis Urban Development Corporation and a member of the Memphis and Shelby County Democratic Executive Committee. Mr. Cody was the first President of the Lamar Society and has been instrumental in the creation of the Society's public interest law firm.

Biographical Notes

JAMES S. FERGUSON, Chancellor of the University of North Carolina at Greensboro, was born in Anguilla, Mississippi, in 1916. He holds history degrees from Millsaps College, Louisiana State University, and the University of North Carolina at Chapel Hill, and has published articles in several journals of Southern history. Dr. Ferguson is a member of the Lamar Society and a board member of the Greensboro Chamber of Commerce and United Community Services of Greensboro.

JOEL FLEISHMAN, a native of Fayetteville, North Carolina, is a 1955 graduate of the University of North Carolina at Chapel Hill and holds a J.D. degree from the University of North Carolina and an LL.M. degree from Yale University. Now Vice-Chancellor for Public Policy Education and Research at Duke University, Mr. Fleishman was formerly a lecturer in political science and Associate Provost for Urban Studies and Programs at Yale. During Terry Sanford's term as Governor of North Carolina, Mr. Fleishman served as his legal assistant. He is a member of the Committee on Negro Colleges of the Southern Education Foundation, a consultant to the Office of Economic Opportunity, and a member of the Board of Directors of the Lamar Society.

WAYNE FLYNT is a native of Pontotoc, Mississippi. He was graduated *magna cum laude* from Howard College (now Samford University) in Birmingham in 1961 and studied for his graduate degrees at Florida State University on an NDEA fellowship. Now associate professor of history at Samford University, Dr. Flynt has received the John H. Buchanan Award voted by Samford students to the best teacher in the university. His articles on Southern history have appeared in several journals, and his book on Duncan Fletcher is scheduled for publication in the summer of 1971. Dr. Flynt is a member of the Lamar Society and secretary-treasurer of the Association of Southern Labor Historians.

STEWART GAMMILL III, author of "Expanding Ownership in the Developing South," was born in Jackson, Mississippi, in 1936. He graduated from Millsaps College, where he was editor of the student newspaper, and received his M.S. degree from the University of Mississippi. A past director of the Mississippi Economic Council,

Mr. Gammill is engaged in organization and management of various small businesses under the trade name Interpine. He serves on the Board of Directors of the L.Q.C. Lamar Society.

RICHARD N. GOODWIN, the only non-Southern contributor to *You Can't Eat Magnolias,* is a former special assistant to Presidents John F. Kennedy and Lyndon B. Johnson, and served under President Kennedy as Deputy Assistant Secretary of State for Inter-American Affairs. He was active in the 1962 Presidential campaigns of Senators Eugene McCarthy and Robert F. Kennedy. The author of *Triumph or Tragedy: Reflections on Vietnam,* Mr. Goodwin is presently at work on a second book. His paper, "The End of Reconstruction," was presented at the 1970 Lamar Society symposium in Memphis.

CURTIS GRAVES is a representative in the Texas State Legislature, one of the first blacks elected since Reconstruction. Born in New Orleans in 1938, Mr. Graves was graduated from Texas State University and began his career as a public relations consultant. He has been active in civil rights and higher education legislation in Texas and is currently writing a book on his experience as a Texas state legislator. Mr. Graves is Vice-President of the L.Q.C. Lamar Society.

ROGER HALL, President of the North Carolina School of the Arts Foundation and Executive Director of the School of the Arts, was graduated in 1947 from the University of North Carolina at Chapel Hill with a degree in journalism. Mr. Hall was previously associated with Angel Records, and later with RCA Records in New York as manager of repertory and Red Seal artists. He has worked extensively in the field of symphony orchestra management and is a member of the Lamar Society and the Advisory Music Panel for the National Endowment for the Arts.

Born in 1939 in Orlando, Florida, WILLIAM R. HAMILTON is a graduate of the University of Florida in political science. Now the director of William R. Hamilton and Staff, a division of Independent Research Associates, Mr. Hamilton has conducted political polls in nearly all of the Southern states over tne past three years. He was formerly associated with the Institute for the Compara-

Biographical Notes

tive Study of Political Systems and the metropolitan Dade County government in Miami. Mr. Hamilton is a member of the American Political Science Association and the L.Q.C. Lamar Society.

MAYNARD H. JACKSON, JR., a native of Dallas, Texas, is Vice-Mayor of Atlanta and President of the Atlanta Board of Aldermen. Mr. Jackson was a Ford Foundation Early Admissions Scholar at Morehouse College in Atlanta, from which he was graduated in 1956 at the age of eighteen. He received an LL.B. degree from the North Carolina Central University School of Law and is the recipient of several American Jurisprudence Prizes. Mr. Jackson is a member of the Executive Committee of the Georgia ACLU and the National Council on Crime and Delinquency. A distinguished speaker and member of the Lamar Society Board of Directors, Mr. Jackson delivered a paper entitled "The Emerging South" at the Society's 1970 Memphis symposium.

RAY MARSHALL was born in Oak Grove, Louisiana, in 1928, and is director of the Center for the Study of Human Resources and chairman of the department of economics at the University of Texas at Austin. He was raised in a Baptist orphanage in Jackson, Mississippi, and holds degrees from Millsaps College, Louisiana State University, and the University of California. A former Fulbright scholar in Finland, Dr. Marshall has numerous other research grants and fellowships, and is currently chairman of the Southwest Regional Manpower Advisory Committee to the United States Departments of Labor and of Health, Education and Welfare. He is the author of a number of books on labor and employment policies A member of the L.Q.C. Lamar Society, Dr. Marshall delivered a paper on human resource development to the Southern Governors Conference in Biloxi, Mississippi, in September 1970.

WILLIE MORRIS was born in Yazoo City, Mississippi, in 1935. He was graduated from the University of Texas, where he was editor of the student newspaper, the *Daily Texan.* After four years as a Rhodes scholar at Oxford, he became the editor of the *Texas Observer* and later the youngest editor-in-chief in the 120-year history of *Harper's* Magazine. His first book, *North Toward Home,* was published in 1967; his second, *Yazoo,* appeared in 1971. He is currently writing a novel. Mr. Morris is a member of the Board of Directors of the L.Q.C. Lamar Society.

LUTHER MUNFORD was born in Jackson, Mississippi, in 1949 and is a 1971 graduate of Princeton University in public affairs and political science. He was chairman of the student newspaper, *The Daily Princetonian,* through which he proposed and helped formulate the Princeton Plan for the participation of college students in political campaigns. He is the winner of a scholarship to Oxford University, where he plans to read politics.

THOMAS NAYLOR was born in Jackson, Mississippi, in 1936, and holds degrees from Millsaps College, Columbia University, Indiana University, and Tulane University. Now professor of economics at Duke University, Dr. Naylor has served as an international consultant on economic development in Brazil, Chile, and Asia. He is director of the Center for Southern Studies and the Social System Simulation Program at Duke, and is the author of seven books and over fifty articles on econometrics, managerial economics, and computer simulation. One of the founders and the first Executive Director of the Lamar Society, Dr. Naylor has received a grant from the Twentieth Century Fund for a research project, entitled "The South: A Strategy for Change," for the study of the major political, educational, economic, and social institutions of the South.

Born in Macon, North Carolina, in 1933, REYNOLDS PRICE is a *summa cum laude* graduate of Duke University, where he is now associate professor of English. He was a Rhodes Scholar at Merton College, Oxford, and received the B.Litt. degree in 1958. His first novel, *A Long and Happy Life,* received the William Faulkner Foundation award for a notable first novel and has been translated into eleven languages. In addition, he has published two other novels, two volumes of short stories and novellas, and a book of poems. A former Guggenheim fellow and fellow of the National Endowment for the Arts, Mr. Price is advisory editor of *Shenandoah* and a member of the Lamar Society. His latest book, *Permanent Errors,* was published in 1970.

Born in Meridian, Mississippi, in 1920, FRANK A. ROSE received his undergraduate degree from Transylvania Col-

Biographical Notes

lege and studied at Lexington Theological Seminary and the University of London. A former President of the University of Alabama, Mr. Rose is also a past member of the executive committee of the Southern Regional Education Board and is chairman of the Educational Advisory Committee of the Appalachian Regional Council. He is currently national chairman of the Salk Institute, chairman of the board of University Associates, and a member of the Lamar Society.

TERRY SANFORD, President of Duke University, was born in Laurinburg, North Carolina, in 1917, and was Governor of his native state from 1961 to 1965. During his term of office, Mr. Sanford received national acclaim for his role in the development of several progressive educational programs, among them the Advancement School and the Learning Institute of North Carolina. A former attorney, Mr. Sanford received his undergraduate and J.D. degrees from the University of North Carolina at Chapel Hill, and holds honorary degrees from a number of Southern colleges and universities. He served as director of "A Study of American States," a Ford Foundation and Carnegie Corporation project to study and make recommendations for improvements in the effectiveness of state government. Mr. Sanford is the author of two books, *But What About the People?* and *Storm Over the States,* and is a former chairman of the Southern Regional Education Board. He delivered the keynote address to the 1971 Lamar Society symposium in Atlanta.

FRANK E. SMITH was United States Congressman from his native Mississippi for twelve years and was appointed by President John F. Kennedy to his present position as director of the Tennessee Valley Authority. A graduate of Sunflower Junior College in 1936 and the University of Mississippi in 1941, Mr. Smith is a former newspaperman and the author of several books on the South, among them the well-known *Congressman from Mississippi* and his latest book, *Land Between the Lakes.* Under President Kennedy, he served as director of the Natural Resources Advisory Committee. He is currently a vice-president of the Southern Regional Council and a member of the Board of Directors of the Lamar Society.

EDWIN M. YODER, JR., was born in Greensboro, North Carolina. He received his B.A. in English from the University of

North Carolina at Chapel Hill in 1956 and studied at Oxford University as a Rhodes scholar. Mr. Yoder was a contributor to *South Today,* edited by Willie Morris, and has published articles in *Saturday Review, Harper's Magazine, Book World* and *The New Republic.* Mr. Yoder is now associate editor of the *Greensboro Daily News* and is a member of the Lamar Society.

— END —